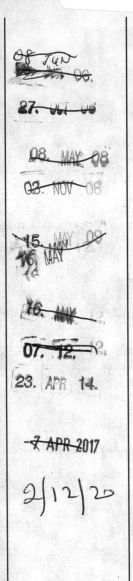

ASSESSMENT METHODS IN RECRUITMENT, SELECTION & PERFORMANCE

ASSESSMENT METHODS IN RECRUITMENT, SELECTION & PERFORMANCE

A manager's guide to psychometric
testing, interviews and assessment centres

Robert Edenborough

KOGAN
PAGE

London and Sterling, VA

To all the people whom I have studied, assessed and counselled over the last 40 years

First published in Great Britain and the United States in 2005 by Kogan Page Limited

Apart from any fair dealing for the purposes of research or private study, or criticism or review, as permitted under the Copyright, Designs and Patents Act 1988, this publication may only be reproduced, stored or transmitted, in any form or by any means, with the prior permission in writing of the publishers, or in the case of reprographic reproduction in accordance with the terms and licences issued by the CLA. Enquiries concerning reproduction outside these terms should be sent to the publishers at the undermentioned addresses:

120 Pentonville Road	22883 Quicksilver Drive
London N1 9JN	Sterling VA 20166-2012
United Kingdom	USA
www.kogan-page.co.uk	

© Robert Edenborough, 2005

The right of Robert Edenborough to be identified as the author of this work has been asserted by him in accordance with the Copyright, Designs and Patents Act 1988.

ISBN 07494 4294 8

British Library Cataloguing-in-Publication Data

A CIP record for this book is available from the British Library.

Library of Congress Cataloging-in-Publication Data

Edenborough, Robert.
    Assessment methods in recruitment, selection, and performance : a manager's guide to psychometric testing, interviews, and assessment centres / Robert Edenborough
        p. cm.
Includes bibliographical references and index.
    ISBN 0-7494-4294-8
    1. Employees--Rating of. 2. Employees--Recruiting. 3. Employees--Psychological testing. 4. Psychometrics. 5. Employment interviewing. I. Title.

HF5549.5.R3E32 2005
658.3'125--dc22

2005005136

Typeset by Datamatics Technologies Ltd, Mumbai, India
Printed and bound in Great Britain by Creative Print and Design (Wales), Ebbw Vale

Contents

Preface

Assessment methods are often separated out into different approaches rather than being joined up into comprehensive means of understanding capability. My own previous books include the different but related subjects of psychometrics and interviewing and, indeed, by writing about these as separate subjects I could be seen as contributing to separation rather than integration of thinking, notwithstanding a degree of cross-referencing that I attempted. Linking these two areas up and adding to them the scope to examine a third related field – that of assessment centre technology – is something that I first discussed at a conference on test use (Edenborough, 1999); the continuing pursuit of that idea is one of the objectives of this book. All of these areas represent 'inputs' to performance, but the outputs or behaviour implied by the various assessment methods but necessarily not directly measured by them and the resultant control or management of performance appear to be worthy of consideration too. Otherwise it is unlikely that a comprehensively organized range of methods will be applied to the whole field of human resource management.

Joined-up methods are, in fact, increasingly sought and considered in a range of fields and one of the organizing principles is that of the application of information technology. This latter has been a continuing theme, of course, for a number of years and I can recall seeing demonstrations of remotely applied test procedures as far back as the early 1970s. Very recently I have been struck by the scope and need for more integration of reference taking with other aspects of assessment in recruitment and in the field of HR due diligence applied to mergers, acquisitions and other major changes. Add to that the ongoing interest in objective understanding of ability, plus integrative philosophies as represented by, among others, Investors in People, the Management Charter Initiative and, indeed, the European Foundation for Quality Management (EFQM) and there seems to be a range of approaches worthy of joint consideration. These views are underpinned by an increasing awareness of the variety of situations in which assessment and performance are meant to be understood together. Work undertaken by firms in the consulting and professional services area is, more and more, reflecting this convergence and it is my own experience in working in several such firms that has provided the final impetus for the present volume.

Acknowledgements

A number of current colleagues at KPMG have contributed in one way or another to this book. However, any errors are mine and the views expressed should not be taken as representing those of KPMG.

Special mention should be made of Caroline Laidlaw, who has assisted enthusiastically with the research and made technical inputs on a number of topics. Ongoing discussions with and specific inputs from Mandy Parker and Gareth Jones have stimulated and challenged some of my thinking and helped shape the scope and expression of ideas in several of the fields covered. Jennie Haigh has been ready with advice to steer me through the intricacies involved in manipulating my text. Tracey Banks has also contributed with inputs derived from her experiences derived from developing her psychometric skills. John Bailey and Liz Stewart provided a number of useful ideas on coaching.

Claire Walsh has coped with the job of assembling and adjusting the written and diagrammatic material, handling spasmodic influxes of text presented in a variety of ways.

My son, Tom, sought out some of the key and sometimes obscure references. My wife, Marion, has provided helpful comment on a number of chapters as well as accommodating my need to spend 'free' time producing the work.

Robert Edenborough
Esher

'Haste still pays haste, and leisure answers leisure;
Like doth quit like, and MEASURE still FOR MEASURE.'

Shakespeare, *Measure for Measure*, Act 5, Scene 1

1

Why selection and performance management?

INTRODUCTION

In presenting my personal credentials I sometimes advise prospective clients that I have been involved in assessment for selection to posts ranging from barmen to spacemen. This is literally true, and reflecting on this breadth of experience it strikes me that there is a very large economic significance in both cases. Select the wrong spacemen and you will have a lack of success in a mission that will cost billions. Apply a better technique to the selection of barmen and you may see an increase in top line of, say, 200 outlets, of anything from 10 to 100 per cent, which could well add up to tens of millions per annum. At a more personal level I was somewhat intrigued by realizing that a former colleague of mine, having had an unhappy marriage that ended in divorce, relied on another member of staff to take his prospective brides through a structured interview process and match their profiles with his. The would-be groom was then advised of their compatibility with himself. He had actually rejected at least two, otherwise seen as very worthy, candidates for his hand on this basis and this again can be seen as a matter of some significance.

Another surprise I experienced was when sitting down with the executive team of a major finance house and finding that they had no clear criteria of what successful performance in their business, at an individual level, actually meant. Some 16 years on, at the time of writing, the press is full of accounts of how their market value has declined by over 75 per cent. Could there be a link between this lack of rigour in considering what makes for successful performance at an individual level and the actual performance of the company as a whole?

SELECTION AND PERFORMANCE MANAGEMENT

A few definitions

Selection can be defined as the combination of processes that lead to the choice of one or more candidates over others for one or more jobs or roles. Assessment is the application of systematic processes to understand the performance of individuals or groups, either currently or in a predictive sense.

Performance management has been defined (Armstrong and Baron, 1998) as 'a strategic and integrated approach to delivering sustained success to organisations by improving the performance of the people who work in them and by developing the capabilities of teams and individual contributors'.

PSYCHOMETRICS, ASSESSMENT CENTRES AND STRUCTURED INTERVIEWS

The order of the items in the above heading is deliberate; it reflects the degree of discipline and recognition of that discipline that is applied to these three areas of assessment. They do overlap each other. And it is also noteworthy that, between them, they cover much of the ground of assessment. Outside them and, to a large extent although not entirely, beyond the scope of this book are fields such as psychophysiological measures, eg the galvanic skin response (the lie-detector technique) and graphology.

While these other approaches have some pretences to scientific system, the field of astrology, as represented by horoscopes, really has no such pretensions. This does not, though, prevent it from capturing the attention of those who might otherwise know better. I have often had the experience, after having presented a comprehensive description of a candidate against a thoroughly developed competency measure, itself established after months of research and with the assessment comprising a mix of methods, of being asked 'So what is his birth sign?' I also had the surprise, not to say embarrassment, when introducing a group of assessors to candidates and seeking to emphasize their professional credentials to find one of them talking about her other interests as a means of lightening the atmosphere of this potentially tense initial introduction and sharing with the candidates the fact that she was a 'trained astrologer'. See also the case in the box below.

The persistence of the fascination with horoscopes in particular was brought home to me very recently. Working on an off-site assessment event with a number of occupational psychologist colleagues, all of whom were very well versed in the strict disciplines of their role, I was surprised to find that an unusually idle moment in the proceedings was filled by my colleagues avidly, albeit tongue-in-cheek, turning to the 'stars' page of the tabloid newspaper that one of them had brought along, and poring over its contents. The fluency of the ensuing discussion suggested to me that this was not a one-off filling of a spare five minutes but was a routine, if not-to-be-taken-wholly-seriously practice. Lest my observation seem too condescending let me admit to feeling uncomfortable if I do not have a piece of wood to hand to touch at appropriately propitiatory moments or if the Scottish play is quoted without due tribute to ever-lurking Nemesis. We psychologists are not immune from displaying irrationality, even if we are ready to recognize it in others!

Let us now bring some of this to life by considering some different situations and circumstances in which more 'proper' approaches are demonstrated and practised.

A RANGE OF SETTINGS

Psychometrics

A small group uses sewing machines, working at stitching two squares of material together to make a pocket shape. A manager sits at a computer terminal, tapping in responses to a series of personality questions. A middle-aged woman completes a series of questions about her preferences for different types of work activity. Sixty students, all due to graduate in a few months' time, are arrayed in a hotel conference suite, which is set out like an examination hall. Under the watchful eyes of a group of administrators they solve problems in verbal reasoning. A scientist studies a long series of numbers and then tries to reproduce them in reverse order.

All of these people are undertaking psychometric tests. Psychometrics literally means mental measurement, and psychometric tests or instruments are measurement devices. The measurement is used to gain understanding of an individual so as to be able to predict behaviour and provide a basis for future action.

Stitching the square of material neatly and accurately will be seen as evidence of ability to train as a machinist in the garment industry. A consultant will write a report on the manager, advising a client as to whether he or she will fit in with a management team. The middle-aged woman will spend time with a counsellor who will use her responses to help guide her decisions about a change of career. Some of the students will be invited on to another stage of selection and a few will be asked to join the graduate programme of a major multinational. If the scientist can repeat the numbers accurately and performs well on a variety of other tasks he will be selected for work conducting experiments in a biosphere.

Thus the applications of psychometrics are various and the benefits arising from their use can include the following:

▌ maximizing an organization's performance by improving accuracy of selection;

▌ improving employee retention by better matching individuals to jobs;

▌ avoiding the financial and personal costs associated, on both sides, with poor recruitment decisions;

▌ optimizing the use of people's capacities by helping focus development activity;

▌ achieving better career management by matching individual aspirations to their organization's opportunities.

In addition to these benefits in the occupational field, clinical use provides scope for assessing, and hence being in a position to deal with, a variety of conditions, including depression. Assessment of educational attainment levels among children and pinpointing the specifics within dyslexia are ways in which the educational field gains from using psychometrics. (Each of these fields is dealt with a little more, though still briefly, in

Chapter 3.) In fact, many people have found psychometric tests to be of very substantial value, but practices in test use are still patchy, variable and often idiosyncratic.

Interviews

A recruitment consultant and candidate sit on comfortable sofas in an office. The consultant refers to a series of notes he has made from the candidate's CV and says: 'I see that you have had experience with XYZ technology, but I'm not clear what your responsibility was for the project that your company was running. Can you tell me a little more?'

A line manager enters a syndicate room in a management training centre, briefly greets an interviewee and enters into a series of questions from a prepared list, covering the competencies of staff development, strategic planning and orientation to change. Occasionally she asks follow-up questions and probes. She makes notes continuously throughout the discussion.

A personnel officer picks up the telephone and explains to the person at the other end that he is working with a prepared interview and would like to record his responses. After agreement the interview proceeds. Occasionally the interviewee asks for clarification, to be told gently: 'However you would like to respond is OK.'

An outplacement counsellor sits and listens while the man before him enters into a diatribe about the organization that has just decided to make him redundant. After a while the counsellor says: 'Your feelings are quite natural and understandable. What we should be working with among other things is helping you to set them in context and so use the energy that you are showing now in relation to your future job search.' He does not intend to take the discussion very much further on that occasion.

A financial consultant explains to a couple in their living room that if she is to advise them professionally she must explore a number of aspects of their background situation and establish their needs. They nod in agreement but at the end of the session she will ask them to sign a form indicating that they have actually understood her role and agree to her advising them.

A group of seven people assemble behind a green-baize-covered table. Five of them, including the chair of the meeting, are elected council representatives with the others being council officers, the director involved and a personnel manager. In an adjacent room a candidate waits knowing that she is the first of three people to be seen that morning. She is invited in, motioned to a chair and the questions begin.

A patient enters a GP's surgery. He looks up: 'Good morning, Mrs X. How are you today?' He has already noted the reddening mark under the patient's left eye and wonders if this will even be mentioned by her and if so if it will be dismissed as 'I walked into a door' and how far he will get in explaining that the 'something' she needs for her nerves is to be as far away as possible from her violent husband.

These, then, form some of the range of interviews experienced variously and commonly in the course of working and everyday existence. Questions, answers and listening are common. They vary in the degree of pre-planning and structure. They are also differentiated one from another in the general form that they will take, the expectations of the parties involved and the skill level of both sides. They are all recognizable as types of interview and as such are themselves only distinguishable by a series of slow degrees from other forms of interaction involving speech. The 'Can I help you?', 'What size do you take?' and 'Can you wait a week for the alteration?' are questions familiar to anyone shopping for a garment. 'Why are your grades so poor?' and 'Would you do better with another French teacher?' are examples relating to a parent interviewing a child on her school report. These shade into the even less structured 'Where have you been?' from the parent, which may signal the start of a lecture, or another 'Can I help you?', this time from an employee, slightly suspicious of the stranger wandering the office corridor.

We ask questions, that is, we *interview*, to find out about other people, their attitudes, behaviours and skills, or to tap into the information they possess. We believe that what people say tells us a lot, an idea neatly encapsulated by Gilbert Wrenn writing in 1949. He said: 'Language is the expression of human personality in words.'

Thus the interview as such is perhaps just a specialized form of what humans spend large proportions of their time doing, ie talking to one another by means of questions and answers. Although specialized, interviews are common. They are themselves a sufficiently significant part of human interaction that interviewing skills may be regarded as a set of fundamental life skills, practised with varying degrees of effectiveness but found at every turn.

Assessment centres

'For a moment I had really thought I was in the office, going through my correspondence on a Saturday morning. I was so surprised when a waiter walked in and then with a jolt I came back to reality and realized that it was a Thursday and I was in a hotel going through an exercise.' So says a candidate confronted by, and evidently engrossed in, an in-basket exercise. Her work in handling the correspondence will be examined by one of a team of assessors, who will share his interpretations with two colleagues, who may well challenge his views and who will themselves present their findings from the tasks that they have observed. These tasks include a group discussion at which they have been present as 'flies on the wall'.

Three senior Royal Air Force NCOs sit astride a pine pole suspended by a rope from a beam in the hangar ceiling in earnest discussion with a fourth – the leader for this exercise – who is standing on an oil drum. How to get two such drums and the whole crew across a space, representing a crocodile-infested river, is the subject of their increasingly animated debate. A flight sergeant on the beam leans out just a bit too far as he gesticulates to the exercise leader and all three fall off, knocking over the oil drum and displacing the one perched there. One of two observing officer assessors shakes his head and turns to his companion remarking, 'The trouble with the SNCOs is that it always turns into a sergeants' mess committee meeting.'

A professional actor makes a scripted remark about health and safety: 'I know they have to say that to cover themselves, but it's really just window dressing. If we paid attention to their rule book every time we would never get anything finished.' An assessor sets down the participant's response, which has challenged the actor and reiterated the standard expected with regard to breaks for people working at screens. Later, as he reviews his script the assessor marks that as positive evidence of the competency: **sets standards for others**.

All of these are examples of the assessment centre method in practice, with multiple exercises covering situations of relevance to the role concerned, using multiple assessors, different exercises and interpretation according to a model of competency developed by a formal job analysis.

INDIVIDUAL DIFFERENCES

These approaches all involve the practical application of a field known as 'individual differences'. This has been defined by Cooper (2002) as 'the branch of psychology that considers how and why people are psychologically very different from one another' and which he goes on to contrast with several other branches, such as social psychology, where it is assumed that people are all much the same.

In this book, psychometrics, structured interviews and assessment centres – three individual differences disciplines – are all considered to help readers see these powerful tools in a broad perspective. The context in which all of these disciplines are used is, in essence, that of understanding and predicting behaviour. As such they interplay with a range of other systematic and less systematic methods. The latter, of course, include the broad sweep of intuitive and largely unconscious devices that we all use in making sense of our fellow beings. The warm smile, the educational background, the manner of speech, the real or supposed slight, arriving five minutes early or five minutes late, all give us day-to-day clues from which we build pictures of friends, colleagues, acquaintances or strangers and which we seek to use to come to conclusions about their enduring behavioural characteristics. The fact that the assessment methods considered here do much the same thing, but through the media of formalized questioning, the manipulation of abstract symbols or prepared exercises, places them among the black arts in the minds of some. But they are not magical; they are, rather, scientific distillations of much practical experience, contained in the convenient form of standardized sets of materials.

Performance management

A group of managers spend a day in a workshop discussing rating systems, how to make their judgements more objective and how to use the full range of the scales available to them. New to some of them is the idea of linking individual objectives to the framework of their company's goals. Their discussion then turns to the question of how far these figures might be related to other sets charting customer satisfaction.

An HR specialist and a medical director pore through the results of assessments made against a suite of performance indicators (PIs), noting the imbalance between 'technical' and 'behavioural' outcomes in the figures before them.

A management consultant reviews a development planning framework with his client, who suspects that a forthcoming senior management team audit will reveal shortcomings in communications and strategic thinking. 'Let's consider the range of development options that the company will back financially,' the consultant suggests and then goes on to say, 'You might contemplate setting up some bespoke training through a business school. But don't let's forget that some of the best development will come through self-driven efforts. We need to ensure that there is a supportive framework, but one in which your people will feel they have scope for choices in the investment they make in their own growth.'

These are all aspects of performance management, not one thing but a mix of approaches supported by an underlying philosophy about the importance of whole organization management. Jones (1995) for instance talks about managing the **context** rather than the performance, while Armstrong and Baron (1998) talk about a range of concerns in the field, including planning, continuous development and improvement, and satisfying stakeholder needs.

INPUTS AND OUTPUTS

Assessments in selection are the inputs used to **predict** future outputs. The inputs may be entirely current in nature, as when a candidate undertakes a group discussion in an assessment centre. Very often, though, they will include aspects of past behaviour. This happens when the same candidate responds to a structured interview in terms of previous successes, say in project management, or reflects habitual preferences in responding to a personality questionnaire item on watching versus performing in a stage production. The same assessments may be reported in terms that cover ideas for working with the candidate if hired, so merging with the field of performance management. In performance management as such as currently practised one uses inputs from past and current behaviour to manage future behaviour relevant to performance. That is, there is more of a focus on controlling outputs. In its antecedents there was less emphasis on the ongoing reviews of performance than is currently the case and more on using historic performance information to determine reward or role. A linking concept in both cases is that of **competency**, which is discussed further below and which is returned to at a number of points throughout this book. Again, a further linking category supporting both these ideas is that of objectivity in measurement, also discussed in this chapter. Some of these ideas are summarized in Figure 1.1.

COMPETENCY

Definitions

The term **competency** sometimes seems to be simply a modern version of what may otherwise be referred to as dimensions, criteria, traits or even themes of behaviour. Its current usage can be attributed to Boyatzis (1982), who defined it as 'a capacity that exists in a person that leads to behaviour that meets the job demands within the parameters of the organizational environment and that, in turn, brings about desired results'. A similar definition from Evarts (1987) will be explored further here. It runs as follows: 'A competency is an underlying characteristic of a person which is causally related to effective or superior performance in a job or role.'

The various aspects of the definition are all of importance. Thus by referring to an underlying characteristic we mean something that is likely to be sustained, repeated and reliable over time. It is not, however, necessarily implied that this should be something absolutely fundamental to

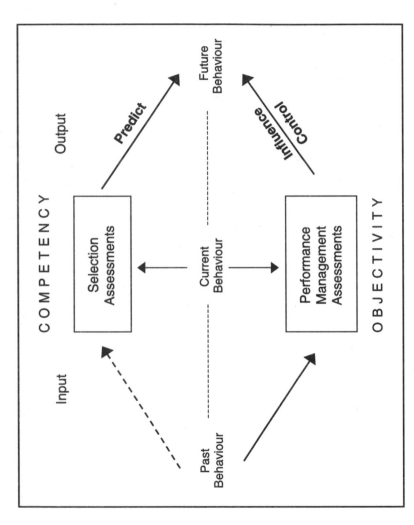

Figure 1.1 Inputs and outputs

the person. Indeed, debates about the various contributions of nature and nurture do not need to be entered into when considering competencies. The term **underlying** and its implication of behaviour that is repeated is meant to remove one from the arena of superficial judgements. For example, the person who appears with a button missing from her jacket at an interview may be habitually scruffy and pay insufficient attention to her personal presentation, or she may have been unfortunate enough to have caught her clothing on a nail while entering the interviewer's office. More information would be needed to determine whether she did in fact possess the competency of appropriate personal presentation. (This is akin to a distinction made by Wernimont and Campbell in 1968 between signs and samples.)

The **causal** part of the competency definition is to distinguish between those many characteristics that may be studied and measured about a person and those aspects that actually do provide a link to relevant behaviour. Thus having acquired a particular academic qualification may or may not be correlated with the capacity to perform a particular job. The qualification is scarcely likely – talisman-like – to cause the capacity for performance. However, a tendency to grasp complexity and to learn new facts and figures may well be part of the causal chain, and the competency would be expressed in these terms, not in terms of the possibly related qualification.

A focus on effective or superior performance is one that we shall return to again in some detail under 'structured psychometric interviews' in Chapters 11 and 12. A moment's consideration may show that in building models of success one is far more concerned with what the successful actually do than with what the unsuccessful fail to do. In seeking to understand competencies required for piano playing one would learn little by watching and listening to an incompetent player striking the wrong notes! By contrast a period of study with an accomplished exponent of the instrument would be likely to expose the relevant characteristics of behaviour far better.

One may be forgiven for thinking that there is nothing very new in competencies and, rather like Moliére's Monsieur Jourdain in *Le Bourgeois Gentilhomme*, who discovered he had been speaking prose for more than 40 years, the discovery of competencies as an idea is not particularly earth-shattering. On the other hand by referring any explicit or implicit model of behaviour to a definition, albeit as simple as that given, one may begin to sort the wheat from the chaff in deciding what range of behaviours and predispositions to behaviour are relevant. This can help avoid the trap of focusing on totally irrelevant or prejudicial aspects or seeking a very broad and over-comprehensive model, covering lots of behavioural possibilities almost on a 'just in case' basis, but with limited usefulness.

Expressing competencies

Competency descriptions may be expressed in a variety of ways. Sometimes they lead to very tight prescriptions, which may apply very much to a particular job or class of jobs. Thus one comes across prescriptions such as 'must be able to draft policy documentation appropriate for consideration of directors of subsidiary companies'. In other cases they are more clearly rooted in behaviour. Two examples are given below. In the first a brief definition is followed by quite a detailed exposition and both positive and negative behavioural indicators are given. In the second, briefer, example only the positive behaviours are shown.

PERSONAL

Control of initiatives

Making decisions and taking charge of events

Executives strong in control of initiatives make a definite decision to proceed with an action or actions. They see themselves as owners of decisions and the actions required to stem from them. They may position a variety of others in representative or supportive roles, for instance using inputs from financial, ops or planning deputies, but they will be clear that it is they who are setting actions in train. They may see their work as a series of projects to be set in motion. They will take initiatives not only in terms of making things happen, but also in the sense of self-management. They will be in control of their own time as a resource and will have distinct means of coping with the stresses of the job. They will be prepared to follow through tenaciously, not letting problems deter them and not succumbing to hostility. This competency is one that will be significant in the leadership style of the executive.

Positive indicators	Negative indicators
Can identify when a decision to proceed was taken	Vague about decision points
Takes charge of a range of activities – calling meetings, briefings, initiatives, planning	Lets activities 'take their course'
In charge of their own time	Event-driven
Statements indicating ownership personally or with or through immediate group	Ownership for actions resting with outsiders, maybe vague 'they'

Reproduced by kind permission of MSL HR Consulting Ltd

DIRECT INFLUENCING

Definition

The ability to convince others to buy something or to support a recommended course of action, and the ability to reach a compromise between two conflicting parties.

Behavioural indicators

▌ Persuades others by pointing out benefits to them.

▌ Uses information or data effectively to persuade others or support a position.

▌ Offers several different arguments to persuade or support a position.

▌ Explains complex ideas by using well-chosen examples from personal experience.

▌ Prepares for presentations with documentation, facts and figures.

▌ Anticipates and prepares for how people will react.

▌ Identifies the most important concerns and issues to others.

▌ Tailors own language to the level of audience.

▌ Makes a special effort to relate to people and their own level of understanding.

▌ Presents own position persuasively.

Reproduced by kind permission of MSL HR Consulting Ltd

THE IMPORTANCE OF OBJECTIVITY

The role of objectivity in assessment and performance management is worthy of some further consideration. If there is not something objective that can be assessed we shall not be involved in assessment as such but into subjectivity, whim or prejudice. Also, without objective measurement there could scarcely be standardization in our understanding of and predictions about individuals and their performance. The Northcote–Trevelyan reforms in the Civil Service emphasized the significance of objectivity in selection as long ago as the 19th century. The history of assessment of performance, formally, is rather later in origin.

Although many accept the significance of the objective approach the picture is not, by any means, straightforward. There was quite a robust debate at a recent conference of the British Psychological Society on the question of clinical, ie relatively **subjective**, versus **objective** judgement, with a number of proponents on either side.

It is by no means 100 per cent clear that objectivity can routinely be applied. Sometimes what is meant by objectivity might better be described as independent judgement when, perhaps, expertise from outside the organization is used and/or standardized tools are employed. The question of objectivity versus subjectivity will be returned to again, notably in Chapter 11 in connection with structured interviewing.

PLAN OF THE BOOK

This chapter has sought to set out some of the general background and rationale for assessment and performance management and has set out a number of key concepts. The next chapter deals with the history of the various assessment disciplines and performance management. Chapters 3 to 8 deal with psychometrics and also introduce some of the statistical ideas relevant to other means of assessment. Assessment centres are dealt with in the following two chapters, and Chapters 11 and 12 cover various aspects of structured interviewing. Performance management is reintroduced in Chapter 13 and its wider scope examined in the following chapter. Chapters 15 and 16 deal respectively with two specialized areas. The first of these concerns relations between supplying consultants and their clients, while the second looks at the various applications of information and communications technology in the assessment and performance field and the associated pitfalls. The last chapter addresses the currently important area of assessing whole teams in relation to a variety of major change scenarios as well as forecasting something of the future of the assessment and performance management fields.

2

Historical perspectives

PSYCHOMETRICS

Early days

Psychometric tests have a history that, although not long, goes back further than is often realized. They originated in work related to education in the latter part of the 19th century, for example by the American Cattell (1890) and the Frenchmen Binet and Henri (1895), with the first published test being produced by Binet and another associate, Simon, in 1905. Earlier foundations can, however, be traced to the work of Wilhelm Wundt. In 1879 he founded a laboratory at Leipzig, devoted to the application of scientific method to behaviour and sensory experience. His work included the systematic examination of a range of aspects of vision and hearing and of reaction times to various stimuli. A physiologist by training, he made the first systematic attempt to describe mental phenomena on a scientific basis. Among the disciplines contributed by these laboratory-based approaches were those of standardization of procedures. These included the same stimuli applied under the same conditions, with set instructions, recording of responses and common methods of interpretation. However, though highly systematic in his approach his work was highly dependent on reported sensations.

Tests as such were taken up in a number of select fields. Notable among these was the work for the US armed forces during the First World War (Yoakum and Yerkes, 1920). Here it was important to identify the abilities of very large numbers of young men quickly, so as to channel them into the most suitable military roles and the most appropriate training. Part of the early scientific interest surrounding tests centred on the way in which intelligence could be described and its structure characterized. There was debate, for instance, on the number of factors into which general intelligence could be divided (eg Spearman, 1904).

The general way in which tests should be applied was set out fairly early on in this process, with scientific and professional standards being progressively laid down. For example, the National Institute of Industrial Psychology (NIIP) in Britain began formally teaching test use and administration in the 1920s. The American Psychological Association (APA) first issued standards for testing in the very early days (1905, as reported by Cronbach, 1966) with progressive development subsequently (APA, 1954; APA, American Educational Research Association and National Council on Measurement in Education, 1974).

The Second World War and onward

In the UK and the United States in particular, development of a number of tests for specific military roles and trades took place during the Second World War. Testing for particular types of civilian occupation had started to be developed in the inter-war period (eg Burt, 1922 – though important parts of his work were later discredited as fraudulent) and this trend continued after the Second World War, with developments such as the publication of the Differential Aptitude Tests (DAT) in the United States (Bennett, Seashore and Wesman, 1947). This was designed to aid occupational guidance and, as such, could be useful to employers and potential employees. It comprised a battery of tests, covering a number of areas from abstract reasoning and abstract spatial relationships to the solution of mechanical problems and spelling.

Small group testing for guidance became more common at this time, whereas prior to the Second World War the more labour-intensive individual testing had been usual. In the UK at the same time, test development research in the occupational field continued to be undertaken, in particular by the National Institute for Industrial Psychology (eg Castle and Garforth, 1951; Vincent, 1955; Stott, 1956). Since then there has been a continued growth of the development and application of testing.

The second edition of Anastasi's book on testing, published as far back as 1961, lists nearly 1,200 references to research on published tests. Since 1941 large numbers of tests have been catalogued and reviewed in the _Mental Measurement Yearbooks_, originally edited by Buros. This enormous output has progressively found its way into commercial and organizational use. In the UK, some large-scale employers such as British Telecom (BT) have or had their own specialist testing departments for many years, developing and applying testing procedures quite broadly.

Back from the present

A British Psychological Society (BPS) 'flyer' produced in the early 1990s cites a 1989 survey indicating use of occupational tests among 73 per cent of major UK companies. Williams (1994), reviewing test use as indicated by a number of surveys, sees a picture of increasing test use. Yet testing has never been anything like universal and has been variable in its application. For example, Bevan and Fryatt (1988) reported much higher evidence of test use in connection with managerial, technical and professional staff than for manual workers and their foremen and supervisors. The present author, while exploring the use of psychometrics among law firms, found reactions ranging from suspicion and amazement that such steps should be contemplated to their application as a matter of routine.

To make what may seem an extreme comparison, despite widespread use psychometric testing has never achieved the currency as a systematic way of looking at people that, say, standard accounting practices have gained for examining the figures and trends within a business. A number of reasons for this state of affairs present themselves. To begin with, many tests – and not just personality measures – have been developed on the basis first of psychological theory and only second in relation to practical applications. This has meant that interpretation has required comprehension of theoretical ideas and material beyond the layperson. The widespread development of training courses in test use for people other than specialists has been a relatively recent phenomenon, going hand in hand with growth in the number of test publishers and distributors. (The 1966 edition of Cronbach's _Essentials of Psychological Testing_ listed 18 leading test publishers and distributors in the United States; nearly as many can be found today serving the much smaller UK market.)

Also, despite the strong academic threads and the evident need for detailed understanding, formal controls on test use have been of relatively late date. For example, the BPS only clarified its standards governing qualification in the use of personality questionnaires in 1995. Thus, poor practices were able to grow up in some areas with tests tending to be subject to a variety of misuses. Although there have, thankfully, been few major scandals, tests became associated in the minds of some with casual rather than professional practices.

There was a spate of litigation in the United States in the 1970s, following the equal employment legislation of the 1960s. This led to extreme wariness on the part of some employers and to their dropping the use of tests. One of the important principles to emerge then was that the intention not to discriminate unfairly was not enough; the practice and outcomes had to be in line with that intention. (See Edenborough, 1994). The parent company of at least one US test publisher withdrew entirely from that business at that time. In the UK, cases such as that of a group of ethnic minority British Rail employees, who successfully contested the use of particular test procedures (Kellett *et al*, 1994), have arisen from time to time.

Clearly there have been boosts to test use, too. One of the more recent has been the competency movement – which is providing a common language, albeit an imperfectly understood one – with its links to initiatives such as the National Vocational Qualifications (NVQs) in the UK. So today, following a chequered history, psychometric tests are extensively but by no means universally in use. Similarly, understanding of their value and potential is widespread, but still patchy.

INTERVIEWS

Ancient roots

The rather relentless questioning of one party by another or others, what we would now call interrogation, is undoubtedly ancient. Among other examples the viva voce examination was, for centuries, the standard way of examining undergraduates in the universities. As well as still being used for this purpose quite generally for higher-level degrees, this methodology has clearly much in common with modern selection interviews, particularly of the formal board or panel interview type.

Formal questioning was, of course, an integral part of the procedures used by the Inquisition set up by Pope Innocent III under the Congregation of the Holy Office in the 13th century. Such processes, although of course often abused, could result in uncovering substantial tracts of information. This is nowhere more vividly indicated than in Ladurie's (1978) account of life in a French village, _Montaillou_. This detailed compilation is based upon inquisitorial examinations conducted by Jacques Fournier, Bishop of Pamiers, at that town and Carcassonne in the late 13th and early 14th centuries. As we have seen, though, the idea of the interview for selection purposes is more modern. Literary accounts of hirings in earlier times are sometimes amusing, as in Dickens's portrayal of Pickwick's acquisition of Samuel Weller, but rarely suggest a comprehensive method for exploring the merits of the candidate.

'We want to know in the first place,' said Mr Pickwick, 'whether you have any reason to be discontented with your present situation.'

'Afore I answer that 'ere question, gen'lm'n,' replied Mr Weller, 'I should like to know, in the first place, whether you're a-goin' to purvide me with a better.'

A sunbeam of placid benevolence played on Mr Pickwick's features as he said, 'I have half made up my mind to engage you myself.'

'Have you though?' said Sam.

Mr Pickwick nodded in the affirmative.

'Wages?' inquired Sam.

'Twelve pounds a year,' replied Mr Pickwick.

'Clothes?'

'Two suits.'

'Work?'

'To attend upon me and travel about with me and these gentlemen here.'

'Take the bill down', said Sam emphatically. 'I'm let to a single gentleman, and the terms is agreed upon.'

The former lack of system in interviewing may, of course, be because patronage and recommendation were at one time a common basis for making hiring decisions. In _The Three Musketeers_, Dumas's account of Dartagnan's candidacy for the King's Musketeers hinges upon a letter of introduction from his father to their captain, M de Treville. The occasion of the theft of the letter en route to Paris is one of the pivots of the novel, and its absence when the hero presents himself to de Treville is a significant mark against him.

It was, in fact, only in the second half of the 19th century that merit rather than patronage was determined to be the criterion for recruitment by as significant an employer as the British Civil Service as noted in

Chapter 1. The Northcote–Trevelyan report of 1853–54 recommended that a Civil Service Commission be set up to oversee recruitment and promotion by competitive examination, ie bringing in an objective system to replace subjectivity and patronage. This was made mandatory in 1870, but even then did not apply to the Foreign Office.

Modern instances

Modern interviewing can be seen as having several strands. The need for formalized techniques in selection was clearly recognized during the two world wars. The first of these gave a boost to paper-and-pencil psychometric instruments, as noted above, but little to interviewing practice. The Second World War saw the origin of the War Office Selection Boards (WOSBs, and see assessment centres below) with their emphasis on an overall system in selection and with associated research flagging problems with unstructured interviews (see Vernon and Parry, 1949). Highly structured interview methods began to appear in the 1950s with the work of Clifton and his associates in the United States. They arose after experimentation with techniques in which perceptions of other people were used to give clues to behaviour patterns (see Clifton, Hollingsworth and Hall, 1952). Specialist selection firms such as Management Selection Limited (MSL) emerged in the same decade, with their professional staff spending much of their time conducting selection interviews.

A significant but not generally acknowledged strand in modern interviewing can be attributed to Sigmund Freud. He considered that much of what people said could be related to unconscious drives and motives, exploring those as day-to-day occurrences in 'The psychopathology of everyday life' (1901). Thus slips of the tongue, the so-called 'Freudian slips' or 'parapraxes', were described by him as telling signs of would-be behaviours.

In terms of counselling and related techniques the work of Carl Rogers is critical. He advocated the importance of objectivity and acceptance in the counselling interview process. His *On Becoming a Person* (1961) is widely regarded as a central work in this connection.

Recommendations on selection interview techniques started appearing in print in the 1950s (eg NIIP, 1952), and there is today a variety of books on the subject (eg Fletcher, 1986; Anderson and Shackleton, 1993). There is also a substantial research literature, with a survey as far back as the 1940s (Wagner, 1949) being sufficiently extensive to have been dubbed by Anderson (1992) 'a major review'. In other uses of interviewing beyond assessment, advisory and research literature has been in existence for decades; for example, Oldfield's (1953) booklet *Fruitful Interviews* gives advice to welfare officers on dealing with their clients.

The use of interviews in staff surveys can be traced back to the 1930s, with Raphael's (1944) paper reflecting 10 years of such work. The 1930s also saw the advent of political polling interviews, with the work of George Gallup in the United States, which then made a significant impact in the UK with the prediction of Winston Churchill's general election defeat in 1945.

Other interviewing developments are more recent; for instance Morgan, writing in 1993, claimed that the focus group technique was virtually unknown to social scientists five years previously. As the various methods and applications unfolded, some developed along crossing or parallel lines, while others diverged.

ASSESSMENT CENTRES

Military origins

Assessment centres provide a means for a fairly direct production of behaviour that is seen as evidence or otherwise of a competency. They have a long history with origins generally ascribed to the methods adopted by the British, German and US armed forces during the Second World War for officer selection. The original US work for the Office of Strategic Services (OSS) is described by Mackinnon (1980). Combinations of tactical planning exercises and outdoor leadership exercises were used. The latter would include tasks such as building bridges from ropes and pine poles, and transporting a team and its equipment across. All this would be done to time, with participants taking it in turn to lead or act as team members, as in the example described in Chapter 1. Officers would observe and rate performance according to preset criteria. Such tasks were seen as fairly direct simulations of what young officers, say those leading an infantry platoon, would be required to do in practice.

In fact, as Anastasi (1961) pointed out, the use of simulation exercises pre-dated those initiatives with the work of Hartshorne, May and others in the 1920s and 1930s in educational settings (Hartshorne and May, 1930; Hartshorne, May and Shuttleworth, 1929).

Civilian applications

The method was taken up in the British Civil Service in the 1940s for its fast-track administrative class entrants. The first commercial applications were in the United States in the 1950s. Today the method is widespread commercially and in the public sector. In the UK, assessment centres are used by many banks and building societies, major supermarkets, information technology firms, food manufacturers, oil companies and central government departments. While much of the work involves 'full-blooded' applications, there are also situations in which an organization will use one or two assessment centre tools, or job simulation exercises as they are termed, perhaps a written analysis exercise and a role-play, which may or may not be linked. (A review of assessment centre work from the very early days on is given by Bray (1985). For more recent expositions see Lee and Beard (1994), Ballantyne and Povah (2004) and Woodruffe (2000). For a long-term follow-up study of Civil Service work see Anstey (1977).)

STANDARD SETTING

There is something of a continuum of standardization, with assessment centres increasingly being subject to similar levels of discipline to those of psychometric tests in their development and use. Another sign of this has been ongoing concern about aspects of discrimination in assessment centre applications, as shown in a review by Scott and Kwiatkowski (1998). However, with interviews standardized practices are far less common than with other methods, although they can in fact quite readily be subject to comparable degrees of rigour, as will be discussed in Chapters 11 and 12.

PERFORMANCE MANAGEMENT

A number of threads can be traced in the origins of performance management, not least because of the breadth of what it encompasses. A few of them will be mentioned here.

Some of the earliest attempts to achieve closer coupling between business requirements and what and how tasks and roles are performed were those of Taylor and his contemporaries. They applied so-called 'scientific' work practices, examining in minute detail just how jobs were performed, capturing the activities of the most skilled (in anticipation of the later subject matter experts – SMEs – discussed at several points in this book) as well as making practical improvements to the execution of tasks including redesigning the physical tools used. (In one of his classically reported studies a manual worker shifted 47 tons of pig-iron daily; the average figure for his co-workers previously had been 12 tons.) Although often maligned as the stimulus for a variety of repressive management practices, the movement started by Taylor – 'Taylorism' as it came to be known – can be seen as one of the elements leading to a number of other movements and practices, from quality management to business process re-engineering.

It was, in fact, an effort to understand what was systematic in behaviour and to codify, classify and measure it arising from Taylor's work that was also one of the strands in the development of assessment methods. One example was the work of W D Scott, whose scale of comparative performance was used to rate US army officers.

In the fast business expansion of the 1950s in the United States there was great enthusiasm for elaborate and multi-purpose 'merit-rating' systems, which can be seen as stimulated by Scott's earlier work. These systems, and their UK performance appraisal equivalents, were complex to run. They were typically conducted on an annual basis and often used as a major determinant for pay awards. At their core was a series of ratings against a number of factors.

However, in the early days these factors appeared often to have been established on a somewhat arbitrary basis by the organizations using them. There was also little research on feedback or follow-up and appraisers were, in fact, often reluctant actually to make the negative ratings that could lead to a range of difficulties in their dealings with their subordinates. Very often the appraisal system was perceived as little more than a ritual, rather than something closely integrated with and essential to the running of a business.

The potential for complexity in the appraisal situation was demonstrated in an early study at General Electric that suggested that, when criticized, employees would either try to improve their performance, lower their levels of aspiration or react defensively. This research involved observation of appraisal interviews and found that employees would react defensively to 50 per cent of the criticism and would rarely be constructive during the interview. Owing to the lack of previous feedback employees usually viewed their performance as above average and in 80 per cent of cases viewed the manager's judgement as too low. Improvement in performance only came from the mutual setting of specific goals and in the case of those with low self-esteem performance would improve if criticisms were kept to a minimum. Praise was deemed as ineffective as it was often viewed as placatory before a barrage of criticism.

Some of the shortcomings of appraisal were crystallized by McGregor (1957). In a classic paper he pointed out the need to engage the subordinate in the process to switch the emphasis from the employees shortcomings to a broader understanding of capability. This would then give greater scope for a concerted approach to the management and development of the person concerned.

Among McGregor's other contributions to the emergent ideas around performance management was his distinction between 'Theory X' and 'Theory Y' approaches to management (McGregor, 1960). Under the former, subordinates were seen as essentially not wanting to work and as requiring close supervision, constraint and cajoling to do so. Under Theory Y, work is seen as potentially fulfilling and something that people want to do well. These ideas can be seen as anticipating the distinction between **transactional** and **transformational** leadership. In the former leadership is effected through processes of command and control, with rewards given for conformance and sanctions applied to transgressors. In the latter the leader consults widely with subordinates, seeking to bring about an alignment between their goals and objectives and those of him/herself and the organization represented.

By the 1970s performance appraisal was becoming accepted as good management practice in the UK. National economic development papers recommended it, and the Institute of Personnel Management (now CIPD) published advice on how to carry it out. However, many appraisal systems still failed to meet expectations and some were abandoned.

Many of the problems of appraisal appear to be related to issues of application as much as design. For example, SHL (1995) noted from a survey that 44 per cent of appraisers claimed to have received no appraisal training, although only 6 per cent of the organizations surveyed said that they provided no such training. Today the use of appraisals is certainly widespread, but there is also a recognition that they are sometimes treated as a 'Cinderella'. Another relatively early strand in performance management was management by objectives, defined by Humble (1972) as 'a dynamic system which seeks to integrate the company's need to clarify and achieve its profit and goals with the manager's need to contribute and develop himself'. Quite widely used at one time and laudable as such a system was seen to be, it was criticized among other things for its complexity and the mass of paperwork that it spawned. That it could sometimes generate confusion, albeit in an unexpected way, is illustrated in the example below, apparently a case of practice not living up to intention.

A CUSTOM MORE HONOURED IN THE BREACH?

It was an annual meeting of psychologists drawn from different divisions in a large UK government department, sometime around 1972. Presenting developments in his own area of responsibility the top psychologist in XYZ division intoned, 'And we have in the last year introduced management by objectives within our own team of psychologists.' Then, with a slight and seemingly placatory nod to the PQR team – minus on this occasion their leader – sitting in the second row, 'Of course, *now* Dr Blank has introduced the same in PQR division.' Dr Blank's number two leapt to his feet. 'Oh, no, he hasn't, or if he has it's the first we've heard of it,' he said. He turned to his divisional colleagues who nodded assent. After a pantomime-style exchange lasting several minutes the number two shrugged his shoulders and resumed his seat. The XYZ man continued his peroration. At the ensuing coffee-break he sought out the number two and, seizing him by the arm, hissed, 'Dr Blank *does* use management by objectives.'

Some of the elements in the overall performance management framework include the Management Charter Initiative (MCI), the competencies movement referred to earlier and 360 degree assessment, covered in Chapter 13. In the UK the Management Charter Initiative (MCI) has had a considerable influence on the promulgation and currency of competencies (or competences in their preferred spelling). It makes a distinction between these and underpinning knowledge and understanding. It sees performance standards, defined as the activities and outcomes that constitute good performance, as depending on both knowledge and understanding and personal competencies.

Today performance management appears well established and applied in a variety of commercial and public sector settings with guidance being given by a range of professional bodies for its use in their fields. For example, the National Association of Head Teachers produced its own guidelines for the practice of performance management some 14 years ago now (NAHT, 1991).

3

Testing explored

As we saw in the first chapter, actions arising from tests could be in a commercial setting supporting a selection or development decision. In educational settings tests are used to help determine actions in fields such as specific learning difficulties, and in counselling and career management they often help shape the direction of guidance being given. Tests are also among the tools used by clinical psychologists in diagnosing a range of abnormal conditions. In all cases the psychometric test serves to provide a method that can be applied in a systematic way by different practitioners. Of the various fields discussed in this book that of psychometric assessment or testing is clearly the most standardized. Psychometrics has been defined (Reber, 1995) as 'Pertaining to mental testing in any of its facets, including assessment of personality, evaluation of intelligence, determining aptitudes.' (The breadth of the definition is worth noting. I have come across a number of managers who seem to equate it solely with personality measurement and a similar number for whom it is identified with ability testing.)

Many of those considering the value of the standardization offered by testing (eg Green, 1981; Eysenck, 1957) have almost immediately emphasized some of the issues and difficulties involved. The principal issues will be examined further in the course of this and the next few chapters. A number of them apply also to assessment centres and structured interviews, discussed later.

Different forms of test

In essence, information is given by a psychometric test through providing those taking the test with the opportunity to respond to a series of items or events that relate directly or indirectly to a particular area of behaviour. The area can be a skill such as reasoning with numbers or an interpersonal behaviour such as a tendency to give support to other people.

Most common and familiar are those psychometric instruments that pose questions with alternative answers. The questions may involve propositions or statements as in the 16 Personality Factor Questionnaire, known as the 16PF (Cattell, Eber and Tatsuoka, 1970), and the OPQ (Occupational Personality Questionnaires) (Saville _et al_, 1984), or can be in a form such as identifying which of a number of diagrams fits a set of other diagrams, eg the Differential Aptitude Tests, abstract spatial relationships test. (The 16PF is now in its fifth edition, the 16PF5. The latest version of the OPQ at the time of writing is the OPQ 32, with 32 referring to the number of scales, ie equivalent to the 16 in the 16PF, rather than the edition.)

Although most of these tests do use questions as such, the more general term for what is presented is 'item'. This broader term encompasses statements to be agreed with or choices between pairs of self-descriptive statements.

In other tests the response required is in the form of an interpretation of pictures. In the well-known Ishihara Colour Blindness Test responses are in the form of recognition of hidden figures. Yet other tests may require responses using wooden blocks or other physical material to match patterns (eg Wechsler, 1955). Psychometric tests involving tasks such as tracking a moving target have long been used in the selection of civil and military aircrews. An early NIIP test for assessing driving ability developed a form of driving simulator. When the candidate driver crashed the vehicle a sandbag was dropped on one end of a pivoted plank. The other end of the plank was thereby forced up to strike the driving seat from below!

Tests have also been delivered using cine-film (see, for example, Ridgway, 1977) and, of course, today increasing numbers are computer driven, with items displayed on a screen. Although at the time of writing paper-and-pencil delivery is probably still the most common method it certainly does not represent the totality of delivery methods. (For further discussion of computer administration of tests see Chapter 16.)

Tests and non-tests

Thus tests vary in form and it is the systematic approach rather than the form itself that is key. Certain standards in the construction of a test are also necessary for it to be truly regarded as a proper psychometric instrument. Such standards are promulgated and supported by bodies such as the British Psychological Society (BPS) or American Psychological Association (APA) and essentially cover the research requirements necessary to set up a psychometric test. These include the development of an appropriate and systematic means of interpretation. Without such standardized methods tests are of little practical use. The BPS also publishes independent reviews of tests, which among other things provide comment on the tests in the light of the standards. It also sets standards for qualification in test use.

This subject of standards will be resumed in the following chapters. However, for now it should be noted that the evidence of such standards does not provide absolute guarantees. Regulation of test design and use has little of the force applied in other areas that impinge upon people, such as food and drugs. A number of tests widely used commercially have from time to time been questioned as to their fitness for use but without any clear responsibility for, and hence little chance of, remedial action. There is, too, still considerable soul-searching among psychologists and others professionally involved in testing as to what procedures and forms of use are proper and representative of best practice. For instance, Feltham (Feltham, Baron and Smith, 1994) claims that bad selection decisions should be more commonly attributed to inappropriate use of tests than to the tests themselves being inherently bad. Gatherings such as the annual Test User Conference in the UK continue to debate such matters. Casually produced sets of questions without appropriate research backing cannot be regarded as psychometric tests as such. However, the fact that in form of presentation what is printed in a magazine looks like a personality questionnaire supported by 20 years of research may well mislead the unwary, particularly when such instruments yield scores, as they often do.

Publication by a reputable publisher, although clearly not a defining characteristic of psychometrics, is one fairly reliable guide. It should be noted though that many effective and respectable testing procedures are also produced within commercial organizations or university departments. Bodies such as the Civil Service have operated with their own test batteries for many years. In all cases the typical pattern has included processes of research to test out the individual items and then gathering these together in a whole test.

Graphology – a persistent case

Of the procedures that should not be regarded as constituting psychometric testing, but which are often wrongly associated with it, graphology is the most common. It is defined as the analysis of the handwriting of an individual in order to infer personality traits and behavioural tendencies.

The means of interpretation used never seems to have been subjected to rigorous statistical treatment, certainly not in a way to accord with the design standards applied to the general body of psychometrics. Eysenck (1957) and Mackenzie Davey over 30 years later (1989), after reviewing research on handwriting analysis, cast doubt on the scientific nature of the approach. (The latter does report research showing it to be an effective guide to gender, but also reports the researcher concerned as being doubtful as to the value of this finding!)

Graphologists believe that idiosyncratic features of a person's handwriting serve as an expression of his or her personality. No standard form of expression is demanded; therefore the result is expressive of the individual. Methods of analysis vary with one broad distinction being between those approaches that concentrate on individual handwriting phenomena and those that look at a sample of handwriting as a whole. The individual handwriting signs that are used include the following: size of letters, slant, width, zones (top, middle and bottom), regularity of letter formation, margin, pressure, stroke, line of letters (upward, straight, downward), connections of letters, form of connection and word and line spacing.

A comprehensive review of the handwriting literature and a series of studies were conducted by Cox and Tapsell (1991). They began their report by pointing out some of the other aspects of handwriting and its significance that may provide further reasons for some of the popularity of the approach. This included the distinguishability of different individuals' handwriting and, clearly linked to that, the use of signatures as indications of identity. (Another associated idea is, perhaps, the popularity of celebrity autographs.) Their review of the literature suggested that the predictions of non-graphologists were at least as good as those of graphologists. They also noted that, when the subjects of the studies were asked to copy standard scripts, rather than writing entirely freely, they did less well. This suggested that graphologists used the content of what was written in addition to the handwriting as such, though they did point out that some researchers saw their research design as potentially leading to an unnatural handwriting style, thereby limiting the scope for validity to be demonstrated. Their own studies included evaluation of graphological assessments of criteria against those emerging from an assessment centre. Although their two graphologist 'judges' were in some measure of agreement between themselves, they did not accurately reproduce the assessment centre ratings. Whilst again pointing out potential limitations in their own experimental design they concluded, along with so many other objective researchers, that there is insufficient positive evidence to support the use of graphology for personnel assessment.

Why graphology has continued to be used at all is a matter for speculation. There is probably an element of 'it would be nice if it did work'. That it continues to command the attention of professional psychologist researchers probably reflects a 'grain of truth' argument. All manifestations of behaviour are linked to some extent. Handwriting patterns could be expected to reflect muscular tension, among other things. Muscular tension might well reflect a general anxiety level. However, the grain of truth fails to reveal itself in any adequate scientific demonstrations.

The British Psychological Society (BPS, 2003) in a short briefing on graphology did leave the door open for further research to prove wrong the studies conducted to date, but for the moment there seems little justification for the use of graphology.

PERSONALITY MEASUREMENT

Questionnaires

The measurement of personality has, as indicated in the last chapter, been a matter of active interest for many years. It has long been recognized that personality is of great importance in people's success in work, no less than in the approach they take to other aspects of their life. Personality measurement is very clearly part of the whole field of testing, but the way in which personality measures are labelled and described varies. The American Psychological Association in its technical recommendations (1954) suggested that the term 'questionnaire' rather than 'test' should be generally used in the title of personality measures. This applied particularly to measures requiring responses to a series of self-descriptive items such as 'I like to attend family gatherings... TRUE, IN BETWEEN, FALSE'.

The argument runs that such instruments do not test behaviour directly, but rather how the respondent chooses to describe his or her behaviour. It has also been argued (eg by Cronbach, 1966) that such question-naires or self-report inventories, as they are sometimes known, indicate typical behaviour. (One corollary to this view is that such behaviour is not very amenable to change.) There are no right or wrong answers as such and these measures are contrasted with ability tests, where there are right and wrong answers, and where the whole focus is upon how high a score can be achieved.

The wisdom of this argument can be questioned in the sense that there certainly are right and wrong personality mixes for certain jobs. However, for the moment it is worth noting that the usage of the term 'question-naire' in titles is common, but not universal, and the term 'test' is widely used in describing such instruments. For example, in Heather Birkett Cattell's excellent guide to _The 16PF: Personality in depth_ (1989), both usages appear on the same page! In this book, the general practice, then, will be to use the term 'questionnaire' in relation to titles and specific ref-erences to self-report personality instruments, but to continue to use the terms 'tests', 'testing' and 'psychometrics' more generally in discussing them.

Traits, types and factors

As just noted, personality measures look at characteristic ways in which individuals behave both on their own and in relation to the world about them. Sometimes these characteristics are referred to as 'traits'. The term 'factors' is also sometimes used, but this tends to be reserved for charac-teristics established by the statistical techniques known as 'factor analysis' (see 'Glossary and technical notes').

Very often such tests are of interest in occupational settings in terms of the behaviour of one person in relation to another or to a group of others. Scales such as 'wanted inclusion' in the FIRO-B (Schutz, 1978), group-ori-ented versus self-reliant in the 16PF5, and 'sociability' in the Gordon Personal Profile are examples. Insights can also be given into such occu-pationally relevant areas as 'conscientiousness' (16PF) or 'need for achievement' (Edwards Personal Preference Schedule – EPPS).

Taken as a whole, such instruments can clearly give clues to managers as to how a particular individual may be best supported or motivated. For example, a person showing a need to be controlled (FIRO-B) will not respond well by being given an entirely free hand.

Many personality questionnaires have been designed on the basis of a psychological theory of personality. For example, the Myers Briggs Type Indicator (MBTI) (see Myers _et al_, 1998) is based upon the theory of psy-chological types expounded by Jung. According to this theory, people's responses to the world, ie their personality, reflect among other things the way in which judgements are made, whether rational or emotional, and the way in which information is perceived. These 'mental functions' operate in conjunction with 'attitudes', which indicate whether energy is outwardly or inwardly directed and whether the outside world is 'judged', either logically or emotionally, or 'perceived', either by sensation or by intuition.

The Edwards Preference Schedule is based on the theory of needs developed by Murray (1938) and lists 15 different need areas, including the need for achievement, the need for autonomy or independence, and the need for affiliation or to be doing things with friends.

The various different theoretical starting points are based on very different views of personality. However, what is becoming increasingly claimed is that a small number of personality dimensions is sufficient to account for much of the variation in behaviour classified under the heading of personality. This number is usually five and the term 'big five' is often applied. Although the labels of the five dimensions vary, one set gaining some degree of agreement is extroversion, agreeableness, conscientiousness, neuroticism and intellect. This relatively simple list may provide a frame of reference for what can be a bewildering array of individual scales and dimensions (32 scales in the OPQ, 15 in the EPPS and 16 of course in the 16PF). However, the finer grain of the larger number of scales will often help important distinctions to be made when comparing and contrasting individuals. We return to this issue a little later on in considering the interpretation of tests.

Projective techniques

Not all personality assessment involves the use of self-report methods. Projective techniques are based on the idea that individuals' perception of the world about them is coloured by their own personality. That is, people project their personality upon the various stimuli that impinge upon them, making sense of the stimuli in at least a partially subjective way. At the level of common discourse, we have optimists characterized as those who see their glass as half-full and pessimists as those who see it as half-empty. The glass and the present amount of its contents are the same in each case, but the personality – optimistic or pessimistic – is projected upon it.

The idea of projection is rooted in the work of Freud and the other 19th-century psychoanalysts. It has given rise to a number of psychometric procedures, such as the Rorschach Test (1942). This is made up of a number of ink blots, to which the person responds by saying what they look like. Responses are scored for a range of attributes, including emotionality and imagination. Despite much research, the validity of this particular test has remained doubtful. Later variants that have stressed a more detailed analysis of the content of responses have appeared more promising (eg Holt, 1958). A detailed introduction is given by Klopfer and Davidson (1962).

Other approaches use pictures with ambiguous situations. For instance, some of these can be interpreted as threatening. Failure to recognize the threats is seen as evidence of a general tendency to cope with threatening situations by denial. Such tendencies can be seen as particularly counter-productive for occupations involving a high degree of risk, such as fast jet pilots or commodity brokers, where threats need to be recognized and accurately weighed up.

Some of the most extensive development with such ambiguous material has been that of Murray with the Thematic Apperception Test (1943). This consists of a series of cards on which the ambiguous pictures are presented. The person being tested is required to make up a story about each picture and the content of this is then subjected to a systematic analysis. This approach has since been developed into the various techniques for analysing motivation and other aspects through looking at the content of responses. A comprehensive handbook (Smith, 1992) lists a number of these. However, these techniques are rarely used in occupational or managerial practice. The interpretation of most projective techniques is highly skilled, with single instruments sometimes requiring months or years of study. They are, therefore, less likely to form part of the routine toolkit of management embarking on assessment than many of the other methods referred to in this book. They have, though, been used routinely in some occupations. The Royal Swedish Air Force, for example, has used the Defence Mechanism Test (DMT), which is based on the perception of risk.

ABILITY, APTITUDE AND ATTAINMENT

Job specific and less specific

The terms 'aptitude' and 'ability' are not always precisely separated. Many tests in these categories are used to look at behaviour, often of an intellectual or cognitive nature, with greater or lesser degrees of specificity. Thus there are tests of general intelligence, which can be regarded as mental horsepower or the general ability to process information, and more specialized tests of particular ability, eg verbal reasoning. The term 'aptitude' is usually reserved for those tests directed at predicting whether skill in a particular area can be acquired. Examples are the Computer Operator Aptitude Battery (COAB) and clerical aptitude batteries such as that in SHL's Personnel Test Battery.

The term 'ability tests' tends to be reserved for measures of less job-specific though often still job-related intellectual characteristics. Examples are the various critical reasoning tests, eg Watson–Glaser Critical Thinking Appraisal, number ability tests (eg GMA-N) and tests of abstract reasoning such as Raven's Progressive Matrices. Although the distinction between ability and aptitude is not always made fully in the description of tests, this whole group is broadly separated from the personality questionnaires by describing them as tests of maximum rather than typical performance.

A range of item formats found in ability tests is shown in Figures 3.1 to 3.3. Different types of problem or task are posed, tapping into different abilities and at different levels of difficulty. Simple items of the type shown in Figure 3.1 might be used in tests for shopfloor selection. Figure 3.2 shows items typical of those used in clerical recruitment. Items requiring extraction of data from complex numerical and verbal material, as illustrated in Figure 3.3, would form reasoning tests such as are used in graduate and managerial selection and development.

Although many tests do focus on particular characteristic abilities there is interest in the issue of how intelligence in general is constituted. Work by Carroll (1980), for instance, has endeavoured to look at how separate intellectual abilities can best be described by examining in detail the types of intellectual task imposed in different types of test. As indicated in Chapter 2, such issues have in fact been an ongoing concern of psychometrics since the early days and have been discussed more recently. (See, for example, Irvine, Dann and Anderson, 1990.)

Attainment tests

Often referred to as achievement tests, these are somewhat more commonly used in relation to educational assessment than in occupational settings. They represent standard ways of assessing the amount of skill currently reached or attained in a particular area. For example, the Foundation Skills Assessment (FSA), which was published by the Psychological Corporation (1988), is designed to measure attainment in numeracy and literacy skills in adults. This battery of four tests is organized at three levels of difficulty for each and with a short initial screening test. The latter means that the appropriate level of difficulty can be chosen for detailed investigation and so the actual level of attainment assessed with some precision.

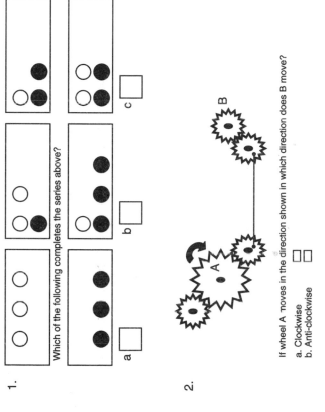

Figure 3.1   Test items in abstract and spatial format

1. ABCDXFGHJ

   ABCDEFGHI ☐
   ABCDEPQRS ☐
   ABECXFGHJ ☐
   ABCDXFGHJ ☐
   ABHDXFGJH ☐

   Tick the series on the right which corresponds exactly to the one on the left

2. John prefers tea to coffee and likes coffee less than mineral water. If offered a choice
   between mineral water and tea, which would he be most likely to choose?

   a ☐   b ☐   c ☐
   Tea   Mineral Water   Can't say

3. Choose the number from the right to complete the series on the left.

   1 5 17 53   161   112   98

Figure 3.2 Simple checking and reasoning items

In the centrally planned state of Rurigaria farmers are given subsidies by the Agriculture Ministry to grow certain crops. If they achieve production quotas they also receive a production bonus. Subsidies and quota levels vary by size of farm and crop grown. The Table shows the amount of money paid out in a four year period. The national unit of currency is the zinka.

Year		Under 200 hectares				200 –1,000 hectares				Over 1,000 hectares			
		1	2	3	4	1	2	3	4	1	2	3	4
Grapes	Subsidy	155	165	360	360	1,000	1,000	1,500	1,600	20	30	10	40
	Bonus	10	25	33	40	10	200	150	200	10	80	90	100
Brassicas	Subsidy	50	60	60	60	45	0	35	0	80	80	80	80
	Bonus	70	30	30	50	30	20	100	110	45	80	70	75
Corn	Subsidy	50	50	0	0	400	600	800	700	50	170	180	200
	Bonus	200	200	70	0	800	1,000	1,200	1,500	300	400	450	600

Notes: 1. All figures in 000,000 zinka
2. Grapes vines planted in Rurigaria take four years to become productive
3. Brassicas and corn can be harvested the year of planting

Answer the following:

	Definitely True	Probably True	Can't Say	Probably False	Definitely False
1. Some farmers grew grapes before the start of the four year plan.	☐	☐	☐	☐	☐
2. There are few large farms	☐	☐	☐	☐	☐
3. The largest amount paid out to was in year 3.	☐	☐	☐	☐	☐

Figure 3.3   Complex reasoning item

In the past many occupational applications of attainment tests have been in relation to blue-collar jobs, for instance to see if remedial educational training was required during initial periods of apprenticeship. However, recently comparable needs have arisen in some other fields. These are not yet evidently addressed by what could be called psychometric methods as such but are, nevertheless, worth noting. The Life Assurance and Unit Trust Regulatory Organisation (LAUTRO) required certain knowledge in those representing financial organizations and gave guidance on how this might be assessed. Some life insurance companies have developed procedures for identifying such knowledge, ie how much of it has been achieved to date, in candidates, taking them through procedures that may be regarded as capable of further formal psychometric development.

Public examinations such as GCSE are also tests of attainment, measuring a combination of knowledge and abilities in manipulating and interpreting knowledge. They are standardized, but not developed according to psychometric criteria as such.

Adaptive testing

The selection of progressive levels of difficulty, as described above in connection with the FSA, is fundamental to adaptive testing. By using computers to score responses instantly, performance levels on tests can be monitored and difficulty levels adjusted. In this way the maximum level of performance can be more finely and more quickly ascertained than with a fixed set of items. After a slow start such tests are being regarded with increasing interest. Variants of the approach, giving detailed feedback on performance, have also been used in individual development.

One of the boosts to this approach in relatively recent years has been 'item response theory', IRT (Cooper, 2002, and see 'Glossary and technical notes'). When this is applied to adaptive testing – often referred to as 'tailored testing' in this context – the adjustment of difficulty levels is made on the basis of responses to individual test items rather than total test scores.

Trainability tests

Trainability tests are designed for use in those situations in which there is a definite and distinct course of training to be undertaken before a job can be executed. They, therefore, constitute one type of aptitude test and tend to have very specific applications. Many of them have been developed in relation to roles in which motor, that is physical, coordination is one requirement. A survey conducted in 1988 in the UK (Bevan and Fryatt, 1988) suggested that, although the bulk of the use of trainability tests lay in manual occupations, there were some applications in managerial fields.

Such tests began to be developed in the 1970s in relation to roles as wide apart as dentists, operators of heavy equipment in forestry and ship-building apprentices. (See, for example, Downs, 1973, and Smith and Downs, 1975.) They have, perhaps, become separated from other forms of aptitude test because of their very close identification with very specific roles, even down to an individual factory, say, employing unique machine configurations. However, it is arguable that an instrument such as a computer programming battery with subtests such as comprehension of flow charts could be viewed in the same way. Thus, effective comprehension would be regarded as an indication of scope to master training involving flow diagrams.

Some trainability tests may also be seen as related to trade tests – measures of attainment – directly simulating samples of work. Examples include tests of stenography such as that produced by Seashore and Bennett as far back as 1948, and more currently the Typing Test For Business (Doppelt, Hartman and Krawchik, 1984), which sets copy-typing tasks.

INTEREST INVENTORIES

A number of psychometric test procedures have been developed specifically for aiding career guidance and career management planning although, in fact, a wide range of tests including personality and ability measures may be relevant. Of the specific tests some look at preferences for particular types of activity and then develop scales that relate these back to occupational groupings. Sometimes their results will suggest occupational areas not previously considered by the person taking the test. In other cases they may help rule out a type of occupation. I can recall a case of a redundant employee in a high-tech company, referred for counselling. The man expressed an interest in farming as a new career. Farming did not, however, feature very highly on the list of likely occupations as revealed by his responses to an occupational interest inventory. Closer examination showed that he had a marked dislike of getting up early in the morning!

With tests cast in a purely abstract format, such as those illustrated in Figure 3.1, the items have no particular topicality. Other tests can, though, have items that relate to everyday life. For example, numerical reasoning tests will often present items in the form of financial figures. Such items are, of course, likely to become dated from time to time.

In the case of occupational interest inventories the issue of obsolescence of items is, though, compounded by the changing nature of occupations. This can happen both in a growth sense, as certain industries decline and others are born, and also in relation to shorter-term cyclical patterns, which will clearly affect the availability of employment in different areas. Thus particular care is required in using such tests for guidance. Test publishers do take trouble to update the inventories themselves and the way in which they are interpreted occupationally. For example, the Strong Inventory, originally published over 60 years ago (see Strong, 1943), has been much updated over the years with the latest edition supported by descriptions of over 100 current occupations.

In practice, occupational interest inventories are often used for careers guidance purposes alongside ability and responsibility measures. The resultant set of instruments may be put together in a uniform battery (eg Armes and Greenaway, 1998). Alternatively, specific groupings of instruments may be used ad hoc, as for example when the feasibility of a career in finance, expressed via an interest inventory, is partly checked out by the use of a numerical reasoning test.

MOTIVATION

There are also a number of tests of motivation. For example, the Motivational Styles Questionnaire (MSQ) (Tarleton, 1997) looks at what an individual wants out of a work situation and how he or she will seek to deal with everyday tasks. The latter include the balance between an operational task focus and seeing the task in terms of personal success. In fact, many test publishers include motivational tests in their listings, and the BPS guide to personality tests (BPS, 2001) has a section on this too. There are, however, a number of potential problems with motivation and, like many other things, it is something about which experts disagree. This is rather vividly illustrated in Reber's (1995) *Dictionary of Psychology* where it is described as an 'extremely important but definitionally elusive term'. This is followed by one of the longest entries in the dictionary, but including a useful reference to it as a general or a specific energizer.

There is debate over the importance of transitory motivators, sometimes indistinguishable from states or moods and those that are enduring or characteristic in the sense of that which can readily be aroused, ie that which can readily provide a specific energizer. For example, a golf enthusiast may find a cocktail party boring, with little beyond polite conventions to keep him involved in small talk. In other words, his motivation for the event is low and he may be thinking of leaving. Finding a fellow enthusiast for the game with the little white ball, however, he happily and energetically engages in discussion, possibly outstaying his welcome at the social occasion.

The idea of the enduring nature here is what has led some (eg Cooper, 2002) to question whether what is really being assessed is, after all, personality. The distinction between motivation and personality seems to become even less if one thinks of those motivations that seem ever present in some people, eg curiosity or need for achievement. The fact that some personality measures have scales labelled in terms like these (eg 'variety' and 'achievement' in the OPQ) is in line with this. Some writers (eg Clifton and Nelson, 1992) have suggested that many personal characteristics – 'themes' in their terminology – are motivational in the sense that exercising them produces positive feelings and denial of the scope to do so produces the opposite.

My own practice has been to take these distinctions on board in assessment, but often to present findings on motivation – drawn from whatever source – somewhat separately. For example, in connection with potential succession in management buyouts and other major changes backed by private equity houses (see also Chapter 17), I have found it helpful to comment on the potential successors' motivations for the top job when the lead person exits with his or her money in two years' time.

EDUCATIONAL TESTING

Some test use in the educational field is essentially occupational in nature, as when tests are used in connection with the employment of teachers or school heads (see, for example, Abrams, Edenborough and Harley, 1998). However, the term 'educational testing' is more commonly used to describe assessments of children and teenagers in connection with the educational process. (It may be remembered from Chapter 2 that the 19th-century origins of psychometric testing lay in education.) There are also some links with the occupational field, as when tests of educational attainment are used in connection with entry or streaming in apprentice programmes or those associated with basic training for other ranks in the military. However, for the most part edcational testing, though a large and important field in its own right, is outside the scope of this book.

CLINICAL TESTING AND ITS RELATION TO PERFORMANCE

Some of the relatively early developments in clinical testing included instruments aimed at assessing aspects of mental impairment such as might arise from brain damage. One such was the Bender Visual Motor Gestalt Test (1938). Errors made in copying abstract designs formed the basis of assessment. In addition to modern equivalents of such instruments, clinical psychologists today make use of psychometric tests aimed at specific conditions. As with educational testing this important field is largely outside the scope of this book. However, there are some overlaps with the occupational field that are worth considering. A number of personality measures have their origins in clinical testing and seek to relate clinical dimensions to behaviours in the non-clinical world. One general result of this is the presence of anxiety, emotional stability or stress-tolerance scales in standard personality measures, such as the 16PF in its various forms, the OPQ and Gordon's Personal Profile and Inventory.

A typical application of these concepts occupationally is to consider if there is an appropriate match between a candidate's capacity to handle stress and the amount of stress offering in a particular job or role. Although the link is not always made, a useful concept here is the Yerkes–Dodson law according to which an initially benign and positive relationship between stress and performance is followed by a performance plateau as stress increases and then by a performance collapse. The particular course of the relationship between the stressor and the performance graph will vary from person to person and with the particular stressor or combinations of stressors being applied.

There is another overlap between clinical and occupational testing in the increasingly recognized field of post-traumatic stress. Stemming from the realization that those who come across stressful events in the course of their work may need some support has been the development of various measures of the effects of stress. One such is the Measures in Post Traumatic Stress Disorder (PTSD) (Turner and Lee, 1998). Such instruments are used as aids to diagnosis and hence as precursors to treatment or management of the condition. Additionally, output from some measures, such as the PTSD one, may provide evidence in support of litigation.

A SPECIAL CASE: INTEGRITY TESTING

An area that has provoked increased interest in recent years, though still not attaining to a major movement in the UK, is that of integrity testing. It has long been practised in one form or another in the United States. (The difference in practice between the two sides of the Atlantic was sufficiently marked that, when asked to undertake some revisions to a US book on testing for the UK market (Jones, 1994), my main contribution was to reduce the amount of integrity testing material included. My grounds were that this was not a characteristic part of the British testing scene.) However, assessments of honesty, integrity and dependability are of interest to organizations because workplace dishonesty including theft, fraud and embezzlement is on the up and so they are explored in outline below.

At the time of writing (summer 2004) there is increased interest in the so-called lie detector tests in the UK in connection with monitoring known paedophiles. Very controversial in the United States where their extensive use originated, they are often referred to as 'polygraph tests'. They are based on the so-called Galvanic Skin Reflex (GSR) measuring the electrical conductivity of the skin's surface. It is claimed that when someone tells a lie there is an increase in sweating, increasing the conductivity of the skin and it is this that is measured.

There are essentially two types of integrity tests, overt and covert. Overt assess attitudes and past 'integrity' behaviours directly. Covert tests assess specific personality traits of respondents thought to relate to 'integrity' (typically conscientiousness). Integrity, unlike other aspects of personality, does not appear to be stable over time or contexts. Situational influences interact with individual predispositions to determine a degree of honesty. Thus integrity in the workplace is not just a selection issue.

Sackett and Harris (1984) found two contrasting viewpoints for and against integrity testing in a review of relevant research. Against integrity testing they noted that any studies that made comparisons with polygraph judgements should be dismissed as it is a criterion that is questioned in the scientific community and so cannot serve as meaningful evaluation for new instruments. They also noted that studies relying on admissions of past behaviour are flawed, as correlations in such studies are inflated by social desirability, which both inhibits admissions and heightens honesty scores. Thus past behaviour may predict future behaviour with regard to integrity, but the relationship is questionable. They also commented that mean test score differences between convicts and applicants are not persuasive evidence of validity or of resistance to faking: differences may be the result of the demand characteristics of the two situations.

They also noted that, while true predictive studies are the most persuasive, most studies to date are flawed by the fact that only a very small number of, for example, thieves have been caught.

Points in favour of integrity testing have included consistency of positive findings across tests and across validation strategies.

A number of ethical concerns have also been raised in connection with integrity tests. One is that they are seen as an invasion of privacy. Also, depending on which test cut-off is used, between 25 and 75 per cent of people will fail the test, but owing to less than perfect validity innocent people will be wrongly denied jobs. On the other hand it can be argued that the test is only unethical if it is invalid, as it is fair enough for an employer to want honest employees.

Also, selection procedures with modest validities (see Chapter 4) are the best that we have been able to create so far, so errors are made with any test.

HOW PSYCHOMETRIC TESTS ARE USED IN SELECTION TODAY

In selection, tests are commonly used as part of a chain of activity, but their positioning in the chain may vary substantially. At one extreme is their use as an early-stage screening process in procedures such as apprentice or graduate recruitment. The idea is to pass on those with a relatively high chance of success for further examination. At the other extreme is their use at much later stages. For example, executive recruitment firms will often suggest psychometric procedures be applied to shortlist candidates to extend information already available on them. This might be particularly to see how the candidates would fit in with other members of the team or to explore particular issues of concern, or particular characteristics such as 'thinking outside the box' not very readily assessed by the other procedures applied. Results of tests may also be used at this stage to inform the explorations made by a final appointing panel.

Test results may also be applied within an organization in ways comparable to those used in external recruitment. The results of tests used in these circumstances will be seen as part of the information to aid management in making a decision as to the suitability of an internal appointee and may be seen particularly as contributing visibly to the objectivity of the process.

INTRODUCTION TO PRACTICAL ISSUES IN CONTROL AND INTERPRETATION

Copyright to driving tests

As indicated at the beginning of this chapter, the control of psychometric use has tended to increase over the years. In the UK test publishers have progressively been tightening their standards on distribution, for instance. There has been a series of successful prosecutions under breaches of copyright law and the BPS has continued to develop standards for competency in test use.

As with many areas of professional usage and practice, however, the issue of decay of skills and keeping up to date with new developments has scarcely begun to be addressed. Thus we have the driving test phenomenon, whereby someone initially and effectively trained may not in fact practise interpretation or administration very frequently, and may not have his or her ongoing ability to perform at defined skill levels checked. In general, though, the professional position is tighter than it used to be and it seems not too optimistic to suppose that abuses will be progressively eradicated as the understanding of tests increases.

Own specialists or consultants?

Organizations embarking on a programme of psychometric application will need to decide whether to spend time and money on having their own people trained in psychometrics or, alternatively, to use the services of a qualified consultant. The latter are listed in the appropriate registers such as those held by the BPS (eg the Register of Competence in Occupational Testing) and will give firms access to a wide range of instruments.

Even for those organizations having their own staff trained, there is a question of explanation of test results to others in the organization who may well have a legitimate interest in them but will not have undergone training in test use. There are guidelines for this, such as those issued by the Institute of Personnel Management (IPM, 1993) and its successor organization, the Chartered Institute of Personnel and Development (CIPD, 1997). These matters are addressed further in later chapters.

SUMMARY

1. Psychometric tests are mental measurement devices.

2. They consist of series of questions or items to which people respond.

3. Proper tests are well researched and standardized, so that they can be interpreted on a consistent basis.

4. Graphology, the study of handwriting, does not accord with psychometric standards.

5. Occupational uses of tests include selection, development, vocational guidance, career management and identification of suitability for training.

6. Tests are also used by professionals working in clinical and educational fields.

4

Statistics and standards in psychometrics I

INTRODUCTION

Many of those using psychometrics, occupational and other psychologists among them, bemoan the fact that they have to get to grips with a certain amount of statistics. Yet without having some statistical principles and, though arguably less importantly, a few statistical methods under one's belt, the standards and objectivity underpinning the use of psychometrics can scarcely be applied. The same is true of assessment centres and structured interviews although statistical approaches are somewhat less commonly applied in those two fields. (For those who do undertake, but may struggle with, some computations themselves it may or may not give comfort to reflect on the fact that early statistical work was inevitably conducted without the benefit of calculators, let alone computers.)

The concepts of validity and reliability presented here underlie what are some of the essentials of psychometrics; the ideas about norms are key to test interpretation while regulation covered in the following chapter is about using best practice. Finally in the section on test construction there is a brief foray into the design methods that themselves reflect the other ideas addressed in this part of the book.

VALIDITY AND RELIABILITY

Much of what has been said in Chapter 3 in relation to what is and what is not a test can be illustrated further through the exploration of test validity and reliability. Validity refers to whether a test measures what it is supposed to measure. Reliability refers to whether the measurement provided is consistent. Within these simple propositions, though, are a host of complications and traps for the unwary. Detailed requirements for test validity and associated matters are given in professional publications such as those issued by the American Psychological Association (1954). Some of these issues will be returned to in greater detail at specific points in the forthcoming chapters. For the moment the main types of validity will be addressed and explained briefly. Referring to Figure 4.1 may help the reader in understanding these important ideas.

Predictive validity

Very often tests are used to help determine suitability for a particular role. Thus, inherent in their use is the idea of predicting behaviour and hence performance in the future. The predictive validity of a test is the extent to which it predicts future behaviour. To establish predictive validity requires scope for effective, controlled research over a period of time. This in turn implies fairly large numbers in the research samples, and some stability of roles and performance measures. Regrettably, performance criteria are often wholly or partly undefined, subject to change over time and/or not supported by complete records. These issues were a fairly early concern (eg Stott, 1950), but they do not go away. In practice, predictive validity studies tend only to be conducted by or with the cooperation of very large and relatively stable employers. Another difficulty is the question of how predictive a test needs to be for it to be effective. This question will be returned to in Chapters 7 and 8. For the moment it may be worth noting that even low levels of predictive validity can be useful in cases where the numbers to be selected are very small in relation to those being tested.

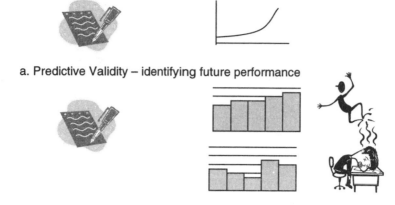

a. Predictive Validity – identifying future performance

b. Concurrent Validity – distinguishing higher and lower performers

c. Content Validity – reflecting relevant material in the test

d. Face Validity – appearing credible

Numerical
Reasoning

e. Construct Validity – measuring what it is supposed to measure

Figure 4.1   The different types of validity

Concurrent validity

Given the difficulties of establishing predictive validity effectively, organizations more often undertake validation in the here and now. If a group of individuals established as high performers on a job are found to produce high scores on a test, with the low job performers producing correspondingly low test scores, effective concurrent validity has been established. Thus, concurrent validity is the extent to which a test score differentiates individuals in relation to a criterion or standard of performance external to the test. As with predictive validity, the criterion itself has to be established. However, what is required minimally is agreement on who should fit into which of two fairly extreme groups. This is less demanding than considering what a person's score should be on some criterion measure as would ideally be the case with predictive validity. Nor is concurrent validity itself affected by minor changes in criteria of performance over time. (However, if these criteria change markedly, concurrent validity will have to be re-established in the changed circumstances.)

Content validity

This form of validity indicates the way in which what is in the test directly represents aspects of a role or job. This again seems straightforward on the surface. However, in the field of personality assessment the items cannot be over-transparent if, for example, the respondent is not to be able simply to project a socially desirable image. Hence the content validity of such items may be hard to establish.

Credibility and acceptance – face validity

Some of the controversies picked up from time to time in the press have focused on particular items from personality questionnaires that appear to be fanciful. Concern of this sort is concern for face validity, a particular aspect of content validity. If those responding to items find them bizarre they may fail to treat the whole process seriously. Whether this happens or not will depend in some measure not only on the item itself but also the manner and setting in which the whole testing process is conducted. Thus good administration may well enhance face validity.

By the same token, of course, an unprofessional demeanour on the part of those delivering the test will detract from the face validity of the whole process, regardless of the particular items. Lack of face validity from whatever source, leading to a casual or overly cynical approach on the part of those undertaking the procedure, can clearly have a negative impact on other forms of validity. However, as with these other forms of validity, face validity cannot just be assumed and nor can its absence. I have seen old NIIP tests with items depicting women in Victorian crinoline dresses being used with complete acceptance for the selection of railway clerks in a developing country.

Construct validity

Construct validity is the extent to which a test measures a particular construct or characteristic. While predictive validity is concerned with the test in relation to an external criterion of performance, construct validity is, in effect, concerned with looking at the test itself. If a test is intended to measure, say, numerical reasoning, can evidence be found that suggests it is this that is being measured – is the construct of numerical reasoning as covered by the test valid? Such evidence might come from a number of sources.

One aspect of construct validity is the way in which the different test items in effect hang together. It should be possible to show that items do fit in with one or other particular construct. For example, if a test has 20 items relating to the scale extroversion versus introversion, people endorsing an extroverted response on any one item should tend to endorse responses in the same direction on other items.

Establishing construct validity will often involve quite extensive studies, typically cross-referring to other tests. Staying with extroversion for the moment, part of establishing the construct validity of a new test of that characteristic would be to compare scores of individuals on that new test with their scores on one or more existing and well-established tests of extroversion.

INTERPRETING TEST RESULTS

The idea of norms

Very often a test result is interpreted for an individual in terms of how that individual stands relative to the scores achieved by a group on whom that test was standardized – the so-called norm group. The group may be identified as a large part of the population, eg UK adult males, or could be a subgroup of particular interest, eg sales managers in high-technology companies or direct-entry graduates. In either case the comparison yields a numerical score. The most common way in which this is expressed is as a percentile. For example, to say that someone is at the 80th percentile means that he or she produced a score in excess of that produced by 80 per cent of the comparison group and that 20 per cent of the comparison group scored higher. Thus, the higher the percentile the higher the standing on the test concerned.

Such comparisons are very commonly made in the case of ability tests, and norms are available for many personality questionnaires too. These latter are typically made up of a number of dimensions or scales and so the norm tables give relevant figures for each scale. Again, these norms may relate to general population groups or be developed for particular categories, such as managers. For example, Bartram (1992) produced norms for the 16PF (version 4) for shortlisted managerial candidates. They provide a common way of thinking about relative scores among individuals on a single test and a language for relating scores of one individual from one test to another. On their own, though, they do not say very much. Even a percentile comparison related to a specific occupational group, eg sales managers, again does not give a very direct indication of the likely effectiveness of the managerial candidate concerned. What it does tell us is, first, simply that person's standing vis-à-vis others in a similar occupational group, eg in the top 10 per cent or bottom 10 per cent. Second, provided the test has been shown to have some predictive or concurrent validity, it indicates that the higher the score the higher the relative chance of effective performance against the criterion of success used in the validation.

The normal curve

A number of other fundamental statistical ideas need to be introduced to help understand comparisons among test scores further. One of these is the normal curve. This curve (see Figure 4.2) describes the relationship between a set of observations or measures and their frequency of occurrence. Observations could be height, weight or, as in the case of interest here, scores on psychometric tests. The very wide range of application of the curve in relation to the study of people was originally explored by the 19th-century scientist Francis Galton. Interpreted simply and obviously it indicates that, on many things one might care to measure, a few people will produce extremely high scores, a few extremely low and there will be a large bulk in the middle.

In Figure 4.3 percentiles have been plotted in relation to the normal curve. The 50th percentile point lies at the middle of the normal distribution so that half the area under the curve lies to the left and half to the right of that point. (See 'Glossary and technical notes' for further discussion of the normal curve.)

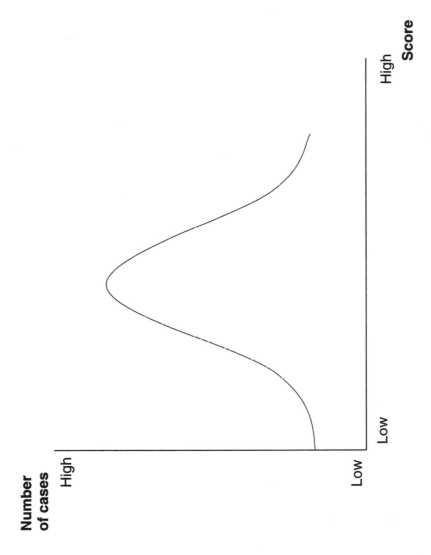

Figure 4.2 The normal curve

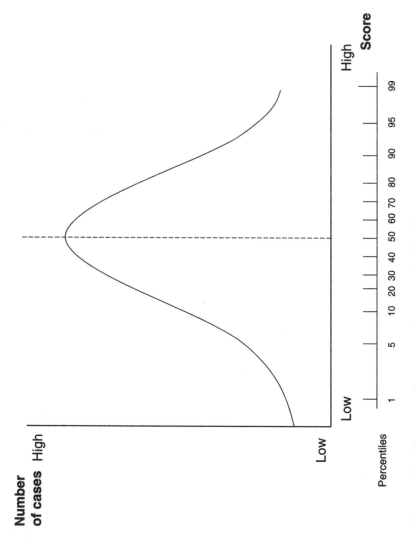

Figure 4.3 The normal curve and percentile distribution

The importance of variability

Test results are also very often interpreted in terms of units that are related to the variability found within the scores of the norm group. Let us say that on a 40-item reasoning test two different individuals got 28 and 32 right respectively – we say these were their raw scores. Let us also suppose that the mean or average score for a large number of individuals was 30. In order to make sense of this four-point difference we would need to know how widely the scores varied in our normative group. Although the general bell shape of the normal curve should apply, it could be relatively flat as in Figure 4.4 or relatively steep as in Figure 4.5. In Figure 4.4 there is much more variability among the scores in general, so a four-point difference would be less indicative of a real difference in effective performance than in the case represented in Figure 4.5. There, with tight clustering of scores, a four-point difference is much more meaningful. A far larger number of individuals would lie between 28 and 32 in this second case, so that the score difference would represent a greater difference in percentile terms.

Thus, just knowing that the scores were respectively two points above and two points below the mean does not tell us what we learn by taking variability into account. A test score recalibrated in terms of variability is called a derived score and such scores ease the making of comparisons among different results.

A range of derived scores

The basic measure of variability used is the standard deviation (for a more detailed explanation see 'Glossary and technical notes'). Standard scores indicate how far a person's score is from the mean score expressed in standard deviation units. These are sometimes known as z scores. Thus +1z is one standard deviation above the mean and −1z is one standard deviation below the mean, and the mean itself is represented by zero. These can be related to percentiles. Thus a score of one standard deviation unit, one z unit, above the mean equates approximately to the 84th percentile.

Unfortunately for the practically minded, rather than the merely curious, test user, a number of other derived scores, all based on means and standard deviations, have arisen over the years. The most common of these are stanines and stens. All of these derived scores can be related back to the normal curve as shown in Figure 4.6.

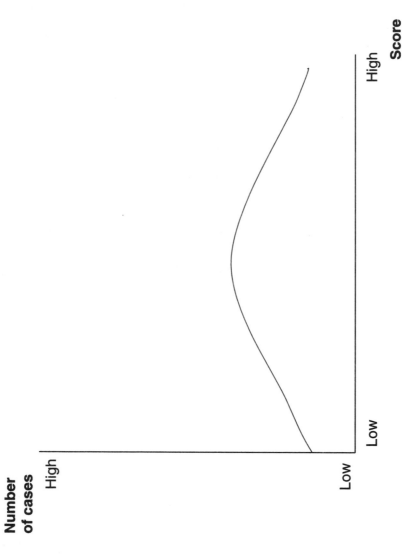

Figure 4.4   Flattened normal curve – scores spread

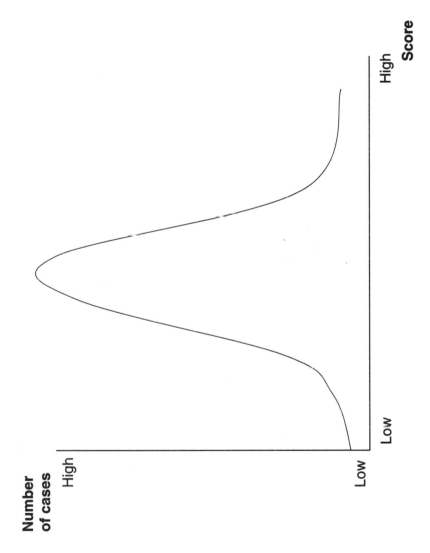

Figure 4.5 Steep normal curve – scores clustered

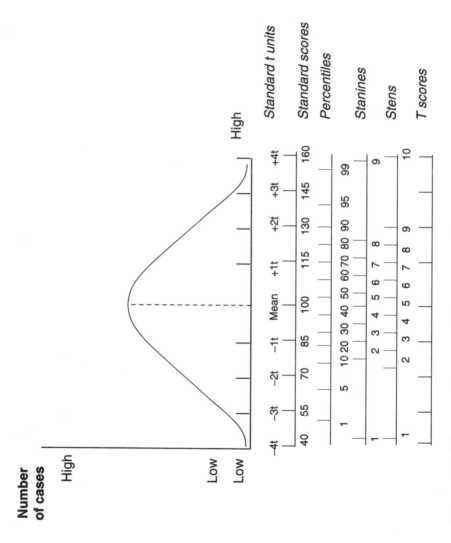

Figure 4.6 The normal curve and derivative scales

The following box summarizes the various derived scores.

▌ z scores express scores in standard deviation units.

▌ Standard scores with a mean of 100 and 15 points are used sometimes, particularly in intelligence tests.

▌ Stanine is a contraction of 'standard nine'. It has nine points, uses a mean of 5 and assigns one point to each half standard deviation unit.

▌ 'Stens', now more commonly used than stanines, have a mean of 5.5 and similarly assign one point to each half standard deviation unit. The term means 'standard ten' and the scale has 10 points.

▌ T scores have a mean of 50 and assign 10 points to each full standard deviation unit.

Percentiles may be more readily comprehensible to the layperson than scores based on standard deviations. However, they only show relative standing amongst different individuals and not the amount of the differences.

Skewed distributions

As well as being relatively flat (Figure 4.4) or relatively steep (Figure 4.5), in practice the distribution curve may be distorted or skewed to the left or right. Figure 4.7 shows a case of what is known as negative skew. There are lots of high scores and few low ones. The test is relatively easy and might fail to give useful differentiation among those taking it. This could occur with a test, say, of spatial reasoning ability, developed and normed with a general population sample but applied to a group of astronaut candidates. If the group had been pre-screened on ability to pilot an aircraft the remaining candidates might well all perform near the top end of the test, limiting its value as an effectively discriminating aid to selection.

The opposite situation, positive skew, is shown in Figure 4.8. Here the test scores are crowded towards the bottom end – most of those taking the test found it too difficult. These particular terms often give rise to confusion, not least amongst those who are quite regular and long-standing users of tests. They are repeated here as they are part of the currency of discourse on test use. Personally I have made a point of avoiding them in reporting test results, especially to those with no psychometric training

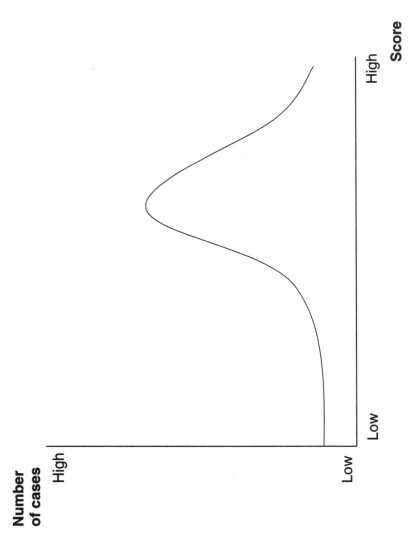

Figure 4.7 Negative skew

themselves, for whom they may seem counter-intuitive. Another way to describe skewed findings is in terms of 'floor' and 'ceiling' effects. The distribution shown in Figure 4.7 does not have enough 'ceiling' while for that in Figure 4.8 the 'floor' can be seen as too high.

Interpreting multiple scores

For those aptitude and ability tests arranged in batteries, eg the Computer Programmer Aptitude Battery (CPAB), interpretation will involve reference to norms for each of the constituent tests. Interpreting the resultant patterns of scores may include considering how far a particular weakness can be compensated for by a particular strength.

Multiple scores can also be obtained from individual ability tests divided into subtests. One example is the Watson–Glaser Critical Thinking Appraisal (1991), which is made up of five separate subtests posing different types of complex verbal reasoning tasks. Here, however, the usual guidance is to concentrate on overall rather than subtest scores. There are two reasons for this. First, there may be insufficient information in the relatively small number of items in the subtest to give a reliable, that is repeatable, score indication. Second, with those tests that are timed – as many are – some people will just not get as far as the later subtests. Guidance on whether or not subtest scores should be used is typically given in test manuals.

Scoring personality questionnaires

As indicated already, multiple scores also arise in relation to the various scales of personality questionnaires. Very often, items on such questionnaires are arranged so that choices are made among alternative statements. Of a pair of such alternatives one will favour one scale and the other a second. Such arrangements mean that the scales are, of course, not independent. This method of combining items leads to what is called ipsative scaling. This is contrasted with the so-called normative scaling, in which strength of agreement to each item is rated separately (see Figure 4.9).

It is commonly said of ipsative measures that interpretation should be based on looking at patterns among the different scales, solely on an individual basis, rather than by reference to norms and their related statistics. Despite such criticisms, which have sometimes been strongly expressed (eg Johnson, Wood and Blinkhorn, 1988), it is common for ipsative personality measures, as well as those based on normative items, to have published scale norms associated with them. The debate will no doubt continue, with some writers (eg Saville and Wilson, 1991) arguing strongly for the worth of both scaling approaches.

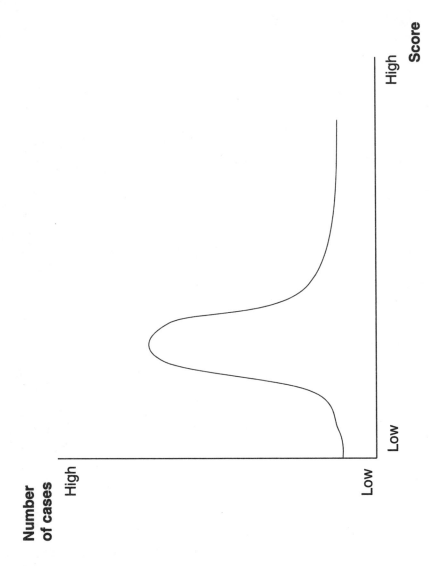

Figure 4.8 Positive skew

Tick which box describes you best

	Yes	In between	No
1. I like to spend time outdoors	☐	☐	☐
2. I prefer my own company	☐	☐	☐
3. I like a good laugh	☐	☐	☐

a. Normative Scaling

1.1 I am sometimes aggressive to others ☐
1.2 I can work hard when necessary ☐

2.1 I dislike detail ☐
2.2 I stick to my point in debate ☐

3.1 I want to spend time with clever people ☐
3.2 I dislike people who make critical remarks ☐

Tick which one of each pair describes you best.

b. Ipsative Scaling

Figure 4.9   Normative and ipsative items

Trade-offs and patterns in personality measurement

Certainly, personality measures do require very careful interpretation, with an examination of patterns among the scales. Consider the following case. Suppose that two of the scales of a personality questionnaire related to a preference for handling detail and an orientation to service respectively. Let us say that we were using the questionnaire to assist in recruitment for order processing clerks responding to incoming customer telephone calls. A person low on the former scale and high on the latter might be disappointing. The intention to provide good service would not be followed through in practice. A person high on detail handling but low on service orientation might fail to convince customers that he or she was actually going to respond to their needs, even though execution of specific clerical tasks might be perfect.

Again, consider executive candidates being looked at in relation to a business turnround situation. People high on tough-mindedness, dominant and forthright as revealed by the 16PF, would be likely to start to make things happen. Whether they carried others with them or not, and so effectively sustained their initial impetus, might depend on their also being high in terms of warmth, tendency to trust and having a controlled, self-disciplined approach. Candidates with the latter but not the former group of strengths might create good feeling but few results.

Gaining an effective mastery of the interpretation of such patterns – typically of course with far more scales than in the examples just given – will take considerable training and practice. In order to reduce the complexity to manageable proportions there have been some interesting short-cut developments. Krug (1981), working with the 16PF, pointed out that, if each of the 16 scales is presented as a sten value, then there are 10 to the power 16 or 10,000 billion possible combinations. In order to reduce the resultant complexity to less astronomical proportions he chose to work with four higher-order accumulations of the 16 scales. He then reduced the sten scale to low, middle and high bands (stens 1–3, 4–7 and 8–10 respectively) giving him 3 to the power 4 = 81 combinations. Word descriptions of each of these were then produced, indicating the interplay among the four higher-order scales in each case.

Test scores and performance

The various types of validity discussed earlier in this chapter and the ways of comparing test scores through norms are all relevant to the question of using tests to predict future performance. Note that validity cannot be regarded as established once and for all or universally for any particular test. Predictive validity would be a most effective guide in those cases in which another group was being recruited to do the same job under very similar circumstances as those upon whom the predictive study had been conducted. However, strong predictive validity in one case would not by any means ensure that in another case it could still be assumed. This could be so even within the same organization and in relation to jobs with the same titles, studied at different periods of time. Consider the case of word processing in the box below.

From the mid- to the late 1980s many organizations increased their use of information technology by leaps and bounds. One manifestation of this was in word processing. Such systems typically include a 'spell-check'. A test of secretarial aptitude including spelling items might well have shown predictive validity – it might have predicted secretarial performance – prior to this innovation, but not thereafter.

During the transition to the new technology some people might well have been apprehensive about it (a condition known as technophobia). A measure of attitudes to change in general or to technology in particular might well have been more predictive of success at that time than the secretarial aptitude test. Later, as this technology becomes more commonplace, with a growing generation of the early computer-literate, such a measure again would fail to predict success.

In fact, concurrent validity studies in periods of transition showing statistical separation between higher and lower performers might not only be the best that could be managed but actually the most appropriate.

Some practical issues in the use of norms

Ideally a validity study should always have been undertaken in the occupational area of interest. However, if norms have been established for an occupational group of relevance and, in particular, if these are clearly differentiated from the general population norm then, even without a specific validity study as such, there are grounds for believing the test to be valid for the occupation concerned. The existence of such relatively local norms do not, though, give direct grounds for selecting any particular score as a cut-off level (that is, a test score used as a decision point with those below it being rejected and those above it being passed on for further consideration).

In practice, the gathering of norms can be tricky. One does not routinely have ready access to the relevant groups and for many occupations in any one firm or organization numbers may be small. Even when people are available in numbers large enough to allow the necessary statistics to be computed, this is no guarantee of the representativeness of the sample used. In fact, so-called general population norms have rather rarely been developed on the basis of a strict reflection of a population. (One exception has been the 16PF. In its original UK norming (Saville, 1972) and its current version (16PF5) care has been taken to sample according to strict population parameters. In both cases the Office of Population Censuses and Surveys was used to support the work.)

One trap that it is easy to fall into arises in connection with tests set up with the **intention** of providing discrimination in a 'high-level' group, such as graduates and senior managers. Thus the designers will aim to produce an unskewed normal curve with its central tendency coinciding with the middle of that group, rather than at the middle of the whole population. If the norm group has been chosen to represent, say, the top 10 per cent of the **whole** population then there can be a temptation to give some solace to those who perform relatively poorly on the test by referring to that fact and further to imply that they are at least ahead of 90 per cent of the whole population. Without having specific reference to a general population norm group it is not actually possible to determine that.

SUMMARY

1. Validity means whether a test measures what it is supposed to measure.

2. Reliability refers to the consistency of measurement.

3. Tests can be interpreted by comparing individual results with norms based on large numbers of respondents.

4. A variety of scores can be used to describe test results. These reflect variations from average scores benchmarked against overall variability.

5. In ability tests it is important for difficulty levels to reflect the levels of discrimination required among the people being assessed and to report results in terms of the actual norm group used.

6. Personality questionnaires may be designed with normative scoring or 'ipsatively' to show degrees of prominence of different characteristics within one person.

5

Statistics and standards in psychometrics II

REGULATORY ISSUES

The need for regulation

The regulation of psychometric tests has been somewhat chequered in the UK, but now seems to be settling down to a set pattern. There are justifiable concerns that tests that have been poorly prepared can give misleading information. There are also concerns about competence in use of tests including issues such as test choice, administration and interpretation. Some of these matters have been related to ideas of value for money on the part of those purchasing psychometric tests and testing services. There is also the need for those undertaking tests to be treated fairly and with due personal consideration.

These issues have been reflected in a general tightening of standards in the field of training for test use, covering both interpreters of tests and those charged with their administration. Test publishers have also been concerned to see enforcement of copyright. Not only does this tend to safeguard their commercial interests, but it also underpins proper professional usage.

Regulatory concerns in the United States

Many of these concerns have from time to time been focused as a result of litigation, much of it regarding equal opportunities, and some of this was briefly touched on in Chapter 2. In the United States in the 1970s, equal opportunities cases had reached such a pitch that many organizations abandoned the use of psychometric tests altogether. However, there now seems to be a prevalence of wiser counsels suggesting this might have been throwing the baby out with the bathwater, particularly when what was left was a set of unspecified procedures typically defaulting to conventional interviewing.

The peak of the anxiety over testing reflected in the 1970s was not by any means entirely new. Haney (1981) traced a series of social concerns over the use of tests in the United States. These ranged from a furore over mental age interpretations of intelligence tests as far back as the 1920s (see 'Glossary and technical notes' for the definition of mental age) to worries over the superficiality of multiple choice tests in the 1960s and on to fairness issues in the 1970s. Novick (1981) traced a shift of focus in the US technical and professional standards for psychometrics. He pointed out that the 1954 standards (APA, 1954) were chiefly concerned to see that test users were provided with enough information by the test publisher to help them in their professional use of the test. Twenty years later (APA, American Educational Research Association and National Council on Measurement in Education, 1974), the main point of concern had shifted to competency in testing practice such as the obligation on the test user to avoid bias. (The requirement for adequate information still remained.) Currently it still appears that litigation represents a form of control in test use in the United States to a far greater degree than in the UK.

The test practitioner as guardian

In the UK today, concerns with avoiding bias in testing are evident. So, too, is consideration of detailed and specific standards of competency in test use. The generality of these concerns is well attested to by the (1999) adoption by the International Test Commission (ITC) of a set of international guidelines for the development of test-user performance standards.

Of course, testing does not take place in a vacuum. The individuals charged with the practicalities of test use in an organization may not be the same as those with responsibility for associated policy matters. Even such mundane questions as the provision of quiet rooms for testing, secure storage facilities for test materials and results require decisions on resources. The test user must first know what standards are proper and then ensure adherence to them, by education, persuasion and cajoling.

Over the years I have had a number of conversations along the following lines:

'Why can't we just photocopy the stuff?'
'Because it's dishonest, illegal and unprofessional.'
'But no one would ever know.'
'Well, supposing I suggested that you should have pirated that new bought-ledger software you've just installed or that we wind back the clocks on the company vehicles.'
'Oh, we couldn't do that. It's dishonest... oh, I see what you mean.'

Each of the issues raised will now be addressed in a little more detail. The specific context here, as in the rest of this book, is occupational. To that end many of the points made, such as those about qualifications and equal opportunities, are particular to that context. However, other comments such as those on copyright are germane to any sphere of psychometric testing, or other means of assessment.

COMPETENCE AND QUALIFICATIONS

Background to the BPS scheme

The issue of qualifications in test use has been evolving in the UK in recent years and the present system was, in fact, introduced a step at a time. (This has produced some anomalies and discontinuities. For example, some test users suddenly found themselves debarred from tests that were previously available to them, because they had not undergone the training that was not in fact in place when the tests concerned were originally developed!)

The development of clearer standards was not before time. Some years ago one test publisher was seeking to define its own standards for access to a certain range of test materials. It set a qualification level as membership of the Division of Occupational Psychology (DOP) of the BPS or eligibility for such membership. It was taken to task by the then chairperson of the DOP for presuming to determine whom the division might or might not admit to membership!

Test publishers have, in fact, been heavily involved in the BPS Steering Committee on Test Standards, and have clearly seen the need for appropriate understanding and competence in test use. Without such skills on the part of users, the test itself – and hence its publisher or distributor – gets a bad name, and the value of its products and services can be adversely impacted.

The need for qualification controls has, of course, been evident for a long time (reference was made in Chapter 2 to the first courses in test use and administration run by the NIIP in the 1920s). Prior to the current arrangements, the BPS operated a system of approval of courses in occupational testing. Completion of such a course typically led to eligibility to purchase and use a wide range of ability tests, interest inventories and careers guidance materials, but not personality questionnaires.

Eligibility with regard to the latter could be achieved in a number of different ways depending on the instrument concerned. Commonly it was through attendance at a specific course on a particular questionnaire run by the publisher or distributor concerned, but other factors would be taken into account, such as, latterly, being a chartered psychologist.

Level 'A'

Under the current arrangements, the BPS is now operating a two-tier certificated qualification system. The first tier, known as level 'A', qualifies people in the use of ability, aptitude and attainment instruments – the so-called tests of maximum rather than typical performance. Qualification at this level requires competencies in seven main areas as follows:

 defining assessment needs;

 basic principles of scaling and standardization;

 reliability and validity;

 deciding when tests should be used;

 administering and scoring tests;

 making appropriate use of test results;

 maintaining security and confidentiality.

These seven areas are subdivided into no fewer than 97 elements of competence, all of which are required to be achieved for the overall level 'A' standard to be fulfilled. Those who have fulfilled the overall standard may be awarded the BPS Certificate of Competence in Occupational Testing Level (A).

One of the expressed aims of this scheme is to permit organizations considering the use of tests to assure themselves of the competence of those who might operate testing procedures on their behalf. To this end, those certificated are placed on an online database register, which can be used for such enquiries into the competence of individual test users.

The level 'A' scheme has been in operation since 1991. It has been generally positively received and has gained considerable currency among those involved in occupational testing in the UK. Its development has necessitated various transitional arrangements. Under these, those who were already trained occupational test users when the scheme was introduced were able to apply for a level 'A' statement of competence. Both statement and certificate are seen by the BPS as recognizing equivalent levels of competence, with both permitting entry on the register.

How to achieve competence

The scheme was set up originally without specification of how or what training should be carried out to help people achieve the various elements of competence. Chartered psychologists who themselves held either the statement or certificate of competence were able to sign an affirmation of competence for the test user concerned, which was regarded as adequate proof of competence for a certificate to be issued.

This procedure has now been strengthened by a process of verification. This involves a verifier checking on the standards used by those signing affirmation statements. These checks are twofold. First is a follow-up of those affirmed to see that they are, in fact, competent. Second is the examination of the processes used in assessing competence. This refinement of the process involves a group of verifiers whose activities in checking on standards are now well established.

Regulation in test administration

For some time test administration as such was not systematically regulated. Although test manuals would make some recommendations, it was assumed that test interpreters would learn test administration as part of their training. It was also tacitly recognized by many organizations that people other than test interpreters, such as administrative staff or other assistants, would actually conduct the tests.

As with any other professional procedures, though, there are key general requirements in administration and there may be traps for the unwary. For example, the administration of certain ability tests such as verbal reasoning requires explanation of particular sample items. While the generally experienced and knowledgeable test interpreter might be able to do this on the fly, this would not be encouraged and could be quite challenging for a junior assistant. Difficulty, hesitation or confusion on the part of this person, as well as confusing participants, might give them justifiable doubts as to the professionalism of the whole procedure.

This state of affairs is not, of course, helped by those organizations in which, sometimes after a good intention of specific professional training of administrators initially, further test administrators are trained by the first group of trainees – and so on down a slippery slope!

Fortunately, the carefully worked-out standards for level 'A' include as a whole the area of administering and scoring tests, as indicated above. This covers 12 separate elements, including arrangement of an appropriate quiet location for testing, use of standard instructions and dealing with candidate questions. Although a formal qualification in this aspect was not previously required or recognized within the BPS scheme, there is now a move to doing just this with scope for specific certification in test administration.

Personality questionnaires – level 'B'

The second stage of the BPS scheme of qualification is the level 'B' certification process, intended to build upon level 'A', extending the scope of competence to cover personality assessment and the use of tests of typical performance. This was launched in 1995.

As this part of the scheme has evolved it has become apparent that the diversity of instruments covered precludes a qualification as general as that at level 'A'. This has led to the idea of a qualification based on relevant general knowledge and core skills plus evidence of ability to realize these in relation to specific personality instruments.

Three broad aspects of competence have been identified, covering nine separate units of competence. The aspects are: foundation, covering fundamental assessment issues in personality; test use, to do with practical skills in administration, interpretation and feedback; and choice and evaluation, covering selection among personality instruments and their formal evaluation. Weights are assigned to the different units of competence indicating their relative importance. The scheme provides for an intermediate level 'B' certificate, which can be converted to a full level 'B' certificate as additional test use and choice and evaluation units are accumulated. Again, as with level 'A', there has been provision for interim arrangements involving statements of competence for those chartered psychologists able to demonstrate existing competence.

The current situation

The BPS scheme is not obligatory upon test publishers. However, many of them have been intimately associated with it and have given it their support. The BPS themselves have encouraged them to limit test supply to those with the appropriate certificate or statement of competence.

Publishers may, of course, continue to set their own standards and may seek to do so particularly in the personality field. Nevertheless, given the level 'B' requirement for realization of competence with identified instruments and given that the test publishers themselves tend to be the ones conducting training in such instruments, as well as being involved in setting standards, it should not be optimistic to hope that any difficulties or conflicts can be solved.

At present though there are some variations as can be seen by reference to test publishers' catalogues. Publishers vary in the extent of recognition that they actually give to training by other bodies and often use their own nomenclature, eg level 1 and level 2 alongside or instead of the level A and B labels. Again, a publication (Lee and Beard, 1994) that dealt extensively with the use of tests in the particular context of development centres (see Chapter 10) described the level 'A' part of the scheme without explicitly referring to it and used the level 1, level 2 terminology.

Despite all this, the way ahead in the UK seems to lie with the BPS scheme. Because the scheme focuses on behaviours required of the test user it also seems likely to give scope for appropriate refresher training and extension-of-skills courses to be developed. Such developments would go some way to minimize the decay of skills or 'driving test phenomenon', flagged in Chapter 3. In fact, both the level A and level B arrangements are now sufficiently far advanced to be undergoing some revision.

DATA PROTECTION

The Data Protection Act 1984 made provision for the control of data on individuals held on electronic media. This could include data generated in that way, through computer administration of a test, or data originated in paper-and-pencil format, but fed into a computer subsequently for analysis. Significant though these provisions were for test users they are less encompassing than those of the Data Protection Act 1998, which has superseded the earlier Act.

The 1998 Act came into effect in early 1999, but with various transitional arrangements up to 2007. It is based on the European Data Protection Directive. It covers data howsoever stored, so it includes paper and microfiche records as well as electronic media. Thus it applies equally to psychometric records held only on paper as to those held on computer. Organizations are obliged to have a data controller (DC), which can in fact be the organization as such. The DC decides how the data are processed and for what purpose or purposes. Fair and lawful processing of data includes knowledge on the part of the subject of the data as to the identity of the DC and the purpose for which data gathered on him or her are to be used. In psychometric applications this would be covered by pre-briefing and/or within administration of the instrument(s). The purposes of use of the data have to be compatible with those identified at the time of gathering the data. For example, test results gathered to help inform a promotion decision only could not then be used to determine who should be made redundant.

Another provision is that data shall be accurate and if the accuracy is challenged the data should indicate this. This underlines the importance of feedback of psychometric results and of noting any areas where a candidate or other participant feels they do not adequately represent the true him or her.

Data are not to be kept longer than necessary for the purpose for which they were gathered. How long would vary from purpose to purpose and could itself be a matter of discussion. For example, it could be argued that a report referring to a candidate's personality with explicit implications for how the candidate should be managed if employed would be of enduring relevance to an employer throughout that candidate's employment. On the other hand, psychometric data used to plan a programme of development, as in a development centre, might be held as only relevant for purposes of cross-referral during the course of the development programme.

There are also provisions regarding authorized access to information, with the reliability of the staff involved being important. Considerations of access also include physical and electronic security, as well as secure disposal.

The subjects of information do have a right of access to information held on them, but there are certain restrictions and limitations on this. Thus a fee (currently £10) has to be paid. The information has to be in permanent and intelligible form. This would seem to imply, as far as psychometrics are concerned, that information in a form that would require psychometric training to interpret, such as a scale read-out in standard score format, should not be supplied, or not supplied without narrative comment. The significance of narrative comment on reporting is also suggested in connection with an exception in the case of automated processing of information. Where such processing is the sole basis for any decision affecting a candidate, he or she can demand to be informed of the logic involved in the decision making. However, information that is a trade secret, which might include equations used in interpreting a personality measure, can be excepted. Thus, again, a narrative report might be covered, insofar as it could be held to indicate the logic without divulging a trade secret, and be seen by both parties as a satisfactory form of disclosure.

Among exemptions to subject access are data processed for management forecasting and planning. This suggests that, say, ability test results used to aid decisions about staff redeployment or promotion would not be covered. Of course, good psychometric practice would still suggest giving feedback in such cases, but this might not, and under the terms of the Act would not have to, include indicating any cut-off level used.

Data subjects can object to decisions based on automatic data processing alone, and require the decision to be made on a different basis. However, recruitment and promotion decisions may be excepted if certain other conditions are fulfilled. With regard to a test, these conditions would include consideration of the existence of norms and its general appropriateness.

The Act also requires that personal data shall not be transferred outside the European Economic Area, unless the country concerned ensures an adequate level of protection in respect of the processing of personal data.

Altogether these provisions are complex and the picture as to just what should and should not be done with regard to generating and handling psychometric data is still emerging.

It may require the development of a body of case law before reliable interpretations can be made. Thus, the above comments should be taken as general guidance to some of the issues raised by the Act with regard to psychometric and other assessment data, but not as definitive with regard to what actions would or would not represent compliance with the Act. Psychometric users would do well to seek legal advice when in doubt about any of the provisions or implications of the Act.

EQUAL OPPORTUNITIES

Direct and indirect discrimination

The overall picture with regard to equal opportunities is complex, but, briefly, British legislation provides that individuals should not be discriminated against in employment either directly or indirectly on the grounds of race or gender or, more recently, disability. Direct discrimination arises where membership of a particular category is used by an employer as a direct means of either admitting or debarring an individual. For example, to refuse to employ or promote a woman because she is a woman would be illegal on these grounds. Indirect discrimination arises when a procedure used to make or assist in an employment or promotion decision favours one group as opposed to another without the basis of favouring being related to the capability to do the job. This would apply if candidates living in a particular area were excluded and that area included a disproportionate number of members of an ethnic minority.

Direct and indirect discrimination are to be distinguished from positive action in which steps are taken to see that opportunities for an under-represented group are optimized, and which also requires the use of fair and objective processes. For example, in the UK there was a campaign termed Opportunity 2000 aimed at increasing the quantity and quality of women's participation in the workforce. Many businesses joined the campaign, as did the National Health Service (NHS). Their action points in this connection (NHS Management Executive, 1992) included monitoring of selection procedures to take account of equal opportunities, helping guard against direct and indirect discrimination.

There is the possibility – not unknown in practice – of an unscrupulous employer actually practising direct discrimination and seeking to hide behind psychometric test results to justify the following disproportionately low numbers of members of a minority group hired – described as adverse impact. Everyone will have some area of limitation, and a wide enough battery of tests would point to at least one area of mismatch to a job in any one person. Thus, such an employer could find some weakness in test score to seek to obscure what, in fact, would be direct discrimination. Fortunately, such extreme abuses are rare and it appears to be much more likely that indirect discrimination will be associated with test use, and that that will tend to arise through error and lack of adequate consideration of all the issues involved. It is, in fact, in the field of indirect discrimination that psychometric tests have sometimes been implicated.

Litigation

Two cases in the UK involving indirect discrimination have been described by Kellett et al (1994) and were briefly referred to in Chapter 2. Both occurred in the transport industry – one concerned British Rail and the other London Underground. Both cases were actually settled out of court. In the British Rail case there were differences in average scores on tests between white and ethnic minority applicants for drivers' jobs. However, validity evidence indicating that such differences reflected actual differences in performance was lacking and there was, in fact, no satisfactory explanation for the differences found. Subsequent adjustments to the selection process have included variations in the trade-offs allowed between different test scores. By relating these to the standard errors of the scores rather than to score points alone it has been possible to find a rational basis for effecting a relative increase in the number of ethnic minority candidates passing the test battery.

In another case involving a test of English language ability an employer had claimed that the test would indicate whether or not applicants could read and comprehend factory safety regulations. The prosecution successfully held that the test used was one of high-grade language capability, which did not directly measure language skills at the relevant level. It therefore discriminated unfairly against those whose first language was not English, and the employer concerned was fined. (If the employer had used a test procedure more directly related to the content of the safety regulations then the prosecution would have had a more difficult case to prove. Indeed, the likelihood is that the ethnic minority workers would have found themselves employed in numbers not dissimilar from their English mother tongue counterparts. Hence, no discrimination would have arisen and there would have been no case to answer.)

One seminal US case was *Griggs* v *Duke Power Co* (1971). The use of general ability tests in selection was challenged on the ground that a relatively small number of black people were hired, that is that the tests had an adverse impact on this particular minority. The defendants' contention that they had not intended this discrimination was thrown out by the court. In the UK, too, it has been actual practice rather than intention that has been seen as critical.

The issue of validity

Most cases involving tests have usually turned on the question of content rather than predictive validity (see Chapter 4), as in the factory case cited above. Of course, with many personality questionnaires, the content is manifestly and purposely somewhat obscure, but the test may successfully distinguish between higher and lower performers! Thus, there may be some degree of conflict between the technical requirements of a test and its ability to stand up in a court of law.

As we have seen already (Chapter 4), predictive validity is often a tricky proposition in any case. In relation to discrimination, one issue is that no one seems to be able to state just how predictive a particular test should be for it to be seen as a fair instrument. As noted earlier, with a high enough cut-off even a test of relatively low predictive power may be of use to the employer. Applied with such a cut-off the test may well have some element of inappropriate discrimination against a minority group, that is allow them through in a smaller proportion than the majority group. It would also, though, clearly be discriminating against many of those in a majority group who could actually do the job but who would not be in a position to bring litigation to bear in the same way as the minority! This idea is illustrated in Figure 5.1.

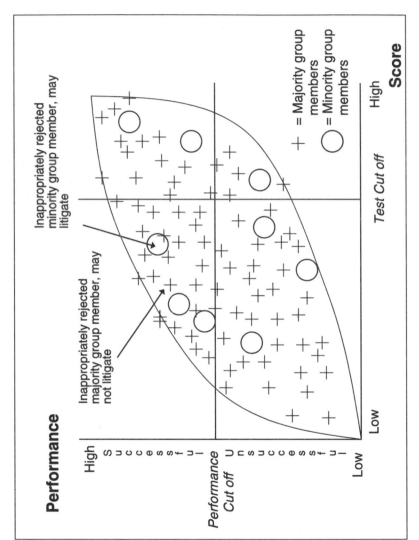

Figure 5.1 Weak predictor and discrimination

The complexity of such issues is reflected in the fact of cases continuing to arise even when there are apparently good intentions on the part of the employer involved. It seems that yet more exploration of the issues, more education and probably more probing of boundaries through case law will be required before employers cease to trip themselves up. An independent view or, indeed, a full independent audit of current practice may help an employer avoid serious problems.

DISABILITIES

People with disabilities may also be discriminated against by injudicious or poorly thought-out use of tests. In the UK, any company employing more than 20 people used to be obliged to recruit registered disabled people if it had not already fulfilled its quota of 3 per cent registered disabled.

If tests are being used in recruitment, but their use is not adjusted to take account of disability, then they could become implicated in a failure to meet quota. Under the Disability Discrimination Act 1995 the quota provision was abolished, but an obligation was placed upon employers not to discriminate against the disabled. Adjustments necessary to psychometric procedures would vary depending on the nature of the job. For example, in a job with a primarily intellectual content a disabled person with motor impairment could be inappropriately disadvantaged through the use of a speeded test of cognitive ability. Adjustments could include extending the time, widening the band of acceptable performance, scoring according to number correct out of those items completed or moving to a test with norms established on an untimed basis. Specialist professional guidance is likely to be needed to suit the particular case. Guidelines for testing people with disabilities have been published by SHL (Clark and Baron, 1992) and ASE (1998).

COPYRIGHT

As with other written materials, copyright is vested in the originator of a test, assessment centre exercise or structured interview. Test publishers have been quite rigorous in pursuing breaches of copyright, committed either by users through practices such as photocopying test materials or through other firms passing off material as their own. It is still, though, not uncommon to find illegally photocopied materials in use (I came across a case in the same week as preparing the final draft of an earlier book). Often it seems that this practice is based on ignorance. It may have been fuelled to some degree by the lack of controls exerted in the past.

The scope of copyright is, in fact, very wide, extending for example to charts and profile documents used in summarizing test results. It applies, too, regardless of the medium used. In an out-of-court settlement, Saville & Holdsworth Ltd gained agreement from another firm that the latter would remove an outline SHL profile chart from their software.

Passing off

Passing off occurs when a person represents, directly or indirectly, work originated by someone else as his or her own. This is also described as plagiarism. As in other forms of copyright breach it will often involve copying someone else's original material, typically with the removal of copyright marks or other identifiers as to the source. Where such breaches lead to integration of another's material with fresh material originated by the plagiarist, they can be hard to detect. Disputes in this area are often lengthy and complex. Besides straightforward theft of other people's material as mentioned above, such disputes can reflect questions such as disagreements between two collaborators who have subsequently parted, in terms of who had an idea in the first place, particularly if each has incorporated the idea in documentation.

TEST DESIGN AND CONSTRUCTION

Similar standards apply on both sides of the Atlantic with regard to construction. In the UK the major regulatory body in test use is the BPS, operating through its Steering Committee on Test Standards. The BPS has laid down standards for the design and construction of tests. These are directed first at ensuring adequate validity and reliability, along the lines outlined in Chapter 4. They also involve the standardization of tests to produce norms. These norms, together with the reliability and validity data, should be presented in a manual. This provides the test user with the necessary data for informed use.

Such standards do not have the direct force of law and, indeed, there is a grey area in relation to the extent to which they are seen as required to be fulfilled by regulatory bodies. Independent and objective review leading to entry in Buros's *Mental Measurement Yearbook* implies adequacy of design without guaranteeing it. The BPS produced its own review publication for ability and aptitude tests (Bartram, 1997) and another one for personality questionnaires (Lindley, 1993), now both incorporated into online versions. It is also evident that the technical merits of some tests may sometimes be matters of dispute. Reference has already been made in Chapter 4 to the debate surrounding normative and ipsative tests in which some well-known British psychologists were involved.

Cook (1992) wrote an article generally critical of the DISC/Personal Profile Analysis – a short personality measure used in salesforce selection. Among other things, he referred to limited data in the technical manual for the instrument and cited its absence from the *Mental Measurement Yearbook*. However, the DISC instrument continues to have many advocates among sales managers and is widely used. This is not just perversity; in a recent discussion I found a personnel manager recently converted to the DISC system, unaware that there had been any question as to its stature as a psychometric instrument.

There are perhaps no absolute guarantees with or without regulation, but competence in test use will help more organizations choose better which tests to use.

AFTERTHOUGHT ON REGULATION

At the end of the day regulation of various sorts is essentially for the protection of all involved. This includes those being tested, those using tests or commissioning their use, or others such as test publishers working in the testing field. Some companies concerned with their compliance with best professional standards will take the trouble to audit their test use, employing external professionals on some occasions or otherwise using their own internal staff. I came across the following situation when conducting one such audit.

A largely independent subsidiary of a major manufacturing group used ability tests to help select some of its operatives. The tests had been used for a number of years and the same administrator had been employed for a long time, with the test administration forming a large part of his work. Over the years he had become blasé about his scoring procedures, claiming that he knew the right answers and no longer needed to use the stencil scoring key.

His management reacted to this in a novel but unenlightened way. They – by scissors, paste and photocopying – rearranged the order of the items in the test so that a number of early items were placed later and vice versa. This also, of course, involved rearranging the scoring key, which the administrator now had to use, being no longer able to rely on his memory in relation to the changed question order. The test was timed. It was originally designed with easier items coming first and moving progressively to more difficult ones. Thus changing the order of questions drastically changed the performance on the test and made the published norms completely inappropriate!

Regulation, of all sorts, although not yet necessarily perfect, is clearly desirable.

SUMMARY

1. Regulation of testing covers a range of issues from test design to competence in test use, the avoidance of discrimination and protection of copyright.

2. Specific concerns have varied from time to time, as different regulatory issues have come to the fore. In the United States and the UK these have been reflected in different points of emphasis in regulatory guidelines.

3. Standards in test design and use do not have the direct force of law, but poorly applied standards may involve the user in litigation.

4. In the UK there is a comprehensive scheme for qualification in test use, with clear standards for a range of practical issues, developed under the auspices of the BPS.

5. The Data Protection Act requires access by the subject to data held about him or her, which would often include test results. Consideration of the most appropriate means of providing access is bound up with the wider issue of feedback of test results.

6. Equal opportunities issues are particularly focused on indirect discrimination in which use of a test leads to an unjustified adverse impact on a particular group.

7. Especial care is required when setting up psychometric procedures for those with disabilities, so that their actual capabilities do not become masked.

6

Tests and selection – the developing context

MASS TESTING TO TRIAL BY SHERRY

The use of psychometric tests in external selection represents the largest category of application in work-related situations. Practices vary greatly but a number of broad patterns of usage emerge. Some of these can be seen to have their roots in the earliest days of testing. In particular, mass application of tests to large groups of candidates is still quite common-place with echoes of the earliest US military experience, referred to in Chapter 2. In all cases there is at least implicit the idea that the test is providing information of value to the selection process. However, the role and status of that information, and its links with other sources, are rarely clearly stated and perhaps even more rarely understood.

One of the reasons why there is often confusion in the role of tests stems from a lack of clarity in the overall information-gathering process being undertaken in selection and hence how they contribute to that process. It is, for example, by no means uncommon for one or more arbitrary procedures to be added into the total flow of information gathered without any very distinct view of how these themselves can contribute. Unstructured semi-social events, dubbed in some quarters 'trial by sherry', are often seen as important and worthwhile parts of a selection process. Calling a candidate back for an extra meeting – perhaps the finance director should see him or her after all – is also by no means uncommon. In such hazy arrangements it is not surprising that the contribution of any particular element, not least psychometric tests, will be unclear!

It will be an aim of this chapter to consider what information is commonly gathered in selection situations and how it is used. Later, in Chapter 8, we look in more detail at how information from tests as such can function in selection.

We shall look first at the elements alongside which tests are often deployed, considering a number of areas of personal specification and reviewing their place in the selection process.

SOME FAVOURITE MEASURES – CLUB MEMBERSHIP TO AGE

The purpose of any procedure used in selection is to find out something about the candidate or candidates that will be of relevance to their functioning in the job or role concerned. Note that this statement, for the moment, carefully avoids reference to functioning successfully or to objectively measured performance on the job. Such considerations are not always implicit in the minds of those making the selection! In fact it is evident that in many selection situations a primary consideration is getting someone who is 'one of us' or 'who I can get on with' without any specific identification of how such criteria are likely to be reflected in performance as such.

It is perhaps because such notions are representative of muddled and non-specific, rather than wrong, thinking that they are rather difficult to understand and shift. Thus an implicit model of 'one of us' could have a fundamentally sound basis and be capable of representation in terms of behaviour. Consider, for example, a successful team of financial consultants dealing routinely face to face with customers to advise them on their affairs. An absence of particular superficial characteristics of speech (both accent and vocabulary), manner and style of dress could immediately brand the candidate as not 'one of us'. This lack could also impact upon the clientele in such a way that, in fact, the candidate would be unsuccessful in the role.

Rarely, if ever, is this formally researched and the extent to which the possession of other qualities such as work rate, a positive attitude and ability with figures could compensate may never be entertained or explored. This may be the case, even though in such circumstances it would be recognized that those lacking these other qualities – eminently capable of investigation by psychometrics – would fail.

Fiction and prejudice

Also, being 'one of us' is not only part of the implicit model of success but also may reflect feelings of discomfort, not necessarily voiced directly, that would arise by admitting to employment, and hence to what is in effect a social group, those with differing styles and mores. Maintaining the comfort factor by control of group membership is a powerful, if often unspoken, motivation. Fiction, from Shaw's *Pygmalion* to Mark Twain's *A Connecticut Yankee at King Arthur's Court,* has often projected the idea of the outsider making good through the use of capacities of real relevance to successful performance in the role. In such fiction these capacities are various, including ingenuity, tenacity and honesty. However, the players in such dramas tend to battle against tremendous odds and the comic structure of such stories is one of the ways in which they can, comfortingly, be set apart from real life.

The power of implicit models is vividly illustrated in a lecture given by C S Myers, a grand old man of British psychology, over 80 years ago (Myers, 1920). In a comment made without explanation, let alone apology or mitigation, reference is made by the doyen to the higher and lower races. The thinking supporting this view of the world – the implicit model – is clearly deeply embedded.

The experience trap

Over millennia, the philosophically minded have commented wisely about the misleading nature of experience. Thus, Hippocrates, 'Life is short… experience treacherous', or Plato in relation to evil and the judge, 'Knowledge should be his guide, not personal experience.' More recently there is Wilde, 'Experience is the name most people give to their mistakes', and perhaps most appositely Shaw, 'Men are wise in proportion not to their experience, but to their capacity for experience.'

Yet in selection situations a number of years' experience of a particular role or activity is often equated with successful performance and comes to be regarded as an absolutely essential criterion.

Inputs and outputs

In practice, what is happening here is that experience, either in terms of a number of years or in relation perhaps to association with a particular procedure or process, is treated as an output behaviour equivalent to, say, communications skills or ability to manage. In fact, it is, rather, a piece of input information.

The fact that the information will, in many cases, have a poor power of prediction is not considered, perhaps partly because it is not understood to be functioning as a predictor of performance but is treated as if it were the performance itself. As a predictor, it stands at best as a rough short-hand for past performance. Past performance may or may not be an effective predictor for future performance, depending among other things on the similarity between the target job and those in which the performance was demonstrated. (See Figure 6.1 for an illustration of these points.) If the reader will tolerate yet another quotation, consider Coleridge: 'Experience is like the stern lights of a ship, which illumine only the tracks they have passed.'

Like the mariners of old in their explorations, most people seeking new jobs are looking for career development. Ongoing job satisfaction is very often bound up with personal growth and self-actualization. This usually means a move on to something bigger, better and different. If candidates were totally experienced in the job they were seeking to fill, one would rightly be inclined to question their motivation. A new job is inevitably a new experience to a greater or lesser degree. The selector has to predict future performance.

The whole picture is complicated further by the fact that some organizations see specific experiences as counter-indicators, which if not absolute will still weigh against a candidate. An example is that of salespeople in the insurance industry. Some employers will argue that, in an industry with such a high staff turnover, the unsuccessful move on and the successful stay. Thus, anybody now seeking to work in such a role, who has done so previously, is bound to be one of the unsuccessful ones!

Experience versus psychometrics

Where experience is more clearly seen as input, rather than output, it is still often regarded as a separate entity from anything that might be measured by psychometrics. In fact, though, there is considerable scope for psychometric procedures or psychometric considerations to be brought into play here. For example, if the role is considered to require the ability

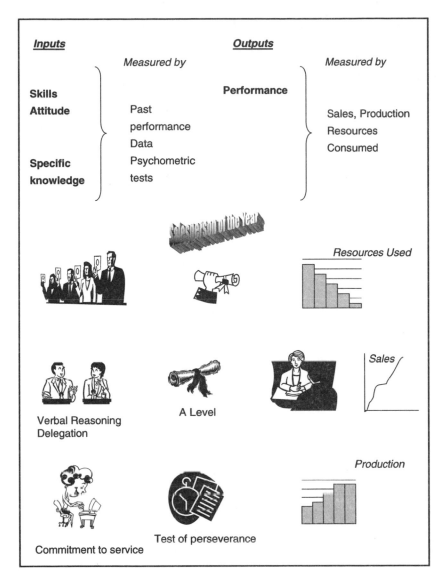

Figure 6.1 Determining performance

to apply experience in novel ways then tests relating to creativity (eg the Cree Questionnaire originally distributed by Science Research Associates, or use of one of the scales derived from the 16PF) may be useful.

Experience is often taken, of course, for a sign of explicit knowledge. Some organizations have gone down the track of actually testing such knowledge directly in what are, as referred to in Chapter 3, in intention, if not in a strict scientific practice, tests of attainment. By a systematic application of such procedures, the relevant knowledge is more fully explored than, say, in a conventional interview.

In many selection situations, of course, activities are taken stepwise. Evidence of experience from a CV or application form means that that experience may be explored further in a later stage, very often an interview. Such exploration may, again, be related to the knowledge base of experience – which as just argued may be better explored by a more formalized method. It is also used to investigate other characteristics, in effect using the experience as the vehicle through which the candidate may demonstrate particular capacities, as in the following box.

'I see that you had a group of six people reporting to you when you were in the XYZ company. Tell me something about how you helped them to succeed.'

'Working on the ABC project in Ruritania sounds interesting. What were the most difficult situations that you encountered there?'

The first of these passages indicates an interest in and concern for others and for staff development – capable of exploration through psychometric procedures such as FIRO-B or the Edwards Personal Preference Scale (EPPS). The second may be seeking evidence on handling complex information or attitude to work. Complex information handling could be measured through instruments such as the Graduate and Managerial Assessment (GMA) Reasoning Tests (Psychometric Research Unit, Hatfield Polytechnic, 1992), while a tendency to be deeply involved in work and to drive through against difficulties could be assessed through the Jenkins Activity Survey (Jenkins, Zyzanski and Roseman, 1979).

This is not, for the moment, to argue that these particular psychometrics would necessarily do a better job than the interview questions, but rather that information derived from experience is by no means the only way in which such evidence could be gathered!

The role of unstructured interviews

We have already referred to the idea of a comfort factor; an unstructured interview may supply this and as indicated above comfort is not necessarily wholly irrelevant in a consideration of someone joining an organization.

Let us dwell for a moment on how a conventional unstructured interview may contribute to the whole picture. (Structured interviews, as described in Chapters 11 and 12, will add more than comfort.) If an interview is conducted by the person for whom the candidate will be working directly, it is likely to give indications of personal liking or rapport, or its absence. These indications may not be formally acknowledged and reflected in any competency description, which will tend to relate to a class of job rather than a specific one in many circumstances. Certainly, once recruited, people often fail in their work because they fail to get on with their bosses and it may quite often be more realistic for interviewing managers to recognize that they actually do or do not like the candidate before them than to be told they should or should not like him or her on the basis of a personality instrument.

However, liking is not a guarantee of success. Very often subordinates will need to have a complementary pattern rather than be cast in the same mould as their superiors and they will, too, have to fit in with a number of other team members. Successive interviews with different interviewers may be popular largely because they often give different team members an opportunity to decide whether or not they would feel comfortable with the candidate joining the team.

Short-term factors

The unstructured interview as an information-gathering exercise is likely to be most effective in determining some of the aspects of the candidate that may be relatively transitory. Present circumstances, motivations and financial expectations are much more amenable to this type of interaction than are elements of personality or higher-level mental functioning. Conversely, information on personality or reasoning, although pointing to behaviour such as competitiveness and practical problem solving, will not address the specific personal circumstances, which the interview can.

Candidates will, too, tend to have a variety of questions to ask of an employer and will often wish to form a view as to their level of liking of the interviewer as an individual and as a representative of the hiring organization.

For the moment, note that it is a commonplace that all drivers think they are excellent drivers and all interviewers excellent interviewers. Although I have experienced the wry smiles and knowing nods that greet this proposition when included in discussions with management groups, I can only recall one manager ever who volunteered that he was, in fact, a poor interviewer! We are all apparently experts on people, with many of us having gained our expertise in the great University of Life.

Age

The specification of age in selection situations is not yet illegal in the UK, though seems likely to be so in the future. It is in the United States and Canada, while in France recruitment advertisements may not by law state an upper age restriction. Like other discriminators, such as race and sex, the use of which are now outlawed, age is quite apparently and conveniently determined. Just like experience, age seems to carry with it implications of behaviour. However, also like experience it is at best an input to behaviour but is often confused with behavioural outputs.

Some organizations claim to have established that only individuals in certain age bands – sometimes defined as narrowly as a period of four years – have been found to succeed in the role concerned. Figures are rarely quoted in support of such assertions. One frequent argument is that only individuals over a certain age will have the necessary experience but, of course, this falls back upon the arguments relating to experience once more. In fact, if age is only working through experience it will be a weaker predictor than is that weak predictor.

JOB DEFINITIONS

The role of job definitions

Defining the job in terms of duties and responsibilities or in terms of outputs, performance and accountabilities has often been helpful in thinking about the appropriate use of tests in selection. Such statements will often define what is required to be done in the job and/or may indicate qualities and capacities necessary to perform successfully. Sometimes the statements of what is required are quite detailed. Where standards of performance, rather than vaguely expressed areas of operation, are indicated they may give quite a ready read-across to the way in which measurement may be carried out. This is illustrated in the extract from the job definition below.

Job title: Senior Engineering Manager.
  Dimensions: Factory operations on three sites.
  Budgeted spend: £12m.
  Total strength: 180 personnel.

Direct reports: 5 engineering managers, quality manager, head of materials purchasing, secretary.

Special considerations: After the recent rundown and the concentration of manufacturing on the present three sites from five previously, there is a need to rebuild morale among the engineering workforce. The company has identified total quality management (TQM) as a spearhead initiative in continuing to drive down on costs and to increase competitiveness through enhanced customer service at all levels.

The person appointed must:

▌ be able to translate the company's TQM policy into effective action through identifying appropriate techniques and critical areas for their initial application;

▌ be able to build a team quickly;

▌ be quick to identify strategic implications of variances from the cost containment plans;

▌ have the energy and sense of responsibility to put in extra effort to 'pump-prime' the necessary new initiatives.

Broad-band personality questionnaires such as the 16PF or SHL's OPQ would yield information on many of these areas – team building, innovation, a rational approach to data could all be covered. The special considerations section indicates the importance of customer service, and those instruments and scales indicating conscientiousness would be relevant here. The liveliness scale of the 16PF would be relevant in considering the rebuilding of morale, and forward planning in the OPQ would be of relevance in translating TQM policy into action.

The reasoning skills indicated might be assessed by an instrument such as the Watson–Glaser Critical Thinking Appraisal.

Checklists

Sometimes in developing a job definition use is made of a checklist of characteristics such as the one below:

■ Individual characteristics:
  - achievement drive;
  - entrepreneurial inclination;
  - personal commitment;
  - energy;
  - self-confidence;
  - flexibility.

■ Interpersonal characteristics:
  - listening;
  - negotiation skills;
  - oral communications;
  - written communications;
  - service orientation.

■ Intellectual characteristics:
  - rapid learning;
  - strategic conceptualization;
  - pattern recognition;
  - verbal reasoning;
  - numerical reasoning;
  - innovation.

■ Managerial characteristics:
  - staff development;
  - operational control;
  - planning;
  - commercial awareness.

Such lists can be helpful but need to be carefully applied. Their use can lead to an over-inclusive wish list of characteristics, which if accepted could result in an unwieldy psychometric battery. In fact, where characteristics are poorly specified there is a temptation to fall back on seeking to measure experience.

Before proceeding further the reader may like to consider the case of the Acme Engineering and Plastics Company.

THE ACME ENGINEERING AND PLASTICS COMPANY – EPISODE 1

Tom Evans, site manager of the Acme Engineering and Plastics Company's main plant and office complex in Welchester, sat at his desk in the firm's 'mahogany row'. He was waiting for a meeting with Will Stevens, the company's new young personnel manager.

As he waited, Evans mused. They were getting together to discuss the recruitment of a new administration manager for the site. There seemed such a lot of fuss about these things today. On the phone Stevens had muttered something about 'profiles' and 'psychometrics'. He said he thought it was important that they worked on a competency description for the job. In the old days, Tom had had one of the senior secretaries ring around a few agencies and ask for some suitable people. If there was a need to put an ad in the paper he would usually write the copy himself and he would get one of the draughtsmen to do a line drawing of the factory.

He usually had a good idea of the type of person he wanted. An administrator obviously had to be experienced. That had seemed to be one of the major appeals of the previous incumbent. You would think somebody who had been a company secretary with a chemical subsidiary of one of the big oil companies would have been able to cope quite well with the work at Acme. Still, the fellow had never seemed to want to get involved in any of the real details and although he had known before he joined that his department was only three people he seemed to expect them to carry out everything themselves.

Of course you could not have a youngster in a position like this one. He was going to have to interface with the senior management and board further down the corridor on the one hand, and also be able to deal with the engineering department managers and shopfloor supervisors. All of them were pretty long in the tooth. But he didn't want somebody who was just waiting for his pension either. There were things to be done and someone with some new ideas who would still have a feel for the way in which a traditional firm like Acme wanted to work would probably be best. So probably no more than 50 and no younger than, say, 44. In addition to administrative experience, maybe an administrative qualification would be a good idea. Perhaps going for an ex-company secretary had been a bit too high-flying, even though the chap had seemed happy to take the salary.

He had heard that some of these tests could tell how a person fitted in. He really was not sure how that could possibly work. Maybe he ought to put something about flexibility in the ad. They had had some trouble, hadn't they, with the administrative supervisor before last, the senior position reporting into the managerial post. He remembered how the whole place had gone into overdrive when they had received a large export order with a very short turnaround period. Administration needed to throw themselves into supporting the commercial department in a whole range of things, including shipping arrangements to Eastern Europe. Then they found themselves involved in the translation and printing of the necessary brochures. He smiled ruefully again. Geoff had said that he had not seen it as part of his job to do that and he wasn't going to miss his kendo class two weeks running. Still, perhaps the right manager could have handled it better. Sometimes you really did need a person who could combine firmness and tact.

Then there was the new software to get to grips with. Naturally it was accounts driven but administration had to understand what it could do for them. The last chap had never seemed to comprehend how the production spreadsheets would be part of his concern. Probably a bit slow on the uptake on the numbers side, thought Evans. Funny, he had never thought of asking him about that. He prided himself, of course, on the way his engineering training had always helped him in his own work. Better to have someone with some solid numerical background to his education: an A level in maths or maybe even sticking out for a graduate in one of the more analytical subjects rather than just a graduate of any sort. He would have to be careful he didn't end up with an accountant though. He'd never found one of them who didn't get on his nerves after a while – too pernickety a lot of them were. In this type of operation there is detail and detail. You needed to know what was important and then to follow that through hard, but not chase every last figure through to the ultimate limit.

He was beginning to feel depressed talking to himself like this when Stevens finally walked in.

'Good afternoon, Tom,' he said. 'I've been thinking about your administration manager post and I've downloaded the old job description. I think it will give us some clues to the type of person we want, but a lot of it is a bit vague. However, you seem to have some ideas yourself from what you put in your e-mail, even though there may be one or two question marks in your mind. I have drawn up a preliminary list of characteristics. You'll see that I've indicated flexibility, a rapid learning style and numerical reasoning ability. We could probably cover that in a personality questionnaire and one of the standard ability tests. By the way, the old JD referred to graduate qualifications, but I can't quite see why.

'There was also a quaint reference to professional institution membership but without any clarity as to which professional body was concerned. There doesn't seem to be any legal requirement of that nature, so I propose to ignore it. There is also a reference to 20 years' commercial business experience, preferably in the manufacturing sector, but of course for the right person who fits the specification in terms of behaviour it doesn't matter if he or she has got 20 years' or 20 weeks' experience. The same applies to age…'

Evans wasn't quite sure yet whether his day was improving or not. Could this fellow have the answers?

SUMMARY

1. The specification of information flows in selection is rarely clear.

2. Models used are often implicit rather than explicit.

3. The use of experience and ages and over-reliance on conventional interviews may be based on mistaken views as to their contribution and effectiveness. Much of the ground intended to be covered by such means may, in fact, be better addressed by psychometrics.

4. Job definitions will aid the specification of required characteristics in ways amenable to psychometric testing.

7

Psychometrics and selection – the practice

In this chapter we look at some broad types of selection situation, from high volumes sourced externally to cases of internal selection. In conjunction with these areas we consider a number of issues of general relevance in psychometric applications, including addressing again the questions of the interplay among different tests, introduced in Chapter 4.

LARGE-VOLUME RECRUITMENT APPLICATIONS

Where large numbers of individuals need to be recruited into a company at any one time it is common for ability or aptitude tests to be applied either singly, in pairs or in whole batteries. In these situations, personality testing would usually be excluded at the initial stage because of the necessary complexity of interpretation. Examples of large-volume recruitment roles include graduate entry schemes, retail management and sales staff, and financial consultants in the insurance industry. Relocation of offices or opening of new factories also often occasion high-volume recruitment.

Use of norms

The very idea of large-scale recruitment raises the possibility of scope for local (that is, specific to the recruiting organization) validity studies to be conducted. Where this is so, the results of such studies can be used to determine where cut-offs on the test or tests should best be placed. In practice, such specific studies will only rarely have been carried out in advance of establishing the need to recruit. By that time there is hardly ever the time available – and not usually the money either – to undertake such a study. One is then obliged to rely on a set of norms developed elsewhere. As discussed in Chapter 4, the norms available may be general population or, if one is lucky, drawn from a similar occupational group to the target. (For example, in one recruitment application in which I was involved I was able to recommend the use of a norm table for clerical staff in financial services when recruiting clerical staff for a financial services company!)

The strength of relationship

If the test has some validity then there will be a positive degree of relationship between performance on the test and performance in the job. In a perfect relationship, if each individual's score on the test were plotted against his or her performance in the job all the points would lie in a straight line, as in Figure 7.1. In practice, of course, such relationships are not found. They would, in fact, be the equivalent of translating inches to centimetres or pounds to kilograms.

Where tests are positive predictors, then in general those scoring higher on the test perform better in the job. In such cases, plots linking test scores and performance for individuals are scattered within a roughly elliptical shape, such as that illustrated in Figure 7.2. While in general a higher test score is associated with higher performance, there are some individuals who do not perform very well in the job despite having a high test score and, conversely, there are some with a lower test score whose job performance would be effective.

The closer the clustering of points around the straight line, the more effective the test will be in predicting performance. As prediction becomes less and less effective, the more the boundary in which the individual

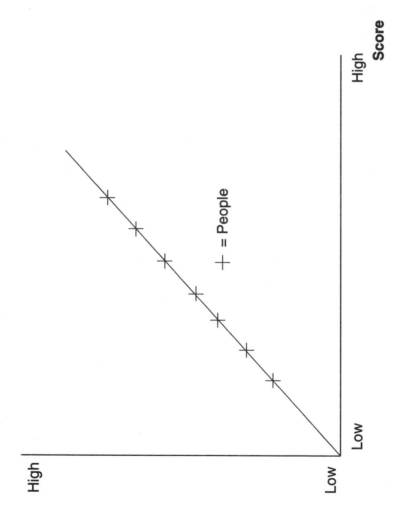

Figure 7.1   The perfect test – performance predicted with certainty

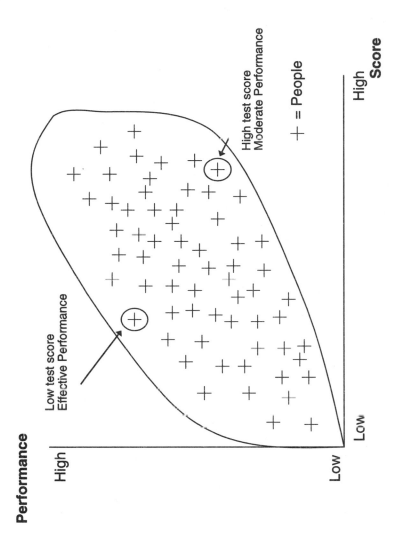

Figure 7.2 A positive predictor but some errors

plots fall moves outwards, bulging the ellipse. The ultimate is where there is no relation whatsoever between the test and performance on the job. Then, for any test score, any level of performance is as likely as any other. The distribution of individuals when test score and performance are plotted together is then bounded not by an ellipse but by a rectangle (see Figure 7.3).

The correlation coefficient

These relationships are captured statistically in the concept of correlation and expressed in the correlation coefficient r. This is a number that can range from +1 down to –1. An r of +1 would result from the straight-line relationship as shown in Figure 7.1. Figure 7.3, with the distribution showing no relationship, would give us an r of zero. For a perfect negative relationship with an r of –1, scores on one dimension would diminish with perfect predictability as those on the other increased. This is shown in Figure 7.4. This could be illustrated by the careful schoolboy with £7 holiday pocket money, spending it at the rate of 70p at a time to furnish himself with one ice-cream per day throughout his 10-day visit to the seaside.

The numbers game

Sometimes tests – and indeed other procedures – are applied without any consideration at all of the form of relationship between their indications and performance on the job. Such procedures may still have a certain superficial attraction for two reasons. They may seem to be giving some further insights, perhaps because the words that are produced in describing results seem to tie in with what is understood about the job or because they have some cachet of the rigorous about them. Second, and with equal scepticism, one may say that they are often attractive because they provide a means – albeit one not rooted in any real truth – of making decisions about whom to take on board or process further. Thus, if there is a score a cut-off may be applied to it and there will, therefore, be a means of making a decision and spending any further investigative time on a smaller group than those originally considered.

If the relationship between the test measure and performance on the job is random then the use of the procedure will have added no other value whatsoever than that of reducing the number of candidates to be processed in a way that could have been achieved by tossing a coin.

This simple fact is illustrated further in Figure 7.5. This indicates the situation where (a) there is no relationship between the score on the test

Performance

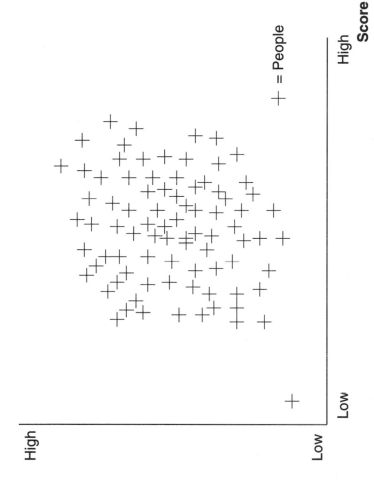

High

Low

+ = People

Low   High
                    Score

Figure 7.3   The pointless test – no predictive power

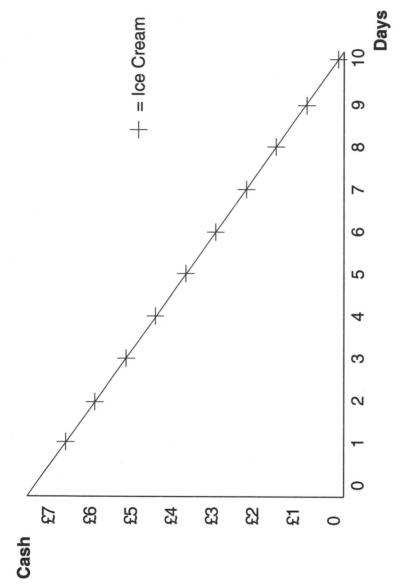

Figure 7.4   Perfect negative correlation the effects of ice-cream purchasing upon cash

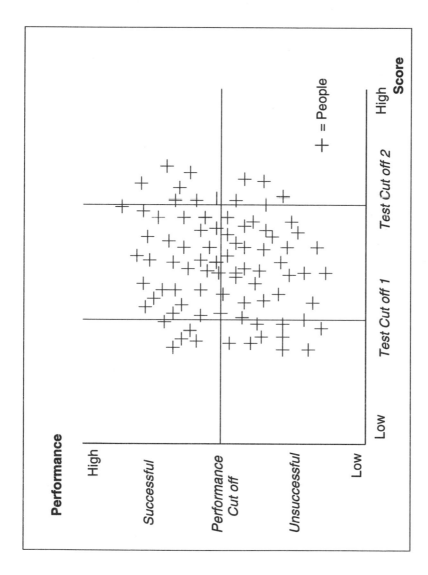

Figure 7.5 A pointless exercise applying cut-offs to a test with zero correlation with performance

measure and performance on the job, and (b) it is possible to think of performance on the job in relation to success or failure. It can be seen that as the cut-off level on the test is shifted from level 1 to level 2 the proportion of those succeeding and those failing remains constant even though, of course, the numbers change. It is the numbers changing that gives the spurious impression that something useful is being accomplished.

For many jobs, of course, the dividing line between successful and unsuccessful performance will be blurred. However, there are situations, for instance those involving training after selection whether it be for, say, a heavy goods vehicle driver or for an accountancy qualification, where a more distinct line of success will be indicated.

False positives and false negatives

The extreme case of zero correlation is, perhaps, relatively rare and the practical picture is complicated by a number of other issues. Consider now a case such as that shown in Figure 7.6. In this situation, the test is a rather poor predictor of success but there is still some degree of relationship. Thus, on the whole, those with a higher score tend to do better on the job than those with a lower score, but there are many discrepancies. If, again, a cut-off is applied to the test score then it will be found that those taken on will tend to do better than if those with scores below the cut-off had been taken on or if people had been chosen at random. Thus the test has some value to add.

Of course, a poor predictor means that some mistakes will be made. There will be some false positives or false selections and some false negatives or false rejections. That is, there will be some individuals achieving above the test cut-off who will not succeed in the job. There will also be a number of those below the cut-off, who were rejected but who could have done the job perfectly effectively. However, the proportion of these will be smaller than the proportion correctly selected and correctly rejected. The more the shape tends towards the straight-line relationship, as in Figure 7.7, the smaller the proportion of the false positives and false negatives.

Leveraging the weak predictor

Note, though, that providing there is a positive correlation then, other things being equal, the highest possible cut-off is desirable. It is doubtless this that employers grope towards when they set higher academic standards. The relationship between such standards and performance in a job may be slight, but if it is present at all then the chances of a successful job outcome by hiring those with, say, first-class degrees rather than those

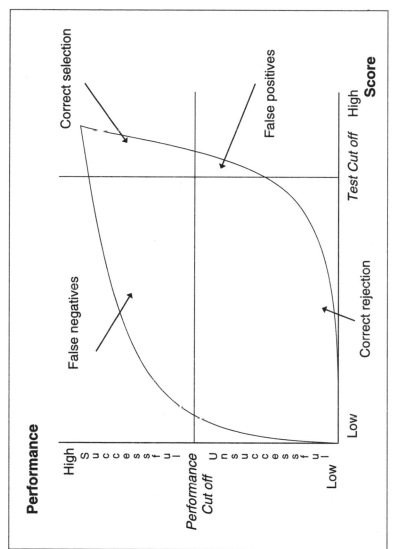

Figure 7.6 Applying a cut-off to a weakly predictive test

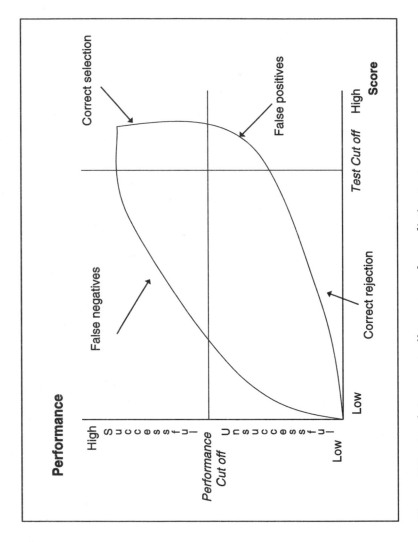

Figure 7.7 Applying a cut-off to a strongly predictive test

with second-class degrees is evident. However, marketplaces are dynamic; first-class degree candidates know their market worth and may well require higher salaries, complicating the picture further. A better procedure might well be to seek to introduce a higher degree of prediction by substituting a test procedure for the academic standard!

The question of cost also emerges within the testing field as such. More, better research to define competencies better or to refine and tailor the test procedures rather than take them off the shelf will all tend to shift the shape of the relationship between the test and job success closer to the straight line ($r = 1$), making it more like the safe task of estimating centimetres from inches. However, such work clearly takes time and money, and even a relatively weak predictor can be leveraged further.

Figure 7.8 shows a case when cut-offs are set progressively higher still with the same relatively poor test predictor. The proportion of unsuccessful selections progressively diminishes and the proportion of the successful increases. Of course, at the same time the absolute number of people taken on board at all and the absolute number of successful ones also reduce. Therefore, for such a system to yield sufficient numbers the pool of applicants needs to be extended. The proportion of people tested who are selected is known as the selection ratio. If the pool of applicants can be extended then the selection ratio can be kept low and only the best appointed.

To increase correlation or candidate numbers?

If we consider what is implied by all of this we can see that there may be two broad options to think about. The first is to increase the predictive accuracy of the test, which requires investment. The second is to increase the pool of applicants, which also implies expenditure in capturing and/or processing them. Which approach to adopt will vary with circumstances.

Attempts to state the relationships among the different issues and variables involved have been going on for many years. For example, over 60 years ago Taylor and Russell (1939) devised tables linking expected successes for different levels of correlation, taking into account numbers of successful performers found without the use of tests. Later treatments of the same issues have tended to regard such early attempts at cost–benefit evaluations as primitive, but still fail to give really comprehensive guidance.

Increasing a pool of applicants will lead to more rejected and hence disappointed candidates, and if the relationship between test score and performance is very weak could lead to an increased likelihood of discrimination in some cases (see also Chapter 5).

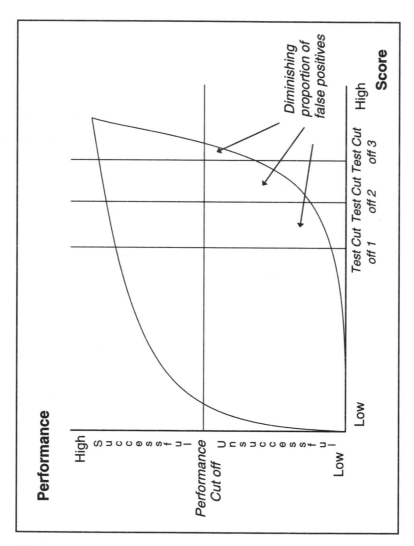

Figure 7.8 Effect of various cut-offs with a weakly predictive test

On the whole, my recommendation would be to opt for methods likely to give some increased accuracy in prediction. Sometimes the time, money and effort spent in improving predictive capability can be borrowed from that which might otherwise go on arbitrary or inaccurate procedures at some other stages of the process. It will always tend to militate against candidate disappointment and risk of prosecution.

What comes next?

Very often, of course, the psychometric procedures in mass selection are set in a chain of activities. Sometimes this chain involves a further review, after the psychometric testing of candidates falling just below the cut-off. This is not altogether unreasonable. It is evident from consideration of the dynamics of the processes, as explained above, that any test is an imperfect predictor and that there will be some people below the cut-off who will, in fact, have a chance of succeeding (quite a lot of people in a case such as that shown in Figure 7.8).

The wisdom and likely success of such a way of proceeding will depend on several factors though. First there is the question of how far below the original cut-off should be regarded as 'just below' and second there are the procedures used for the further investigations. If the revised or provisional level below the original cut-off is very close to the original, so that a relatively narrow band of scores is yielded for further consideration, then the overall chance of success would not be much different from that with the higher-level cut-off. (Of course, this also implies that not many more individuals will be considered.) As the cut-off is shifted further and further away, although the number of potential successful applicants increases so does the number and the proportion of the unsuccessful. At the ultimate, such a proceeding amounts to abandonment of the test altogether.

Another statistic: the standard error of measurement

Just what constitutes a narrow band of revision of scores does not have to be regarded arbitrarily. Reference can be made to the standard error of measurement. Derived from the reliability studies on the test and typically reported in test manuals, the standard error indicates the expected range of variability of a test score. If it is relatively large then the true test score can be expected to lie in a wider range than if it is narrow. Hence, with a large standard error relatively large shifts in the cut-off score could be regarded as still within the original basis of decision. (Standard errors are explained further in 'Glossary and technical notes'.)

Let us consider now the further review of candidates in the provisional band below the original cut-off score. If the procedure now to be applied is arbitrary and itself not a predictor at all or a very weak predictor, such as, say, having passed GCSE Geography, then this amounts to a random choice among that next group considered, in effect making a pretence of a systematic approach to selection for this group. On the other hand, if this group is now subjected to a more accurate process, there will still be a cost but the overall accuracy of selection will have been enhanced.

It is now time to look in again on the further tribulations of the Acme Engineering and Plastics Company, to which we were introduced in the last chapter.

THE ACME ENGINEERING AND PLASTICS COMPANY – EPISODE 2

Will Stevens was faced with a problem. The recruitment programme for computer programming staff for the company's administration centre was just not getting enough people through. The programme had been set up prior to Will's arrival and the arrangements were sufficiently far advanced that after a brief check on what was to be done he decided to let it run.

The young personnel officer there had been an enthusiast for psychometrics and had introduced a test from a well-known publisher involving logical reasoning, numerical calculations and flow diagramming skills. Hardly anybody seemed to be getting through it. The personnel officer wondered if the original cut-off set had been too high. He had sent Will some figures that suggested that if they lowered the acceptable score by 2 points they would get an extra 20 per cent of people through.

Will decided it was time to take a closer look. He unlocked a filing cabinet and took out his test manual.

Multiple testing

So far in this chapter we have considered only the case of a single test with a single cut-off to be taken into account at any one time. But what of the case when several different tests are used, either completely separate ones or forming part of a battery? In the latter case, for instance, with batteries such as the Differential Aptitude Test (DAT, referred to in Chapter 2) or the General Ability Test (GAT), which comprises separate verbal, non-verbal, numerical and spatial tests, there is usually the advantage of a common set of norms for the whole battery. This gives some basis for comparisons among the different tests used. If tests are drawn from different sources then the norms available will often reflect widely differing samples, limiting the scope either to combine or trade off scores.

Combining test scores

When there is scope to do the necessary research, test scores can be combined to give a weighted sum, in what is known as a multiple regression equation.

Such an equation gives a direct read-out of predicted performance. This approach is attractive and in one sense ideal; test scores are put in and performance on the job comes out! In practice, life is not so simple. There is, of course, the problem of the criterion of performance, which multiple regression shares with other means of interpretation of test scores. (As suggested earlier, this is, in effect, side-stepped by making comparisons on a normative basis.) There is then the question, again mentioned before, of gaining adequate data for research. It is usually just not a practical proposition to do this in conjunction with a selection or recruitment programme and so one often relies on offline studies reported in the test manuals or research literature.

Again, the apparent simplicity of the idea of combining weighted scores can be questioned. Inherent in it is the idea that a high score on one test can offset a low score on another. Although this may be so in general, it may gloss over the negative impact of very low scores. For example, a battery used for clerical selection might include a clerical checking test (with items such as shown in Figure 3.2). Someone scoring very low on such a test might be so inaccurate that all their work would have to be checked and in effect reworked. High performance in other aspects of their work, as predicted by other tests in the battery, would not compensate. The multiple regression approach would tend to mask the impossibility of adequate compensation for the area of limitation.

Another approach to the use of multiple test scores is the use of multiple cut-offs. A minimum score is decided on each of the tests, so that only those above each of these minima is considered further. Sometimes further consideration is in terms of another process entirely, such as an assessment centre (see Chapters 9 and 10), and sometimes it is in terms of, in effect, combining scores. Thus, a score level averaged over the various tests is sometimes set. Without specific research there will be a degree of arbitrariness about any of these approaches to multiple tests, with the existence of relevant norms often the firmest foundation available. (For some further comment on multiple regression and multiple cut-offs see 'Glossary and technical notes'.) It is also worth noting in this connection that considerable management effort may be required in working with someone whose profile of characteristics is made up of extremes. One needs in such cases to be constantly considering whether enough support is being given to cover the areas of relative deficit, and if enough leeway is being provided for the strengths to have full scope to demonstrate themselves. Managing someone with a more consistently average profile is likely to be a less demanding, if also less exciting, proposition.

Some guidelines

Overall, the guidance to intending recruiters here will be as follows:

▌ Consider competencies and choose tests accordingly. If there is insufficient information to do this do not just launch into a recruitment advertising campaign and arbitrary test procedures, but be prepared to spend more time in researching and building some form of competency description.

▌ Consider the numbers of people that you are prepared to process and organize your procedures accordingly. (In many situations, precise numbers will be difficult to gauge but if you are overflowing with candidates you will be tempted to apply more or less arbitrary procedures rather than use effective psychometric methods.)

▌ Consider cut-offs and if you are tempted to lower or to raise them think about whether this amounts to degrading or enhancing your original testing process.

ONE-OFF AND SHORTLIST ASSESSMENT

Consultant's report

In many circumstances psychometric tests are applied in occasional rather than large-scale applications. This may happen, for example, for middle or senior management posts, or in relation to the replacement of key functional staff. Again, the existence or creation of job definitions or, better still, competency models and the avoidance of arbitrary selection on the basis of irrelevant or very weak predictors such as age and educational qualifications are to be encouraged.

Sometimes, the use of psychometrics in these circumstances takes the form of reference to an internal or more often external consultant in effect with a view to finding out things that have not been thrown up in earlier procedures. These would often have consisted of sifting of CVs and the use of conventional interviews, both of which relate largely to experience. In such cases there is a recognition that psychometric procedures may save the costs of expensive hiring mistakes, which could have a negative impact on the hiring organization in general and particularly on the hiring executive. Giving clues to the most appropriate way of managing the candidate, if hired, can also help optimize his or her contribution.

Sometimes in these cases the competency requirements may not be made as explicit as elsewhere, particularly in the case of an external reference to a consultant who may use a more or less standard battery, often including a fairly broad-band personality questionnaire. (The idea that there may be something else to find out about the candidate reflects an implicit appreciation of the fact that the procedures likely to have been used earlier – even though an enormous amount of time and money may have been spent up to this point – are, in effect, weak predictors!)

The potential interaction and complementarity between personality and ability tests such as those measuring high-level reasoning can also be seen as coming into play here. A relaxed individual may not in general feel stressed by high workloads but, if his or her cognitive reasoning abilities are weak, he or she may still fail to cope effectively. Conversely, a more tense person with a high reasoning capacity may be able to cope more effectively. A sample consultant's report weighing up the information from a short battery of this nature follows.

A REPORT ON JOHN JONES, MANAGERIAL CANDIDATE FOR COMPANY Z

Brief description of tests and questionnaires used

1. Test of reasoning ability

   Two tests from the Graduate and Managerial Assessment Series have been used to assess the level of intellectual effectiveness. The tests measure verbal reasoning and abstract reasoning ability and are designed to discriminate levels of ability among graduate-level managerial candidates. Abstract reasoning skills would indicate an ability to recognize patterns and trends and to be able to switch easily between different contexts and levels of analysis.

Comparisons are made with a norm population of graduate-level managers and are expressed in percentile terms.

2. 16 Personality Factor Questionnaire version five (16PF5)

This is a well-researched and documented questionnaire and provides a comprehensive picture of an individual's basic personality. As the name implies, 16 different and independent personality dimensions are measured. Interpretation of the information focuses on aspects of behaviour known to be closely associated with managerial effectiveness, and in particular the key competencies identified as being significant for this particular post.

It should be noted that, although likely to provide a useful guide to performance, psychometric measures are not infallible. For decision-making purposes they should therefore not be used alone but in conjunction with other sources of information.

Findings

Pattern of interpersonal relationships

A strongly goal-oriented individual, he will readily and easily work as part of a team, where he will actively and assertively seek out a leadership role. He displays a need to have control of the circumstances in which he finds himself and, while he will be prepared to delegate, he will maintain a high level of vigilance to ensure that progress towards a given objective is maintained.

He is naturally disposed to be open and frank in his communication with others and will prefer to 'get on with the job'. He recognizes that this approach does not always agree with others and this is an aspect of his behaviour that he constantly tries to moderate.

He will display a high level of social confidence and quickly be at ease in any work or social situation although he may become impatient in a culture that becomes preoccupied with the means rather than the end.

His social confidence is underpinned by a natural gregariousness and to be effective he will need to have a team around him, in part to act as a sounding board for his ideas but also to be the means of implementing his decisions. He will always initially seek for others to critique his own ideas and arrive at a consensus on a course of action. He will, however, have no compunction in imposing his will if agreement is not readily reached. It is critical that those working for him adopt the same high standards as those that he sets for himself as he is unwilling to 'carry passengers'.

It is interesting to note that while he will display an assertiveness and an independence of mind his continuing effectiveness will be dependent on a substantial level of positive feedback and stroking.

Problem solving/decision making

Faced with a decision he will be diligent in seeking out all the pertinent essential information that relates to that particular issue. He will be analytical in endeavouring to understand the causes rather than the phenomenon itself and having gained his understanding of the causes will use these to synthesize a solution and a decision. When arriving at a decision, it is important not only that the logic should be sound but, to use his own words, that it should 'smell right'. If a decision does not 'smell right' he is unlikely to go with it and by the same token if others present to him decisions that do not have the same intuitive appeal then he will challenge them and press hard for justification.

His problem solving will be typified by a systematic approach and it is improbable that his decisions will break with conventional wisdom. Having arrived at a decision, he will hold to it tenaciously, almost to the point of stubbornness, relinquishing his position only in the face of extremely well-reasoned, logical argument, which must also have an intuitive appeal for him.

Coping with stress

There is nothing within the profile to suggest that he cannot cope adequately with the stresses of operating in a senior position. It is, however, worthy of note that he may on occasions experience a mild degree of frustration as he gets too close to a particular problem and such frustration will be readily and quickly vented.

Work style

A natural team player, his optimum contribution will come when he has the opportunity to take leadership of a team of competent and able subordinates. His particular strength will lie not necessarily in the development of strategy, but rather in the interpretation of strategy into detailed plans of implementation. He will then action this through a relentless drive towards the objectives.

Thus, such reports set out the various balances in the profile of ability and personality, and can help focus on areas where the candidate may prove to be a liability.

Sometimes the consultant will be briefed very explicitly in terms of the requisite competencies and will shape the report as in the sample extract above. 'Quality orientation' might be a competency required generally in an organization embarked upon a total quality management (TQM) initiative, or it could relate to a requirement in a specific role with a quality focus.

The scope for tailoring such reports quite finely to reflect the pattern of likely behaviour in relation to the role means that consultants and their clients will often prefer to work in this way rather than to use expert system reports, which are discussed in Chapter 16.

Sometimes there is a temptation to set aside the unpalatable indications that can come out from testing individual candidates. This seems to be the more so, not surprisingly, the more the psychometric procedure is seen as merely confirmatory and, perhaps very particularly, where a number of people in the firm have seen the candidate and felt comfortable with him or her. Their own observations may be subjective and their conclusions the result of a halo effect – someone judged good in one aspect of relevance, such as assertiveness, is judged good in all. Such circumstances often build up a weight of inertia that can tell heavily against the test findings. These cases then become equivalent to the procedure of lowering the cut-off discussed above under mass applications. Then the consultant may have to be particularly vociferous or extreme in his or her comments for any misgivings about a candidate to carry the day. The more closely integrated the testing process is, and the clearer the model of requirements against which the consultant is working, the more scope there is for an informed comment that is likely to add value to the decision-making process. With greater integration there is less likelihood of the psychometric findings – or those from any of the other systematic procedures discussed in this book – just being set aside.

Further exploration – follow-up and feedback

Sometimes testing used for one-off appointments is seen as throwing up ideas for further exploration. It is frankly not clear that this process is always used to best effect. At its best it will, in effect, add to the accuracy of the test process itself, being equivalent to narrowing the distribution of scores ever more closely to the single straight-line prediction. A skilled consultant with detailed knowledge of the target role and expertise in the tests used will be able to probe and explore effectively, giving a sound basis for the detailed elaboration of a report and adding considerable value. (For example, whether or not a tense person with a high reasoning capacity has, in fact, been able to cope with high workloads could be established in this way.)

At the other extreme, though, the follow-up process may invite substitution of a less accurate measure for one over which considerable care and trouble has been taken – the psychometric test or battery. Consider, for instance, the case in which a candidate going through the Gordon Personal Profile and Inventory is described, among other things, as unlikely to invest heavily in personal relations, though having effective superficial sociability. (This would reflect just two of the scales in that instrument.) If the former indication is considered by a panel of interviewers as worthy of further exploration they are more likely, in fact, to be able to gather information relating to the latter characteristic of sociability, concluding that they should set aside the test finding.

A skilled test interpreter is more likely to be able to probe for information at a level that could actually enhance the accuracy of the overall picture. In doing so he or she may, in fact, also undertake feedback to the candidate. Feedback of test results is in general recommended (see, for example, the IPM – now CIPD – Code on Psychological Testing, 1993).

If integrated into the whole testing and selection process itself, feedback can, however, be two-edged. On the one hand, discussion with candidates in which the profile or elements of it are displayed for their comment can elicit illustrative information as just indicated to confirm or refute the test findings. Feedback can, though, also forewarn candidates, perhaps encouraging them to make an extra effort in a later face-to-face interview situation. For example, someone who would not, by nature of personality, routinely project warmth in the way that might actually be required in a job might still be able to do so for relatively short periods. Similarly, given feedback on a tendency to dominance and over-aggressiveness, this characteristic might be toned down at a later stage of selection.

Clearly, care and thought are required in the follow-up questioning and the feedback process.

PSYCHOMETRICS AND INTERNAL SELECTION

So far the consideration of psychometric testing in selection has been largely directed towards candidates being recruited and brought on board from outside. Similar considerations will apply to those joining from within an organization, that is moving from one part of it to another. Hence this section of the chapter is relatively brief. However, there are one or two special factors to be borne in mind.

Don't they know me?'

First of all it is sometimes questioned when tests are to be used internally whether that is right and proper. The view is often expressed that 'Surely my company knows me?' or 'Surely I know my people?' or 'I've been around in this organization a long time; I don't expect to be tested.' These would, of course, be valid arguments if there were data available to provide the information about the individual's suitability for the role. The obvious limitation to begin with here is that one would necessarily be looking at historical performance in a role different from that now being considered, so that it is likely there would be some further dimensions that would require to be explored by one means or another.

The idea of the Peter Principle, by which people are promoted to the level at which they can no longer function effectively, is a sad reflection of the fact that previous performance in a different job or one at a lower level is an unreliable guide. Sources that one would think could potentially be tapped, such as appraisal data, are rarely seen to supply requisite information. As discussed in Chapter 14, appraisal systems are widely seen as inaccurate, inadequate and/or incomplete. The idea that a test procedure may be intrusive is, of course, not only confined to internal selection. In the habitual absence of objective data from other sources, such as appraisals, the benefits of psychometric information are evident. It is, of course, by no means uncommon for internal and external candidates to apply and be considered together. In such circumstances the objectivity that a psychometric intervention can bring will help underpin and demonstrate the fairness of the proceeding. In my experience, it is about equally common for both internal and external candidates to be a little wary. One group will feel that the insiders might have the advantage of special knowledge, while the others feel that new blood is really being sought. Professionally applied psychometrics can mitigate the effects of any such suspicions, as well as actually supplying the objective data required.

Large-scale internal applications

Massive selection applications internally are relatively unusual. They may sometimes arise in relation to large-scale redundancy situations where those who would otherwise be displaced from the organization are first given the opportunity to apply for jobs inside. In such circumstances, the number of applicants may be large but the number of jobs relatively few. Given the overall emotional climate that will, in any case, attend such circumstances it will be appropriate to proceed carefully. The objectivity of psychometrics is likely to be welcomed. However, it will be important, given the likely small number of vacancies, to shape expectations realistically. Special care may be needed in briefing on the test procedures as such in order to reduce apprehensiveness about what may often be unfamiliar procedures. In these circumstances, too, feedback processes may well need to be linked into other aspects of career counselling that may be undertaken for such individuals.

SUMMARY

1. Ability rather than personality testing is likely to be used in connection with early stages of large-scale selection.

2. Because specific validity studies may not be practicable, use of the most relevant published norm groups may often be indicated.

3. The degree of relation between test score and performance is expressed in the correlation coefficient.

4. Where selection procedures are applied with no consideration for their correlation with success they may give a wholly spurious impression of value.

5. Relatively weak predictors can be made to work by setting high cut-offs, but this carries penalties in terms of numbers required to be processed and potential discrimination.

6. Psychometric results can be degraded by ill-considered shifting of cut-offs or unstructured follow-up procedures.

7. Where several tests are used their practical interpretation may involve the use of multiple regression methods or the setting of multiple cut-offs.

8. Consultants' narrative reports are often used in relatively low-volume selection. For their value to be maximized they need to be integrated into the whole selection process.

9. Tests can be used as an effective basis for a further in-depth analysis of an individual, but such analyses are specialized.

10. In internal selection, psychometric results may often provide information not actually available from sources supposedly of relevance.

11. In recruitment involving a mix of internal and external candidates, tests may underpin objectivity and fairness.

8

Implementing psychometrics

INTRODUCTION

In this chapter we begin by considering the accumulation of information in a psychometric application and then from this consider some of the logical and practical issues involved. This is followed by a checklist of points to take into account in applying psychometric tests.

INFORMATION FLOWS – BUILDING THE PICTURE

Capturing the competencies

As is indicated throughout this book, no one procedure, psychometric test or otherwise, will provide total information about an individual's chance of success in a job or the most appropriate path for development. Many organizations recognize this tacitly at least, but the response of some may be to engage in behaviour that is costly and dysfunctional. One high-tech company, for instance, wanting to be sure that its sales managers were of the right calibre for the organization, insisted on candidates being interviewed by no fewer than 15 executives on some occasions. In that particular case, psychometrics did not actually play any part at all. The company concerned had no systematic way of pooling the data and the poor candidates in effect experienced a similar process 15 times over.

Other organizations are, though, profligate with psychometric procedures themselves. It is not uncommon, but not particularly helpful, for an occupational psychologist working as a consultant to be provided with an array of results from different tests that may have been conducted at different stages of a candidate's recruitment process, or to be told that a referral to him or her was for a second opinion to back up or presumably contradict what the company psychologist or personnel people had already concluded by some other set of procedures.

Nor is it uncommon for organizations to use performance, on the job or during fairly extensive training, as a selection process in itself. There may then be a recognition that, say, 50 per cent failure among trainees is regrettable but sometimes organizations will smugly say, 'Thank goodness we did have such an exacting programme and that we did not have to leave it until the chap was actually working on the job to find out that he couldn't do it.' Obviously a little thought would have resulted in a more effective use of everybody's time, effort and money.

Information mapping

Consider the series of diagrams shown in Figure 8.1. This could represent any job, but for the moment let us imagine it is that of an area manager in a supermarket chain. Success in the job is partly to do with the competencies that the individual brings and partly due to the factors that may interact with these competencies. These could include management style – how supportive or otherwise the regional manager to whom this post reports is; trading conditions – whether the other supermarkets are cutting prices; or business processes used, such as the efficiency or otherwise of the company's just-in-time warehousing. An uninterested regional manager, cut-throat competition and a just-in-time system that turned out to be just too late more often than not would all reduce our friend's success. The application of a psychometric procedure would be used with a view to determining some of what the candidate brought to the job that was of relevance. The test applied might be one of general intelligence designed for use with managerial-level staff. An example would be the AH5 Test, comprising verbal, numerical and diagrammatic items.

In Figure 8.1, the small circle, indicating the test overlapping with the large one indicating success, shows the effectiveness of such a process. In the area of overlap of the two circles the test procedure can be seen to be adding value. The part that is outside is, in effect, noise in the system as far as this application is concerned, that is it distorts the message. How far the person using the selection procedure knows the degree of overlap will probably vary from case to case. It will depend on the general research done on the test and the specific work done in relation to the competencies for the job. It is evident, though, that the test will be more effective if it is chosen on the basis of relevant competencies, if it has itself been well constructed and if appropriate norm groups are chosen.

The same test may, of course, be applied more or less well. The use of inappropriate norm groups, rushed or hurried instruction and poor test conditions would all tend to reduce the degree of overlap between the test and what it was purporting to measure, indicating a movement apart of the two circles as in the first diagram in Figure 8.1. Our area manager candidate might be experiencing a selection process including a visit to a supermarket in the chain. The test might be conducted in the dimly lit assistant manager's office, which is not made too comfortable so as to encourage the assistant manager to spend most of his or her time out front, which doubles as a storeroom and in which the phone rings on and off throughout the test, despite protestations that it should be on divert. Alternatively, a largely inappropriate test might have been chosen, perhaps one just measuring spatial ability in the mistaken belief that merchandising layout would form a very large part of the area manager's job. Such a test might add some value, but less than the broader general intelligence measure.

If the supermarket had been able to develop its own AH5 norms, then the precision of use of the tests might be enhanced, increasing the overlap between test results and success as in the bottom right-hand diagram in Figure 8.1. In other cases it could be extra-skilled interpretation of the test, for example by someone drawing on depth of knowledge to recognize a variety of patterns in a personality questionnaire, that would increase the area of overlap. The use of a follow-up interview specifically related, at least in part, to the output from the test results and probing the findings further may have positive or negative results on the area of overlap.

This has been discussed to some extent in Chapter 7, but to give a further example, again related to the supermarket, in recruiting a clerk the

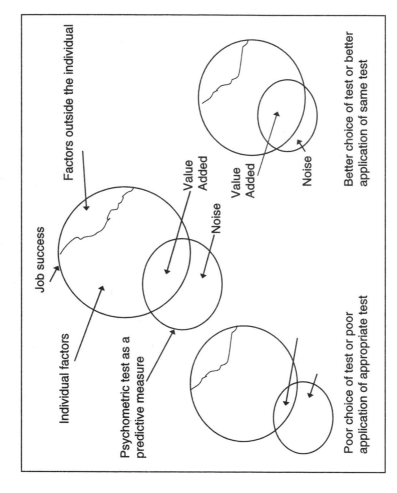

Figure 8.1 Mapping psychometrics on to job success

use of a question as in 'You do not seem to be very conscientious – what do you say to that?' 'I deny it utterly. Why, only last week I stayed behind late every night to finish some filing' might lead to the interpretation that the test result was wrong. However, a further follow-up, 'Why did you need to stay late for filing?', as in 'Well, actually, it had been hanging about for months and months and I thought I might get into trouble if I didn't at last get around to it' might suggest that the original conclusion from the test was accurate. Though this passage may seem a caricature, it should serve to spell out how inept questioning can have an impact on what is gathered from the test results. Appropriate and skilful questioning can, on the other hand, enhance the information gained – in effect increasing the area of overlap of the two circles.

Combining tests

Figure 8.2 shows what may happen when a broad-band personality measure is used, together with an ability test such as, say, numerical reasoning. The area of overlap with the competencies may actually be larger for the personality questionnaire. However, because much of the domain of that measure lies outside the required competency area, looking at the personality test as a whole could be misleading with so much of it functioning as noise. Returning again to the supermarket case, suppose the personality questionnaire used were the Edwards Personal Preference Schedule (EPPS) referred to in Chapter 3. Of its 15 scales, several including achievement, dominance and affiliation might lie in the area of overlap. Other scales would lie in the noise area. These could include exhibition – a preference for being at the centre of attention – and heterosexuality.

It may even be that the increasing focus on big five personality dimensions (see Chapter 3) would compound difficulties here. With such a broad sweep as the big five model gives there may be a compulsion to believe that somehow it is all to some degree relevant in all cases: 'Isn't it nice to have a general description of someone because you might come up with something interesting?' If the competency modelling has been thorough, such a view misses the point. It may also lay the user open to charges of insufficient care in the use of tests. A finer-grain personality read-out does not guarantee that consideration will be given to the question of what is relevant, but at least makes it possible – and effective competency modelling would help determine which areas of the test should be given consideration in interpretation.

Note also that the two tests themselves are seen as not overlapping. Each then adds some unique value to the process. In the supermarket case

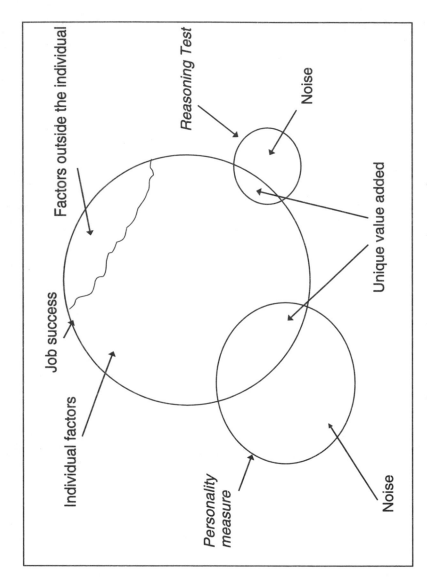

Figure 8.2 Contribution of two dissimilar tests in predicting job success

the EPPS would not throw light on numerical reasoning ability, and a numerical reasoning test would not tell us about motivation. Quite commonly, though, tests do overlap in what they measure, as shown in Figure 8.3. In this case there is some unique value added by the second procedure. There is also some unique noise in each test, which needs to be systematically discounted if the interpretations are not to be misleading. If there is no system for determining what is noise and what is relevant then all the data may be thought to add value. What may be particularly misleading, then, is that which is irrelevant but which has been measured by each test in turn, confirming the existence of something that has no real bearing on success!

Consider our supermarket case again. Suppose we had two test procedures, one measuring verbal, detail-handling and spatial abilities, and the other numerical and detail-handling and spatial abilities.

The area of overlap of the two smaller circles representing the tests within the competency domain is simply a redundant measure, in this case the separate measures of detail handling. However, it may not be recognized as such. Very often test users will take comfort in some degree of confirmation. Usually this is so because the precise area of overlap between what the test measures and what is required is not known perfectly, and it is also recognized that any measure is imperfect. However, there is a temptation to believe that, because the two measures of detail handling yield a high score, not only is competence in this confirmed, but the candidate can be regarded as really having an extra-high ability in this area. In this same case we might be tempted to take extra note of the two indications from the spatial scores, both of which would be largely irrelevant!

The addition of further and further tests or other procedures builds up the multiple picture shown in Figure 8.4. Ultimately, much of the domain of relevance has been measured – the personality characteristics and abilities that make for success in supermarket area management, say, but with much overlapping, confusing, irrelevant data and some of the irrelevant data confirmed by yet further measures!

Competencies and sub-competencies

It is worth noting that the systematic use of multiple measures in the assessment centre movement has, as part of its rationale, the very sound idea that competencies may, in effect, manifest themselves as sub-competencies, operating in different situations or different environments. Thus, someone may be very persuasive in written communications as demonstrated in an in-basket exercise, but far less persuasive in meeting

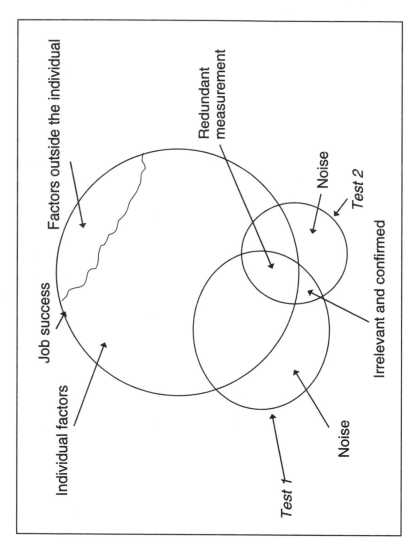

Figure 8.3 Contribution of two similar tests in predicting job success

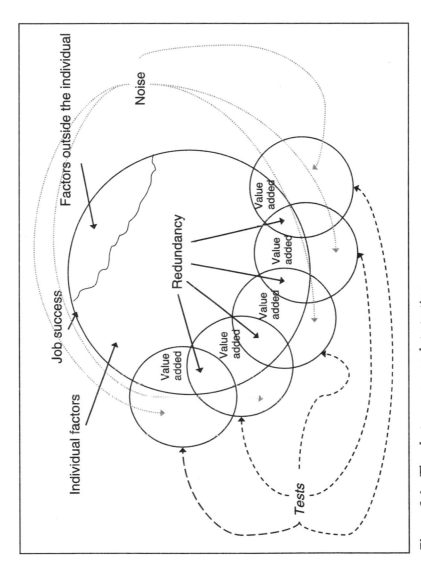

Figure 8.4 The shotgun approach to testing

people face to face as represented in, say, an interview simulation. These situations may then be sufficiently distinct to require an additional measure. This is a different case from increasing measures simply because we are not sure about the validity of the first, second, third, fourth or fifth one.

Making sense

The way through this morass is at least moderately straightforward. Thinking about the domain of competencies, better still doing work to define competencies carefully and considering tests in terms of what they contribute, is an important step on the way. Also note that, as a practical matter of time and cost, relatively few test applications will be able to be undertaken with tests developed on a bespoke basis. Rather, in many situations, off-the-shelf tests will have to be used. This implies the particular need to consider actively what is relevant and what is not. As indicated already this may be particularly germane in the case of personality questionnaires. It is also important to consider the way in which the maximum value can be squeezed out of any one measure. Most benefit can be achieved with attention to appropriate test administration standards and meaningful follow-up questioning.

Arbitrary criteria

The existence of good information from a psychometric test or tests and from follow-up questioning does not guarantee effective use of that information. Even when it is set out against a clearly developed competency model, with the intended contribution of each part clearly displayed, there can be no complete assurance that it will be used effectively.

Anyone working in personnel or human resources must have experienced the candidate, excellent in all known competencies as evidenced by psychometric results of the highest order, rejected out of hand by line managers because of, say, wearing suede shoes to an interview. Particular shoe-wearing behaviour has never, in my experience, been specified in a competency model or job definition and certainly no evidence exists of either positive or negative contribution to job performance. Nevertheless, the candidate gets no further. Painstaking thought about the psychometrics and attention to some of the practical issues outlined in the next but one section all militate against such arbitrariness, but there are no guarantees.

OTHER ASSESSMENT METHODS

Much of what has been said about building the picture could be applied to whatever methods of assessment were under consideration, whether psychometric instruments as such or, say, assessment centre exercises. So, how does one choose when an assessment centre or, say, a critical incident interview should actually be deployed? Inevitably this is like asking the proverbial question about the length of a piece of string. Certainly, with so very many psychometric tests in print there is reason to suppose that most competency domains can be covered. (I have put together test batteries off the shelf for roles as far apart as sales directors, factory managers and public school headmasters.) However, relevant norms will inevitably be lacking in some of the more far-flung applications.

Some form of structured interview may be thought a quick route to a highly focused assessment tool. However, to use the full power of that technology as represented in the structured psychometric interview described in Chapter 12 is to embark on a substantial research and development exercise.

Full assessment centres provide comprehensive information and would be unlikely to be appropriate at, say, the early stages of a recruitment campaign. Because they typically involve multiple participants as well as multiple assessors they are generally not suitable for counselling situations or one-off recruitment. However, individual exercises such as an in-basket may be very powerful information generators in such cases, not least because of the richness of potentially relevant and readily understood information that they may yield. This is discussed further in Chapter 10.

FURTHER PRACTICAL ISSUES

Control and ownership of test results

As indicated in Chapter 5, when test results are held on computer file, then the subject of them has been legally entitled to access and this now applies to assessment results gathered and stored in other ways. It is also important to give consideration as to who else may have access to them. Two criteria usually used are that they should be available only to those with a genuine interest and/or those appropriately trained in interpretation. One category does not, of course, necessarily imply the latter. In many organizations there will be people with appropriate training who have no real business need for knowing a particular set of test results. Conversely, some individuals, eg recruiting managers, with an interest in results may not be skilled in their interpretation. Narrative reports, as discussed in Chapter 5, can be a significant aid if they are appropriately prepared.

There is also the question of where and how such test data should be held. Normally there is a need for some separation from other personnel files, which may be largely managed by personnel administrators, even for tests related to recruitment. Access to such reports also needs to be considered in connection with the requirements of the Data Protection Act and the need to give feedback, as discussed in Chapter 5. In the case of development there is likely to be an ongoing tension between the need to ensure the maximum level of confidentiality and the need to give access to test data on the part of those who may have a genuine interest in the development of their staff or, as discussed in Chapter 5, be functioning in the role of interested third parties. Abuses of access to test data are probably still sufficiently common to err on the side of caution rather than complete openness. You do not have to go very far to hear stories of people attending development centres where confidentiality is being stressed, only to learn that feedback on the supposedly confidential results has gone straight to a potential employing department! The stronger provisions of the Data Protection Act do not necessarily imply that better practice will arrive overnight. The test user may well have to function as champion with regard to this aspect of testing, as with others.

Who should be trained?

Ownership of data and the questions of expertise that this raises lead inevitably to the question of training. We have covered this to some degree in relation to regulation in Chapter 5. The point to be made here, which was touched on in the first chapter, is essentially how far to spread training and how far to rely on specialist staff either internally or externally. There are, of course, pros and cons in either direction.

The use of external consultants in relation to psychometric administration and interpretation was briefly discussed in Chapter 3. It confers the advantage of width and depth of experience, and a likely breadth of knowledge of, and access to, tests. They are also likely to have devoted facilities and trained administrators, and be organized to provide rapid turnaround of results. However, consultancies may themselves develop pet practices with a limited range of psychometric instruments and have some inclination to utilize these, with some justification, but without their necessarily being the ones most apt for the particular purpose. (Other aspects of the use of consultants are discussed in Chapter 15.)

Of course individuals and consultant groups within an organization may suffer from the same or even greater constraints. It does take time and money for training and also extensive use over time to enable even a specialist to master a new test process. The internal person may have limited time and be under pressure to fit in test administration, scoring, feedback to the candidate, and reporting the outcome with other duties and tasks.

The external person also has the advantage of a greater degree of independence, and may underline some of the points on confidentiality and other aspects of good practice. Indeed, he or she may be in a stronger position to walk away from or stand up to pressures from unscrupulous management in relation to inappropriate revelation of data or to requests to adjust reports to be more in keeping with some alternative view of the subject of the report. Such pressures are by no means unknown either in the commercial world or in the public sector.

An issue that can arise in using an external or internal specialist in a psychometric application is that the test or tests concerned may forever remain something of a black box. This will lead to limited comprehension by management of what the test can contribute. It can also lead to the possible disregarding of test results, in the way discussed in Chapter 7 and referred to earlier in this chapter, under arbitrary criteria. This is sometimes thought of as more likely to arise with an external consultant – someone more remote from the organization concerned. However, such a person is in a strong position to produce an authoritative report, indicating likely behaviour and the significance of this in the role under consideration. External consultants will also be in a better position to make their report and analysis truly comprehensive. For example, if they should come across inadequate or conflicting test data they would be expected to make use of further tests as necessary or to complement the test findings with information from, say, a criterion-based interview. They are also more likely to have the business and management knowledge necessary to interpret the test results in a business context than, say, a junior personnel officer, who might function as an internal specialist.

Another issue with regard to using internal consultants or, indeed, of spreading expertise widely is that the practice of test interpretation may become limited. This can happen in one of two ways. In the first case the trained person simply has very little scope for ongoing exposure to tests, perhaps applying a single psychometric procedure only two or three times a year. In the second case a single or narrow range of tests comes to be utilized very frequently and, as raised above with the external consultants, becomes a pet practice of the individual concerned. There is no simple answer to these issues but they remain matters for consideration.

Costs and benefits

I had an experience many years ago with a client who began by stating that he wished to use a particular ability test. The instrument concerned was virtually a museum piece and did not appear to be the most appropriate for the application concerned. When the matter was pursued further the real reason for focusing on the test emerged – 'We've got a cupboard full of them – management won't let me buy any more until they are all used up.' The fact that they had not been used up quickly because there were more modern tests available with more appropriate norms was apparently beside the point!

Times do not necessarily change very fast. Recounting this little story to another client, 15 years later, firm nods of understanding were observed. However, closer enquiry revealed that these were not signs of empathy but simply a signal that the same thing was being experienced by them. This client had a cupboard full of tests too: the consumables had to be consumed and the booklets used to dog-eared and scribbled destruction before further purchases of any materials could be made. Relevance, competencies and standards were clearly not considered important.

Foolish as such situations may seem, they do underline the fact that tests are not free and users will expect a return on their investment before investing further. Thus, it behoves those responsible for deciding upon a psychometric application to consider the benefit of a particular test purchase or particular training expenditure against its requirements in the longer term. Precise costs of psychometrics will vary but in, say, a recruitment application are unlikely to be more than a couple of per cent of a salary. The benefits conferred are likely to dwarf such figures. If an objective psychometric procedure is not used, inappropriate appointments are much more likely. Not only is there considerable anguish on the part of the employer and employee, but ultimately the recruitment process with all its associated expenditure has to be repeated. In the interim, damage may be done commercially to the business both directly and through the adverse effects on the morale of those working for or alongside someone who is inappropriate and may be manifestly failing. The cost of all this can be conservatively estimated as 200 to 300 per cent of salary.

Similarly, in development, the use of psychometrics will make it much more likely that an investment is well thought out, toning down the expensive knee-jerk, 'Let's send him on a training course...'

Physical considerations

Training in test administration will refer, among other things, to the control of the physical environment for testing. One or two other aspects are worthy of consideration. A company operating a large-scale psychometric testing programme on behalf of a government department sought to update their test battery. The test development company that they approached was a little surprised to find that one of their requirements was that the new battery should weigh less than the old one. All became clear, though, when it was realized that test administration took place at continually varying locations around the country and that the test administrators typically travelled by public transport.

Some years ago computers used for test administration would often better be described as luggable rather than portable. Also, where testing is to be conducted at a remote site it may be necessary to make the physical requirements known very explicitly. Space, light, quiet, desks, chairs and even electric power points cannot necessarily be assumed!

Briefing and practice materials

One of the trends in recent years has been the development of an increasing amount of pre-briefing material for psychometric testing. This is of various sorts. First there are books seeking to help individuals pass ability tests, by increasing their familiarity with material quite close to that which may be experienced in the tests themselves. This material is set alongside general guidance on the role and purpose of testing. An example is the 1991 book by Bryon and Modha. It is not clear whether the major contribution of such a volume is in the specific practice opportunity provided or in the general briefing on testing. Fairly clearly, direct practice of actual items is likely to lead to distortions of scores, but so could nervousness or lack of confidence stemming from lack of familiarity. Some employers' groups have opted to provide general briefing, seeking to demystify the testing process and give candidates the greatest opportunity of doing their best. For example, Banking Information Service produced a booklet (1993) particularly aimed at helping young people understand the place of psychometric testing in employment.

A number of test publishers, too, produce specific briefing material on particular tests. These are designed to be sent out in advance, again to help familiarize those due to take the tests with the type of items that they will see and to shape their expectations. An example is given in Figure 8.5. However, the use of such specific materials is very varied in practice. Their development appears to have arisen in response to requests from candidates. Further research and possibly firmer guidelines are needed to ensure a level playing field. It was only in 1971 that Vincent, writing about practical issues in testing from an NIIP perspective, warned against the menace of test sophistication, arising from deliberate coaching of candidates and the effects of test practice. Perhaps the wheel has come half a circle since then. The advice pro tem to test users is at least be consistent to your testees in the briefing materials with which you do or do not provide them.

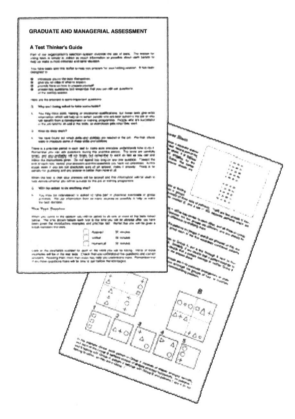

Figure 8.5   Test briefing material

The question of briefing also arises, in effect, in relation to repeated applications of the same test, which was raised in Chapter 7. The development cases considered there would often provide scope for control of instruments used within one organization. However, in recruitment one cannot legislate for what the candidate may or may not have experienced with other organizations. Some tests have parallel forms, that is alternative versions designed to cover the same ground. Parallel forms of ability or aptitude tests are more likely to offer a solution than those for personality instruments, where recent feedback may still be expected to have an impact on responses. In the personality field, moving to a different test than the one experienced recently is likely to provide a better solution.

Tests and stress

As has been reiterated several times throughout this book, tests are designed to give readings that are as stable as possible. Reliability is a key concept in psychometrics and wide random variations in performance are not a desirable characteristic of a psychometric test. However, this stability assumes set and controlled conditions. As mentioned already, tests need to be conducted in a stable and uninterrupted environment. This suggests that, given a test that has been established as adequately reliable in such stable conditions, performance of groups of individuals on the test may be used to determine the effect of the environment as such.

For example, the argument would run that, if a particularly noisy or otherwise physically stressful environment impairs performance on a test, then that environment may also have implications for performance on intellectual or other tasks required to be carried out there. There would be consequent implications for the initial levels of intellect required to perform such tasks under such conditions or for the amount of effort required to maintain performance.

Thus, the use of tests to explore such situations can be helpful in determining how recruitment procedures may be modified and at what level the environmental stress is likely to become wholly dysfunctional. The research necessary to establish such factors is likely to lean more on the experimental than the individually based psychometric tradition and may well require the use of special, laboratory-based facilities. Such research is not particularly common but can be seen as a legitimate application of psychometric procedures and concepts (see, for example, Allnutt, 1970). More common is the use of personality measures in relation to assessing propensity to stress or the deployment of specific measures designed to assess states of stress, as described in Chapter 3.

These are some of the issues to be considered in utilizing tests:

▌ What is the application?
  - Selection:
    - internal?
    - external?
  - Development:
    - current role?
    - future role?
  - Counselling?
  - Auditing individual or team capability?
  - Team building?
  - Other?

▌ Where in the chain of events should the application be made?

▌ What is known about the role/roles concerned?

▌ Competency model?

▌ Job definition?
  - Established or emergent?
  - Does the intended timescale permit further investigation?

▌ Have tests been used before in connection with this role?

▌ Which ones?

▌ When?

▌ Why?

▌ By whom?

▌ Are candidates likely to have experienced the tests envisaged already?

▌ What norms or other interpretative procedures were used?

▌ What norms are available?

▌ What resources are available?

▮ Money?

▮ Trained personnel?

▮ Existing test materials?

▮ Testing cubicles/rooms?

▮ Computers?

▮ Who will have access to results?

▮ Personnel?

▮ Line management?

▮ Subjects of test – who will give feedback and in what form?

▮ With what other data will results be associated?

▮ Appraisals?

▮ Outcome of succession planning discussions?

▮ Assessment centre outputs?

▮ Will external or internal resources be used?

▮ Why?

▮ Who?

▮ Is it feasible to undertake bespoke developments or establish local norms?

▮ Will the Data Protection Act apply?

▮ What other procedures will/should be used?
   - Assessment centre exercises?
   - Interviews:
     - structured/unstructured?
     - criterion based?

       – structured psychometric?
       – panel?
       – sequential?
    – Biodata?

▌ When and how will integration of these different data sets take place?

▌ When, how and by whom will final decisions be made?

▌ How will briefings and other communications be made?

▌ Who is responsible?

9

Assessment centres

SCOPE AND USE

Simulations and multiples

As discussed in Chapter 1, assessment centres use exercises designed as simulations of situations likely to be encountered in a particular job or role. An individual's performance on the exercises, then, is regarded as providing evidence for the likelihood or otherwise of success in the role concerned. In the original military applications, success in the various outdoor leadership exercises was seen as evidence for the likelihood of success in the operational aspects of platoon command.

The approach may be applied in selection or in development. In the latter applications – termed development centres – the results may be used to point the way for development towards success in a specific role or more generally.

Interpretation of the behaviour generated in the exercises is undertaken by trained assessors making their interpretations according to a competency model. Hence a critical element will be the specification of the competencies, based on a job analysis. The exercises themselves will often be supported by participant report forms on which participants comment on the approach taken and may indicate views on particular aspects of the centre. These then provide a secondary source of information for the assessors to use.

Very often assessors are drawn from the ranks of line managers in the organization concerned. They will typically pool the data gathered before their interpretations are finalized. They usually undertake this pooling under the chairpersonship of a separate facilitator, for example a person from the personnel function or an external management consultant. The meeting at which this pooling takes place is described in terms such as 'assessor panel discussion' or, more colloquially and more commonly, the 'assessor wash-up'. This discussion is an important element in standardization in the assessment centre process, something that starts with the definition of the competencies to be assessed. It is discussed further below. Another strand in standardization is the use of assessor guides indicating how a particular competency is expected to be demonstrated in the exercise and what is seen as constituting positive and what negative examples of behaviour. An example is given in Table 9.1.

Another important concept in assessment centre design is that of multiples: multiple competencies are assessed by multiple assessors observing multiple exercises. It is also important that the exercises used cover some of the range of different situations or circumstances that may arise

Table 9.1   Part of assessor guide

Customer and stakeholder orientation	
Pros	**Cons**
Considers end users, ie buying public.	Addresses only narrow constituency of customers.
Makes specific provision for interaction with representatives of particular groups, eg staff affected by reorganization.	Fails to make provision for interaction with representatives of particular groups.
Identifies areas for potential concern to end customers, with at least outline remedial action.	Ignores expressed customer concerns.
Seeks to address likely concerns of stakeholders quite widely. (May do so in participant report form.)	Focuses exclusively on a single group, eg shareholders.

in the type of job in question. Usually, feedback is given whether the centre is for selection or for development purposes. In the latter case it will be very detailed and form a critical step in development planning. The use of psychometric tests as such, in concert with assessment centres, is fairly common, either to supplement or to complement information from the work simulation exercises. However, some have argued that such usage is contrary to the idea of simulating behaviour in circumstances closely resembling the 'real-life' situation. There is a further argument, particularly with regard to the use of personality measures, that participants are in effect delivering their own view of themselves and their typical behaviour, rather than generating the behaviour to be observed. There is a related objection, namely that, whereas the evidence from the exercises, or job simulations, as such is apparent and can be interpreted, albeit with appropriate training, by line managers, the interpretation of the psychometrics requires different and specialized training as discussed in the chapters on psychometrics and so there is a danger of that element of the assessment centre constituting a 'black box', without the appeal of transparency represented in the exercises.

Part of assessment centre design involves determining which competencies are to be covered by which exercises. The principle of multiple coverage and of mixes of interactive and individually conducted exercises is, of course, relevant here. So too is the question of the scope for different exercises to measure different things. As a general rule a larger range of competencies can be covered by the in-basket than by other measures.

Trialling of assessment centre exercises is a part of their design and use. However, as noted in Chapter 1, this may not always be done with the same degree of rigour as for psychometric tests. This is particularly the case for a centre designed for a one-off application, say for a chief executive in a unique agency. In that case one may need to have recourse to run throughs with assessment centre specialists who know the type of role, but have not been directly involved in the design, plus detailed review of the findings with the client's or other subject-matter experts. The outputs of trialling may be used to prepare model, or at least sample, answers to use in training assessors and in refining assessor guidelines. Finally, if scope for trialling is limited, one may have to use ranking rather than absolute cut-off methods in reporting the findings on a shortlist of, say, five candidates.

A typical assessment centre programme, including psychometric testing as such, is shown in Table 9.2; Table 9.3 shows the relation between assessment centre activities and competencies, for the same programme.

Table 9.2 Coverage of competencies by exercises

Competency	In-basket	Role-play performance improvement	Role-play sales call	Analysis exercise	Linked to Group discussion	Numerical reasoning test
Written communications	**			**		
Financial planning	**		*	**		**
Operational control	**	**		**		
Negotiation	*	**	**		**	**
Service orientation	**	*	**	*	*	
Staff coaching	*	**				
Networking	**			**	**	
Perseverance	*	**	**			

* = Competency likely to be demonstrated
** = Competency very likely to be demonstrated

Table 9.3   Assessment centre timetable

Briefing 15 minutes A–F
Numerical reasoning test 40 minutes A–F

Interview simulation
Performance improvement   Analysis exercise
15 minutes preparation   45 minutes
30 minutes role-playing

A	B	C	D	E	F
1P	2Q	3R			

D	E	F	A	B	C
1P	2Q	3R			

Group discussion 45 minutes

A	B	C	D	E	F
3	1	2	3	1	2

Continue in-basket   Interview simulation – sales call
45 minutes   15 minutes preparation
                                                            30 minutes role-play

A	B	C	D	E	F
			2R	3P	1Q

D	E	F	A	B	C
			2R	3P	1Q

All complete in-basket
15 minutes

Legend:
A–F Candidates
1–3 Assessors
P–R Role-players

The most common types of assessment centre exercise are now reviewed.

EXERCISE TYPES

In-basket

An in-basket simulates correspondence relating to a particular role. Over the years, these exercises have been found to be among the most valid of assessment centre exercises (see, for example, Meyer, 1970). They give scope for exploration of a wide range of attitudes and ideas. Typically, the respondent is required suddenly to take over a new role after the previous incumbent has died or become seriously ill. Other commitments mean that only a limited amount of time is available to deal with correspondence before he or she must leave, say to catch a plane. There are no other colleagues around in the office – it may be a Saturday morning – and the phone-lines are not available.

The correspondence is seen as having built up over a period of a couple of weeks. It will usually be a mixture of issues competing for priority. Thus, there may be diary clashes between the visit of an important personage and the requirement to undertake budgetary planning. Sorting out these issues and dealing with other aspects of a short-term nature may sometimes conflict with a need to get a grip on the whole organization. For example, unresolved underlying tensions among the members of a management team are often indicated through a number of the items. The content of such an in-basket has sometimes been described as rather like a soap opera. All the elements present do happen in real life in the job, but typically not in such compressed episodes!

One of the strengths of the method is the scope it gives for exploring specific issues. For example, in the local government field topics such as the private finance initiative, modernization and e-government can be represented. Because the work is all done through correspondence without direct knowledge of the people concerned, the assessors can tell how far candidates can read between the lines of what is presented.

It is also possible to gauge how far they can adjust their style of response to suit a number of different bodies and constituencies. If a subordinate is asking for a lot of support, is he or she given it or just told to get on with the job? If a councillor is asking technical questions for which there may not be an answer to hand, does the candidate make steps to find out the information and send out an effective 'holding' communication to the councillor to advise what is happening?

Issues such as valuing diversity can be addressed at a number of levels. While many candidates may acknowledge blatant discrimination, few will respond effectively and adequately to subtleties such as indications in a background brief reflecting a range of cultural interests, which may have implications, say, for an item on community centres.

Most candidates find working on in-baskets demanding but to some extent fun, and they often comment on the realism of the approach. They can sometimes provide some interesting insights too. For example, in one exercise in which the difficulties of communicating with a number of minority groups was raised again in the local authority field, the candidate came up with the idea of multilingual notices about council services being displayed on the sides of buses.

The **design** of the in-basket is critical and some of the elements in that design are set out in the box below.

NOTE ON DESIGNING IN-BASKETS

▌ Having established the competencies to measure you need to think about the range and volume of correspondence to include. Pack too many items in and you find most candidates delegate or hold over 80 or 90 per cent of the material, making it difficult to evaluate their approach or thought processes.

▌ If you are going to assess candidates from outside the type of organization concerned, care must be taken to see that they are not presented with scenarios requiring minute familiarity with internal operations if a level playing field is to be provided. Of course for some posts detailed and up-to-date knowledge is to be expected, but the trick is to get the balance right for the post and the anticipated candidate pool.

▌ Gather materials and ideas. The relevant organization is likely to be a fruitful source and there is nothing like delving into the actual in-basket of an incumbent, sifting through the contents with him or her and exploring the actions that have been taken to provide useful material. However, in a selection context this approach can be compromised in cases where there are internal and external candidates. This is especially so if one internal candidate is acting up in the role and so would actually be providing material against which he or she would be assessed.

▌ Consider the general form of the in-basket. Electronic delivery or not is one issue here. There is also the question of whether it is to be treated directly as a simulation with participants answering elements of correspondence or whether they are asked to comment on the implications, or to indicate a priority order.

▌ Further variations on the form can be attained by the use via the in-basket interviews or participant report forms or both of these.

▌ Establish if there are any special elements that need to be indicated and explored. This might be a *preparedness* to handle numerical information and as such will be distinguished from a capability with numbers that might be better addressed with numerical tests.

▌ Clarify instructions to candidates, for example pointing out that they actually need to do something with the material rather than simply passing it all on if assessments are going to be able to be broadly founded.

▌ Consider the style and tone of the correspondence. Again, utilization of existing correspondence sources will be an aid here. Other approaches if the designer of the material is not skilled as a pastiche writer will be to use several different authors.

▌ Utilize other sources about the context and operation, eg the internet, professional journals or the wider press.

▌ Determine whether the exercise is to be set as if in the actual organization or a fictional one. There are advantages to the latter, again particularly to provide and to be seen to be providing a level playing field for different participants.

▌ Write items mindful of the scope for each competency to be revealed.

▌ In drafting, consider scope to bring in a variety of different individuals, eg externals, senior management staff, peer-level colleagues. This will give scope for differentiation of responses in communications to these different constituencies and to bring in matters such as staff management and development or political sensitivity.

▌ In preparing an assessor guide as a first cut indicate which competencies most naturally fall out of work on each item and how these could be demonstrated. Then produce a chart indicating how well each competency is covered in the exercise as a whole and make amendments accordingly.

The in-basket approach has been criticized recently as irrelevant to current ways of working, with so much correspondence work being done these days by electronic means. Goodge (2004) has gone so far as to say that they are trivial and 'managers at all levels are engaged in much more serious stuff than shuffling paper'. Of course, this is to miss several points. To begin with, practices with regard to the mix of electronic and paper methods for handling correspondence are by no means uniform; many people will print out even short e-mail messages and/or draft responses on paper. Many more will certainly print out longer documents and use both paper and on-screen means again for framing their responses.

Analysis exercises

These exercises are often based on case studies. The participant has some complex written and/or numerical material to deal with, and will be required to prepare a paper summarizing understanding and making recommendations. They have some similarities with high-level reasoning tests and, indeed, some of the elements within an analysis exercise will look remarkably like reasoning test items on occasion. Because the analysis is conducted as a whole exercise there is unlikely to be the reliability that stems from the item-by-item aspect of a reasoning test as such. On the other hand, the scope to present a participant with a real-life case – in which perhaps only the names have been changed – can be seen as a very powerful content-valid aspect of the approach. Again, though, some degree of artificiality inevitably arises from the need to undertake such an exercise in the assessment centre with more limited time than might be the case in real life and, of course, without reference to external sources of support. Sometimes the information presented will include correspondence and in that sense resembles the task given to the participant in an in-basket exercise. However, the output required is a single coherent document and, although issues involving other individuals may be included, there is unlikely to be so much scope for demonstrating interpersonal competencies. In general the coverage will be narrower for the analysis than for the in-basket (see Table 9.3).

To create an analysis exercise one must begin by deciding if the topic to be covered is, in fact, to be representative of the organization concerned. If so discussion with the subject-matter experts (SMEs) and review of the documentation that they may be handling can provide a fruitful source. Again this may be inappropriate if people from the organization are potential candidates. In such cases I have typically done a rather broad sweep of the same SMEs, but gone elsewhere for specifics. For example, I have made substantial use of company reports from similar-size and same-sector organizations. (In these cases a little design trick that I have applied is to multiply figures in tables by, say, 1.3).

If one chooses to represent a different situation from that directly involved in the real workplace then there is still value in making the situation one to which candidates can relate, rather than what might be perceived as an extreme fiction. Thus in designing analysis exercises for a government department, where the story line might include an aspect of resource management, it will generally be acceptable to set the exercise in another, even non-existent, department. This is usually preferable to making it, say, a case of efficient rationing of food, water and oxygen on a spaceship that has crash-landed on Mars!

Group discussions

Group discussions vary between those dealing with a series of controversial issues, with no definite 'right answer', and those in which roles are assigned. In non-assigned role discussions with a relatively inexperienced group, such as potential graduate entrants, the topics may be general social issues, such as the use of soft drugs, the need for internet censorship or the value or otherwise of extending the number of entrants to higher education. With a managerial group the topics are likely to be managerial issues and problems, eg common grading schemes, difficulties with an IT implementation or a project to gain government funding. An issue that arises is that, particularly in a relatively large group, say six participants, there may be considerable variation in the amount of 'air time' achieved by the different individuals. Although this in itself provides a certain amount of information, particularly on competencies such as dominance, assertiveness and vice versa empathy, it also means that the total amount of information on some participants and hence the scope to rate them at all on some of the competencies becomes severely limited.

Where a role is assigned there is usually some degree of advocacy required, for example bidding for a share of a budget. Thus, negotiating skills are often among the competencies examined in such an exercise. A particular problem with assigned role discussions is that the advocacy becomes seen by the participants as the main point of focus and the discussion becomes simply a bargaining exercise. This limits the scope for behaviours not associated with this aspect of interaction to be observed, again affecting the coverage of competencies in practice.

An alternative to these versions of the group discussion is a format that I started experimenting with in the late 1990s, and which I have found generally effective. Termed the semi-assigned role discussion it requires each participant to lead on one topic, but each is expected to contribute to the whole discussion. Exaggerated advocacy is avoided, though there may be some bargaining, for example about the order in which the different topics are to be addressed or the possibility of linking some of them. Each participant is more nearly guaranteed a reasonable proportion of time than in the assigned role discussion. In addition this approach gives an opportunity for variations of behaviour to be displayed with a frequent move from a phase in which the means of proceeding is discussed to the consideration of the various topics as such. In the first part, competencies such as planning and organizing may come to the fore.

The choice of topics is important as with all assessment centre exercises. In trialling assigned role, and to a lesser extent semi-assigned role, exercises it is important to balance the complexity and the appeal of the cases or topics to be assigned to different centre participants. This may be done partly by seeing if there is a topic that never 'wins' in an exercise about the allocation of funds from, say, a bonus pool and partly by gathering opinions from trial participants about the relative worth and difficulty of the topics represented. If this is not done, even though there may be a substantial amount of evidence, for example from a part of the discussion devoted to deciding how the overall task is to be addressed, participants may not feel that they have been treated fairly and assessors may find themselves struggling to make allowances for differences in opportunity in the differences in performance observed.

Interview simulations and role-plays

These exercises are cast in a one-to-one format. Very often negotiation or some other form of representation of a supposed organization is required. Other scenarios require the participant to undertake a disciplinary interview with a role-player. The role-player's function is to give the participant scope to generate the behaviour required. Thus, the role-player's job is to stay in role and to optimize opportunities for the participant to show his or her capabilities.

Such role-playing requires specific training, as there is a need to give the participant the chance to demonstrate competency. For example, a highly assertive role-play in relation to a non-assertive participant would demonstrate the latter's lack of assertiveness, but would at the same time limit his or her scope to show reasoning or planning. In the same exercise with the same participant, a highly accommodating role-player might help bring out the latter two characteristics, but fail to bring out the lack of assertiveness.

In these interactive situations a choice has to be made as to whether the role-player is someone with specific knowledge of the job or jobs concerned

(which might be an internal assessor or an external consultant) or a professional actor. There are arguments either way: the specific knowledge can be
an advantage, but this can be vitiated if the role-player cannot sustain the
role; the actor may have to fall back on 'I'll have to get back to you on that'
if the participant strays too deep into organizational specifics. In either case
there is an extra level of standardization to be established so that the role-
players are providing a comparable experience and comparable challenge
to each of the participants. Having the same one or very few role-players
for different participants in one or more centres is clearly of assistance in
this connection. Use of training in role-playing and briefing on the particular exercise being used is also important as is the use of specific guides,
which may include information not known to the participant, such as a concern about his or her future career. Where professional actors are not being
used the role-player will sometimes double as assessor. This obviously
places demands on him or her in terms of note-taking whilst performing.
Some sample role-play situations are shown in the box below.

'You are a representative for the Greenspace Care Company, a service
organization that supplies and maintains potted plants in offices. You
are to meet Jean Morris, office manager for the head office of the
South Blankshire Building Society. You have not met Jean before but
you understand that she is interested in regular maintenance of
plants and the provision of cut flowers for main reception areas, a
service that you would have to subcontract.'

'You are Pat Dawson, factory manager of the East Walton plant of
the ACME Fastener Company. You are due to see Lou Smithers, a
supervisor who has been the subject of some complaints from other
staff members. You have a number of documents relating to the situation, which you must read before meeting Lou in 30 minutes' time.'

'You are Jo(e) Diestrait, a partner in the accountancy firm of
Trimble and Trimble. A decision has been taken in principle to merge
with another firm, Wily and Dodge. You are to meet Les Marks, one
of their partners, to find out more about their internal administrative
procedures.'

'You have just taken over as Assistant Personnel Director
(Recruitment) in a large catering company. You have been asked to
meet Astrid Starr, non-executive director, who has recently written to
the Chairman about the company's record on the employment of disabled people.'

In designing role-play exercises some care needs to be taken in the volume of information and the number of sub-topics to be addressed. If the role-play is set for half an hour then a full-scale review of a multimillion pound project with a client is unlikely to be realistic or fair. There is also the question as to whether or not to represent that the participant and role-player have a previous history of working together. If not then, obviously enough, one or other, if not both, of them has to be positioned as new to the organization or the role. This may limit the extent of the interaction. For instance, if the situation of a meeting with a difficult subordinate is posed, a participant may see it as reasonable to spend this notional first meeting as an exercise in getting to know the other person, limiting the extent to which problems are gripped. On the other hand, indicating a history of previous acquaintance may be seen as particularly unrealistic and as posing a demand of unnatural rather than the required natural behaviour on the participant. A halfway house is to suggest that the two parties have met before, but not to create a detailed tale of erstwhile encounters. This seems often to work best in practice, but ideally needs to be tried out as part of the specific design.

Fact-finding exercises

These are also one-to-one interactive exercises, but the form of the interaction is limited. The participant is in role, but the other party – sometimes referred to as a resource person – is not. He or she acts as a repository of information, which can be accessed by the participant. A situation is posed to the latter in which he or she has to make a decision or recommendation about an issue. He or she is given limited information in advance and has to question the resource person to discover more facts on which to base a decision. He or she is typically asked for the rationale for the decision or recommendation made. The efficiency of the questioning, in terms of the range of aspects of the situation explored, the elimination of possibilities and the avoidance of revisiting information already given, provides evidence of analytical competencies. The lines of questioning in terms of whether, for example, people-related issues are explored or not can bear on aspects of interpersonal sensitivity, while the final decision and whether it is supported by a clear rationale can indicate decisiveness and the relative roles of logic and emotion in decision making.

These exercises have, to some extent, fallen out of favour in recent years, with relatively scant attention being given to them in some books on assessment centres. However, as Lee (2004) points out, their potential power is substantial. He notes that effective performance on them cannot be achieved by glib interpersonal skills and that there is a serious analytical task to be done. Their unreality has been challenged, but anyone in, say, management consultancy faced with the job of extracting key information from a chief executive will appreciate how like real life can be a 15- or 20-minute slot with a potential iceberg of information to explore. They are, too, arguably no less real than a non-assigned role group discussion with its relative lack of structure.

The design of fact-finding exercises can be quite complicated. A substantial amount of information does have to be provided to the resource person. Otherwise, particularly if faced with a strongly lateral-thinking participant, he or she may have very frequent resource to the line, 'I have no information on that point.' Although as far as it goes that cues the participant to vary or sharpen his or her line of enquiry it can add to the air of unreality. Training of the resource person is also important if he or she is to provide a sufficiently standardized approach to the provision of information. For example, in response to the question, 'Can you tell me about the budget for the next stage of the project?', responses might be 'Yes' or 'What exactly do you want to know?' or 'It's £100,000.' A range of such questions needs to be anticipated with responses agreed and scripted.

Presentations

Presentations are quite commonly used in selection procedures that would not be regarded as assessment centres, such as final interview panels. However, they also have a part to play in assessment centres as such. A certain degree of popularity of this type of exercise stems from the familiarity that many line managers and other assessors have with receiving them in other contexts. In the setting of the centre they do have one or two potential pitfalls. First, one must be careful to distinguish between the form and the content – the 'how' and the 'what' – of the presentation. This should, in principle, be made clear by reference to the competency model: the 'how' may reflect competencies including communications and planning and organizing, while the 'what' may be seen in strategic thinking and other competencies with an analytical or cognitive component. In practice 'horns' or 'halo' effects may well intervene and, in what may be largely non-interactive exercises, blur the picture. Indeed this may be seen to some extent as inevitably so in some cases, as when the presentation is so curtailed, or so hesitant, or so rambling that the intended message content cannot be effectively received. Sometimes there is more interaction, as when the 'audience' asks questions, which may be wholly or partly scripted to focus on particular competencies. In these cases there is more scope for exploration of content rather than just form.

Because these exercises are similar to those presentations made to final panels, ie outside the rigour of the assessment centre, there is a temptation to use them without all of the disciplines of the true assessment centre. I have come across cases where it has been requested that untrained line managers should receive the presentations. Such pressures should be resisted as there are at least two dangers here. First, it is unlikely that such assessors will do a proper job of assessing the presentation and, second, it is likely that they will concentrate on the impressions gained from the presentations and ignore the other centre evidence, whether or not they have been party to discussions about it.

Interviews within the assessment centre

Interviews can be used in assessment centres in a variety of ways. To begin with there is the in-basket interview, frequently but not invariably used to add further information to that given in the written work. This interview is conducted after a preliminary examination of the work that has been done by the candidate. This examination may take anything up to an hour. The assessor prepares and then asks a range of questions designed to follow up further on the work done. For example, if a number of items have been discarded the interview may shed further light on whether this was deliberate, accidental or a result of lack of time. The in-basket interview can also be used to explore specific competencies. For example, seeking the candidate's views of the various characters depicted in the in-basket may give clues to his or her interpersonal judgement. Candidates will sometimes also offer further information about their typical approach to handling issues akin to those depicted in the in-basket. This then shades into the criterion based interview, discussed at greater length in Chapter 11. Such interviews can be used to help complete the coverage of competencies by the exercises as such and so contribute to the principle of multiples.

Links and overlaps between exercises

Thus, it can be seen that there is a broad but imperfect division in types of exercise as between those where the output behaviours are produced in written form – in-baskets and analyses – and those where there is a direct interaction with one or more other people as in role-plays, group discussions, presentations and fact-finding exercises. These distinctions will often be less than complete in practice, as when an in-basket interview is used. Also, it is usual for assessors to have access to the participants' preparatory notes for group discussions and role-plays, again blurring the distinction as less than absolute and also more closely reproducing real-life operations.

Within a single exercise type, too, there may be variations. Thus a written analysis may include some correspondence within a file of information, and the same exercise may be used to provide the basis of a presentation. Conversely an in-basket may contain one major document on which participants are advised to spend, say, half their time. In a role-play exercise the existence of some facts, eg personal concerns of the role-player, that are not disclosed in the initial brief and that have to be uncovered bring that exercise closer to a fact-find.

The role of the assessor

The objectivity of assessment is supported by several aspects of the assessor's role. A key element is that they follow what has become known as the ORCE process. This stands for:

▌ Observe.

▌ Record.

▌ Classify.

▌ Evaluate.

It identifies a stepwise process that prevents a too-rapid arrival at conclusions, which is the case if such a structure is not followed. Thus the first part is observe, which is just what it says: observation is made of what is going on. This strict emphasis has several implications. In an interactive exercise, such as a group discussion, it is critical that the assessor is seated in such a way that observation is possible, by taking up a position in the room where lines of sight to the participant or participants are good, but without intrusion into what is being observed.

The next stage, record, means that assessors are literally recording what is going on, what they have observed. In a group discussion, again, this will typically mean capturing in writing what is said and what is done. Either a pre-prepared form is used or the assessor will work on an A4 pad. Typically in a group discussion each assessor will be recording the behaviour of two participants, but will also be expected to make some note of when others are speaking. This enables the flow of questions, answers and challenges to and from the assigned participants to be identified, so building up a more comprehensive picture for the next stage.

Observing and recording are demanding tasks and the novice assessor will often complain about the impossibility of doing so, seeking to fall back on an impressionistic summary, which of course loses much of the behaviour that is the assessment centre's focus. Faced with these challenges many will call for video or audio recordings to be made, so that they can go back and check that they have got everything down. In fact although these methods are sometimes used to good effect, they are typically found to be slow and tedious. The answer lies in continued practice of observing and recording.

Having observed and recorded, the next stage is for the assessors to classify the information they have gathered, that is they have to decide which competency each passage of behaviour represents, going through their scripts and annotating them accordingly. Note that both positive and negative examples of behaviour may be gathered. The assessor guides (as illustrated in Table 9.1) will typically exemplify both of these. This represents what is in effect a 'pigeon-holing' of the various parts of what has been observed and recorded. The results are typically transferred to a summary form.

The final stage of evaluation involves deciding on the strength of the information gathered on each competency. Scales for evaluation vary, but a common scheme is to use a five-point one as in the box.

---

5. Very strong: a model example of the competency.

4. Strong: the competency generally exhibited at a level beyond that required for the job or role.

3. Effective: the behaviour represents the competency at the level required in the role.

2. Mixed: the competency demonstrated at a level below that required, albeit with some positive evidence.

1. Limited: weak or non-existent evidence of the competency in the behaviour demonstrated.

Deciding on which evaluation category to apply is, to some extent, a matter of practice and, as indicated above, will be aided by the use of samples or material derived from trialling. Some general rules of thumb may be applied, however. For example, for 'effective' to be decided upon, one would want to see a preponderance of positive over negative behaviour as well as no extreme negative examples. The latter can take the form of a denial of the significance of a behaviour critical to the competency concerned. Thus if someone stated, 'I don't think we should be spending time or money on developing our staff: they should just know what to do', he or she would not be judged as effective on the competency of staff development.

An evaluation of 'mixed' might reflect a wide variation in the pattern of behaviour, possibly in different parts of an exercise. Alternatively, it might reflect a performance systematically falling somewhat short of that required.

Although the ORCE model is indeed a cornerstone of assessment centre technology, its application to written exercises is, in part, notional. Thus there is no direct observation to be undertaken and the recording, being the output of the exercise, is done already.

The assessor panel discussion

Exactly how the assessor panel conducts its deliberations varies somewhat from case to case and from context to context. I have come across sessions where the discussion on a single candidate took over six hours and others where no more than 20 minutes was taken over any one person. A common format is for the assessors to arrive at their individual evaluations and for these to be captured in a chart for all to see. Under the direction of the panel chairperson the evidence supporting these evaluations is presented and debated. As necessary, adjustments are made to the evaluations and it is seen as important that the whole panel agrees the final ratings. The order of proceeding is sometimes on an exercise-by-exercise basis and sometimes competency by competency. The former approach means that each assessor will present on a whole exercise and then a second presents on the next, and so on. This has the advantage of a 'story' emerging about each exercise, but with the concomitant tendency towards whole exercise rating. This is notwithstanding the fact that performance on the exercise will have been reviewed and discussed one competency at a time. Where the discussion proceeds competency by competency each exercise will, of course, be addressed several times.

Some organizations invariably use one approach rather than the other. In my experience it is a matter best left to the discretion of the panel chairperson, basing the decision on the overall pattern of provisional evaluations.

When a group discussion is being reviewed by a panel, there is scope for the others present to contribute on the basis of their own notes and recollections of the meeting. However, one assessor will still have the job of presenting his or her evaluation and _all_ the assessors will still participate in the review.

A less common approach is for the assessors to present their classifications of behaviour and then each assessor gives his or her evaluations, which are then discussed and finalized. This is sometimes seen as a more robust approach, but it is also more time consuming than that previously described. Notes are taken during the panel discussion so that feedback can be given (see next chapter).

The important elements in effective assessment centre operations have been captured recently in guidelines published by the British Psychological Society (BPS, 2003). These have, to some extent, drawn on US guidelines, albeit post-dating these by over 20 years. They include the key elements discussed above and other matters including assessor training, which will be discussed further in the next chapter.

SUMMARY

1. Assessment centres use multiple exercises and multiple assessors to provide evidence against competencies for a job or role.

2. Exercise types include written simulations, such as in-baskets and analytical case studies, and interactive tasks, such as group discussions, fact-finds, role-plays and presentations.

3. Each type of exercise requires careful design and will often involve input from subject-matter experts.

4. Interviews may be used in assessment centres, either as independent sources of information or in connection with in-basket exercises.

5. Assessors may be drawn from line management, HR or specialist consultancies.

6. The assessment process goes through stages of observation, recording, classification and evaluation.

7. At the assessor panel discussion, which is chaired, the inputs from the various assessors are gathered together to form a common view of each participant.

10

Other aspects of assessment centre technology

The application of assessment centre technology is quite diverse and, although the principles are relatively few and very well established, there are many practical and other issues to be taken into account. The example in the box is a fairly unusual one of the approach reaching parts that other methods may not.

I was once asked by a divisional personnel manager to set up and run assessment centres for his division. I explained that I would be glad to do so in principle, but that I needed to be sure that that really was the right way ahead for the division. He acknowledged that, but added that he had a particular reason for seeking to use that methodology; the senior management of the division, who would comprise the assessor team, were habitually at odds with one another. They communicated very little directly among themselves, using the personnel manager as a general intermediary.

Having ascertained that assessment centres were, indeed, a proper way ahead for the division, I duly trained the senior managers as assessors and started to implement the programme. A few months later when the assessment programme was well under way, I received another call from the personnel manager. 'I should like to be trained as an assessor, too,' he said. On enquiring why, he explained that the senior managers, after many long days and late-night sessions wrestling with the mechanics of the assessment centre process, now formed a close, cooperative and cohesive team, from which he was, in large measure, excluded.

ASSESSOR CHOICE AND TRAINING

The essence of assessor training is to produce assessors capable of capturing and interpreting the behaviour generated at the assessment centre. The use of the ORCE process described in the last chapter is at the heart of this and so exposure to that process and practice in using it will typically constitute a significant part of assessor training. Before that can happen, though, the assessors have to be chosen. As indicated in the last chapter, these will often be representatives of line management one or two levels above the posts being recruited for or into which internal candidates will be promoted. Alternatives are external consultants and members of the organization's HR function or a combination of these.

Where line managers *are* involved there is a question of how far they are to be selected for the job. Some organizations see this as providing a major development opportunity in itself and one through which people are rotated as part of aiding their own growth. Even where this is not so clearly emphasized it is quite common for a relatively small group of managers to function as assessors, establishing them as a pool of expertise and efficiency. Where this importance is recognized then there is likely to be considerable attention paid to the issue of how the assessors are to be selected. Where a programme of assessment has been running for some time then it is quite common for the output of previous centres to be used to determine who would be suitable assessors, looking at competencies such as objectivity, analytical ability and interpersonal sensitivity for instance. In other cases one or other or both of volunteering or management nomination are often used. While not perfect, such approaches are generally better than indicating that someone is suitable to be an assessor by virtue of his or her position alone.

Another approach is only to let those who 'pass' assessor training to act as assessors. Given the degree of structure inherent in the whole approach to assessment centres there is plenty of scope for doing this in quite a formal way. However, organizations often shy away from doing this and it is more likely then that the assessor about whom the trainers have doubts will never find him/herself called on to assess in earnest or will realize that he or she has been quietly dropped after one or two sessions.

PREPARATION AND TRAINING PROGRAMMES: ASSESSORS

Quite commonly, assessor training programmes will last one or two days and be run on a residential basis. However, there are considerable variations and a one- or two-day course may well be complemented by some advance work, such as going through an in-basket that they will learn to mark on the event itself.

Time should be spent in explaining the purpose of the particular centre and how the use of the assessment centre fits in with the organization's selection and development policy in general and how it is to be used specifically. In particular, it is important to clarify if it is to function as a definite screen before a final panel process or is to provide collateral information to such a panel. Raising of reports, feedback arrangements and access to centre outputs all should be covered. Even if these points have been addressed in earlier briefings they are nearly always worth reiterating during assessor training. I have also often found it useful to spend some time reviewing the origins of assessment centres and contrasting them with other methods of assessment.

Responsibilities of the various parties involved need to be clearly set out. When an organization is setting out on the use of assessment centres it will often rely on external consultant specialists to run its training, but this will frequently be brought in-house subsequently. Particularly on an initial training event, which may sometimes be treated as a pilot, it may be helpful for a representative of the whole programme's sponsorship to be present. Such a person may have a part to play in answering any questions not previously considered as well as acting as a conduit back to the wider management or sponsorship team, in addition to 'showing the flag' and underpinning the significance attached to the activity by the organization.

It is important to define assessment centres and to ensure that the assessors are familiar with and fully signed up to the principles of objectivity, the idea of multiples, of competencies in general and the particular competencies being used. It is also critical for them to be fully at one with the ORCE process. For this to work effectively it is vital that the assessors should practise all the elements of the process. Without that there is unlikely to be adequate buy-in and certainly insufficient development of the skills. (I have found it very salutary in training after, say, a group discussion session to pose the question when a view is rendered, 'What is your evidence for that?' It soon convinces those who have spent some of the time with their arms folded, when they should have been writing, that their preparation has been inadequate.)

By using the actual exercises to be employed on a particular centre one can ensure familiarity with the materials, which greatly eases the assessment process. In addition, in this way one gives the assessors a degree of understanding of the actual experience that centre participants will undergo.

Typically the training is arranged so that the assessors have the opportunity to assess one another's performance. The trainer will then review with them the various stages of the process. This will include having established at the outset that for all of the interactive exercises the assessors were positioned correctly so as to be able to see and hear without intruding upon the interaction. Recording can then be checked for completeness. There can sometimes be dismay at this point if the assessors find that they have been able to capture relatively little of what has gone on. I usually stress then that recording is very much a practice skill and one characterized by a steep learning curve. (I often suggest some 'offline' practice, such as recording from a television interview.) It is also sometimes found then that certain assessors have summarized or paraphrased what has been said or have even leapt on either one or even two stages to note classifications or evaluations. For this reason it is usually a good idea to make the first piece of practice relatively short, so that the trainees do not end up with, say, 45 minutes of useless material, which can be disheartening. Where, as is usual, others have actually done the job properly, it generally proves relatively easy to get conformity from the rest.

Checking standards of classification can be done by asking for examples from around the trainee assessor group and considering if they have been correctly 'pigeon-holed'. I usually find it better to work with the material actually gathered by the trainee assessors themselves for the interactive exercises, but it is possible to provide them with scripts for them to classify and then to check their classifications against those of established assessors. Typically, though, the use of scripts comes into its own more with written exercises. There the study of 'model' or at least 'sample' exercises can serve two purposes. First is the central one of helping set the standard for classification. Second, it can help indicate what can be done in response to the demands of the exercise. This may be important for assessors who have found the exercise demanding when attempting it themselves and/or who may be inclined to challenge the assessor guidelines in terms of whether the behaviours indicated would be likely to be generated in practice.

In addition to the use of pre-prepared answers to written exercises it is common to get them to assess the work of another trainee assessor.

The results of classification are usually recorded on assessor report forms, which makes for a fairly ready move to evaluation on an individual basis and to a trainer-led discussion amongst the group. The rating scale discussed in the last chapter is quite typically used.

The trainee assessors are also introduced to the assessor panel discussion and will sometimes be led through part of such a discussion. They will also be advised on how any other information, such as that from psychometric instruments, is to be used and where it will be introduced to the assessor panel. (Note in this connection that line managers will usually not have been trained in psychometric interpretation themselves, so this information will require to be introduced by a specialist.)

Training in feedback to assessment centre participants is also often covered, so that the assessors are in a position to provide that. Although the feedback itself is mostly given in a one-to-one setting, the training can be done in part in a 'fish-bowl' arrangement, with trainees taking turns to give part of the feedback. The first assessor introduces the session as well as relaying part of the findings and the last rounds off. This can clearly be quite a demanding experience for the recipient and so it is quite common for one of the training team to be cast in that role. This very visible approach, though, can be powerful, for instance in helping the assessors to realize the deleterious effects of ill-judged language such as 'The role-play was a bit of a disaster all round, wasn't it?' Examples of specific behaviour need to be readily to hand and assessors need practice in marshalling these accordingly.

Consideration will also be given in training to the choice of assessor to give feedback to each candidate. One approach is to base it on the mix of exercises seen by the assessors, and very commonly if an in-basket has been used it is the assessor who has had responsibility for that who will be the one giving the feedback. Trainee assessors are encouraged to emphasize the behavioural evidence that led to the evaluations given and to make participants aware that views have been reached by an assessor panel considering the evidence together. They will also use the competency model and will be advised to check understanding of that, which is likely to vary from situation to situation.

Explaining how the different competencies are covered in the different exercises will also be a part of the feedback process. When the assessment centre is a penultimate stage in a selection process it will also be important to clarify that they are giving feedback on the centre itself and not on, say, a final panel's deliberations. Use of any written reports will also be covered.

Feedback for **development centres**, which are addressed below, will typically be more extensive. However, even for an assessment centre as such, especially one for internal candidates for promotion, there may be a need to pay some attention in feedback to development aspects. Indeed, whether scripted in or not, it is quite likely that participants will seek some such guidance during their feedback. Thus the assessor training will often cover this as well, but with the level of detail varying from suggesting that participants stay in contact with their line manager and/or others in their organization who may be able to help with development to direct involvement in development planning by the assessors themselves.

Even after a diligently applied and received training course, assessors will not usually be fully proficient to begin with. It is therefore a good idea to mix new and existing assessors on any one centre and to be prepared to give the new ones extra attention and support.

Reports

The preparation of written reports is not always covered in much depth in assessor training and is probably something to which more attention should be paid. I have found that relatively few assessors, even if drawn from the ranks of consultants, are really comfortable with or adept at writing comprehensive reports. Often, then, what is presented as output from a centre is rather in note form, though often including the ratings on the five-point or other scale. In training for write-ups it is important to emphasize that even in a short report evidence supporting evaluations, not just the evaluations themselves, needs to be presented. As well as points for development, written reports may often include suggestions for how a participant might be managed, with indications of the most suitable individualized approach to optimizing performance. Thus both the oral feedback and written reports can be seen as forming inputs for performance management purposes.

All of the above applies particularly to those with no previous experience of working as assessors. For those competent in assessment for one centre the skills will be to a greater or lesser degree transferable to another. For such people one may be talking more of a briefing or 'walk-through' of the centre where emphasis will be placed on the specific materials to be used and the 'rules of the game' with regard to where the centre fits in a wider process. Some caution is necessary here, though. Competence with assessing a written analysis exercise will not imply the same with an in-basket and someone who has not used a competency-based interview before will certainly need specific training in that.

PREPARATION FOR OTHER ROLES IN THE ASSESSMENT CENTRE

Chair and centre facilitator

The roles of chairperson of the assessor panel discussion and centre facilitator are sometimes combined and sometimes separated. In the latter case the facilitator role is often undertaken by a support person and the chair is filled by someone already trained as an assessor who may be a consultant, a representative of the HR function or a line manager. Where a support person is facilitating, he or she needs to be familiar with the principles of the assessment centre and, particularly, the details of the timetable and which documents are required by whom and when. He or she will also typically be giving the instructions for the various exercises and activities and practice in doing this. Using scripted introductions is helpful.

The demands of facilitation

Whoever facilitates, it can be useful to have a 'crib sheet' indicating what things may need particular attention. The use of checklists for materials and activities such as venue liaison is also useful. Although the facilitator may not be the person who has put together the timetable for the centre, he or she needs to know exactly how the timetable works and what the scope is for 'running repairs', eg in the case of late arrival of one or more candidates and unplanned interruptions or other unwelcome events. (In one series of centres that I was involved in there were two fire alerts, one complete non-arrival of lunch, one lunch delivered 45 minutes late by a rude waiter, one loss of pre-delivered materials by the centre venue and a participant falling down and breaking his wrist. The facilitator dealt effectively with all the demands that these happenings occasioned!)

Chairing the assessor panel discussion

To chair the assessor panel discussion one needs a thorough grounding in the assessment process. Ideally this will include having worked with and understood other organizations' assessment centres, so that points of comparison can be made and assessors helped with any particularly tricky classifications or evaluations on the basis of precedent. A thorough understanding of the *particular* assessment centre is also essential. Although the panel chairperson may be asked to render views, the prime purpose of the role is to see that the assessors are giving their evidence and rendering their judgements in as objective and fair a way as possible. The requirements of tact and firmness may sound trite, but they are what is needed. The chairperson will also need to see that all the tasks of record keeping and other aspects of document management are covered and that follow-up actions are clearly understood and agreed.

Playing a part

For role-playing and working as a resource person in a fact-finding exercise, again familiarity with the assessment process is necessary, but not necessarily full training as an assessor. A full study of the exercise brief, run-throughs and a chance to ask questions, ideally of the designer of the exercise, all form part of their preparation. Comprehensive briefs, particularly clarifying where latitude is and is not permitted, are helpful.

Assessment centre design

Before the assessment centre can be run it needs to be put together. Some aspects of design in relation to the different exercises were referred to in the last chapter. Those charged with design need to be familiar with all the principles and practices of assessment centres and will almost certainly have undertaken assessor training and have applied their assessment skills in centre operations. The BPS guidelines, referred to in the last chapter (BPS, 2003), note that in addition to the important task of writing exercises the designers need to be trained in job analysis, although they recognize that in practice for any particular application the job analysis may have been undertaken by another person or group.

Training in exercise writing includes understanding how a number of standard scenarios or 'tricks of the trade' can be used. These include diary clashes in in-baskets, changing time and place in editing real material so as to achieve appropriate anonymity, and ambiguities in role-play situations, eg the previously valued subordinate who has recently appeared to have lost direction.

Also covered in centre design is timetabling to ensure an appropriately challenging but still workable day, with different assessors seeing different participants. This latter point is relatively straightforward with the application of a 'who sees whom' matrix (see Table 10.1), but something of a nightmare otherwise.

Very often designers will be occupational psychologists sometimes working for publishers of assessment materials. Some organizations 'have a go' at writing their own exercises on the basis that they know the roles best. They tend to neglect piloting when doing so and typically fail to achieve the appropriate balance of timing or coverage of competencies.

DEVELOPMENT CENTRES

Comparisons and contrasts with assessment centres

Development centres are essentially a form of assessment centre, but they vary in their degree of adherence to the assessment centre principles. At one extreme they would appear largely indistinguishable to the outsider in terms of their operation. They would be distinguished in part by the preparation of reports, which would tend to major on development aspects. They might also involve extensions to the assessor panel discussion to consider practical development activities within the power of an assessor team to recommend, such as secondments. At another extreme there is emphasis on the development aspect throughout, with some organizations claiming that the term 'development centre' should be reserved for those events where development manifestly begins to happen within the centre itself. Although such a centre will still use work-like simulations, these may be explored by the participants themselves as much as or more than by a separate team of assessors.

The BPS guidelines note that it is not possible to be absolutely adamant about what constitutes an assessment centre and go on to note that that is even more the case with development centres. They also note that hybrid assessment/development centres are often run. However, there are some

Table 10.1 Who sees whom

Candidates: A–F; Assessors: 1 and 2								
XYZ COMPANY, SALES DIRECTOR								
	16PF5			**Group discussion**			**Written**	
1	A	C	E	B	D	F	A	C	F
2	B	D	F	A	C	E	B	D	E

distinguishing features including, obviously enough, the emphasis on development in the development centre and the increased length and cost of these events compared with those run 'simply' for assessment. Development centres are not run on a pass–fail basis, which is commonly, though not inevitably, the case with assessment centres. Also of importance is the fact that, whilst for an assessment centre the results are seen as being primarily the property of the organization, in a development centre there is a much greater degree of ownership and access on the part of the participant.

In one series of development centres that I ran for a very large national public sector body, the results were seen as entirely the property of the participants. No central records were kept and although participants were encouraged to share the findings with their immediate managers this was not mandatory. In fact the invitations to the centres came from a specialist HR unit in the organization's headquarters and were not copied to participants' managers. At least one participant took annual leave to come on the centre and her manager was not aware of her attendance. It turned out that she had a poor working relationship with him and part of her motivation in attending was to understand her relationship management capabilities further and to see if she could improve her performance in this area.

Form and content of development centres

In one type of application, termed a **self-insight assessment centre (SIAC)** the participants assess and give feedback to one another under the guidance of consultant facilitators. Such events are relatively lengthy as they need to cover the generation of the behaviour through exercises, the inculcation of the assessing skills amongst the participants and the application of those skills to the behavioural information generated. Feedback and at least a start on development planning also need to be covered, so it is little wonder that such an event may take a full five days to complete.

Whether the centre is for development or selection, comparable methods of assessment are involved, using a range of work-like exercises that are assessed. There may also be a further set of exercises and activities, beyond those where performance is evaluated by assessors, which give participants a chance themselves under guidance to explore and evaluate their potential and developmental inclinations.

Psychometrics may be used in connection with the former, assessed, exercises or linked in with the latter phase of self-exploration. In connection with the assessed exercises they will be seen as either providing data to corroborate the findings from the direct observations in the work-like simulations or as giving additional information about competencies and characteristics not readily measured in these exercises. Personality questionnaires will be commonly used, for instance, and outputs from these will include information on interpersonal style. This is likely to be reflected in behaviour used to influence others, which might have been seen elsewhere in exercises involving negotiation. The corroborative nature of information about behaviour from these two sources and the interplay between them can, if sensibly handled, be powerful in helping the participant to understand the impact of that behaviour. For example, a group discussion exercise might have indicated the participant as being forceful, but tending to lose the initiative to others as the discussion progressed. If the 16PF5 indicated the same person to be dominant but lack ing in warmth, there could be a rationale for an impact that was not sustained. The subsequent feedback might help the person concerned reflect upon whether in real life he or she sometimes failed to carry initiatives through, because he or she had failed to build sufficiently strong relationships with colleagues.

Where personality measurement is likely to be able to go further, though, and enter into development as such is when the questionnaire gives indications of areas of support that may be utilized in development to manage around an area of relative weakness. For example, someone indicated as relatively low on dominance but high on persuasiveness might be encouraged to put his or her persuasive arguments in writing when feasible.

It is in the second stage of self-exploratory exercises that interest inventories such as the Strong Inventory referred to in Chapter 3 may be used. Whereas in the first stage of the development centre psychometric tests will be used alongside exercises assessed by others, here they will be operated alongside a variety of other techniques for generating developmental ideas.

One of these techniques is brainstorming, in which a group of people work together initially to generate suggestions, which are first simply captured and listed without evaluation, and then progressively sorted and grouped for inclusion in plans. Another technique is domain mapping in which people identify areas of importance in their work and in other aspects of their lives individually, and then indicate the current status of each of these domains and where they would like them to be. Links and tensions between the different domains can then be seen and potentially resolved. An example would be when the absence of an accountancy qualification was seen as hindering career progression, but limited time with a partner tended to preclude attendance at evening classes. The resolution here might be to seek a job providing day release or study leave opportunities for the pursuit of the qualification.

Some of the exercises and activities used here might indeed be seen as intermediate between psychometric procedures such as the interest inventories and the more free-format techniques just mentioned. For example, there are questionnaire-based methods for exploring personal values, such as Schein's (1985) Career Anchors. His approach involves the use of a booklet containing a questionnaire and supporting material for a range of activities, including an interview with a partner. It helps the person define his or her self-image, values and areas of strength.

Such questionnaire tools are not claimed to be full psychometric instruments, though their form is similar and they have been designed to provide insights. As such they again represent some blurring of distinctions between different assessment approaches. Other inventories that come into this category and are sometimes used in a development centre context or otherwise in a development context include the Assessment for Training and Employment (ATE) package (1988), which the then Psychological Corporation (now Harcourt Assessment) used to publish. This included a five-scale inventory designed to help clients deliberate on their occupational preferences. This was not – and was not claimed to be – fully standardized psychometrically, but would appear capable of standardization. A domain-mapping exercise, on the other hand, would be less amenable to standardization. Both the inventory and domain mapping are intended as stimuli to thought, but the former has a readier capability for operating as a measure – as a full psychometric procedure.

Positioning of the development centre

Harley (1995) refers to development centres as often being perceived as representing a 'rite of passage'. Thus in the case of director-level assessment centres there may be a view amongst participants that they are undertaking a definite step into the boardroom. However, he further contends that for many what is being offered is a view of the topmost roles, but with a real possibility that it may remain that, just a view. Thus if the competencies are not demonstrated at the requisite level and the necessary follow-up development is not actually feasible, then the next step may never be taken. This can obviously lead to frustration. He makes a related point that prior to the introduction of the development centre process the means of passage to the higher levels was shrouded in mystery. By the explicitness and openness of the process the participant who fails to find him or herself set on the path to promotion has the burden of failure sitting on his or her shoulders, rather than it being something that can be dismissed as one of the mysteries of 'the system'.

A very steep uphill path may be implied and/or the virtual impossibility of gaining the final rung on the ladder, rather than a continuing – if slowly and eventually withering – hope that less explicit processes imply. Appropriate sideways development will sometimes keep the individual on track and motivated but there are not a few for whom the development centre experience provides the occasion for considering their position and moving on.

Feedback in the development centre

In feedback it is particularly important not to get involved in a negotiation on the ratings given but to represent these clearly as the combined opinion of the assessing team. The way to do this is to present the evidence – that is, the observed behaviour – first, followed by the evaluation. If the evaluation is given first this tends to result in defensiveness on the part of the centre participant (the interviewee). By presenting the behavioural evidence first the evaluation given is seen to come naturally, arising logically from what has been presented. In the same way it is not usually a good idea, when giving development centre feedback, to ask participants what they thought of their performance in a particular exercise, or in relation to a particular competency. If the participant's view does not accord with the assessor's, this advance declaration of a position may lead to defensiveness and difficulty in accepting the evidence.

If the feedback interview is to be most effective and worthwhile, careful preparation of the participant is necessary. This will include detailed familiarization with the centre processes – how the observations are made and how evidence is pooled among assessors. The necessary training and briefing for this will often be undertaken during the centre itself while the assessors are holding their deliberations.

Participants also need some explanation and understanding of the competencies. Sometimes briefing on this is undertaken in advance of the centre and this may be particularly so where competencies are common between development centre processes and other aspects of management. In other cases the briefing on competencies is given on the centre itself, while the assessors are undertaking their discussions. The feedback may extend to discussion of possible career options and the implications of those. Part of a development centre feedback interview is shown in the box below.

Assessor: Jack; Participant: Tim

Jack: Well, as you will know by now, I'm here to take you through the results of our observations over the last two days. All the assessors have had a lengthy discussion about all the participants. You know from the in-basket interview that I studied your work on that exercise, but I'm not just reporting on that. I'm going to tell you about the other exercises, too, so what I'm telling you about is the combined view of everyone. Is that clear?

Tim: Yes, that's OK.

Jack: You've seen the competency model and understand the terms used in that and you've also had a look at the whole assessment process that we are using?

Tim: Yes, I'm fairly clear about all that.

Jack: Well, I'm going to begin by talking about the competency called strategic vision. That's the one to do with indicating how far you would have what's sometimes called a 'helicopter view' of the world of the business.

Tim: Yes, I was rather intrigued by that one particularly because I wasn't at all sure how you could possibly find that out from the exercises that we did.

Jack: Well, it will come out to different degrees in each of the exercises. Let's start with the group discussion exercise. You were all working on that problem of the site for the new administrative offices to support the three factories. Your preliminary work had shown that you had paid some attention to the costs and you spoke about those quite a lot during the discussion.

Tim: Yes.

Jack: Now, you did follow on when Ranjit raised a question of the long-term future of the business to say that your cost model might well vary if, as he was suggesting, one of the factories was actually closed down, so you were able to identify with a different future and that's one of the things that we looked for. However, you didn't indicate that you had thought of that in advance. It wasn't in your notes and you actually said, 'Well, if that is a possible scenario…' You also disagreed with Jennifer when she said that it would be important to consider different patterns of working in the future with a lot more people being likely to do their administrative work from home.

Tim: Yes, I remember that. I was really impatient at that point because we only had 10 minutes left and we had spent a lot of time talking about process.

Jack: Yes, a lot of the discussion did go on that. Of course, one way of moving that along would have been for someone earlier – and it could have been you as well as anybody else – to have raised the question of longer-term objectives and the need to consider the future shape of the business within the process for managing the discussion. That could well have had an impact on the approach taken.

Tim: I'm not sure, though, that it's really fair to think of that exercise as something that would really have got us on to a strategic approach. After all, we all knew that we had to get in our threepennyworth somewhere and there was a jostling for position and people were trying to make sure they stated their views rather than it being set out as something with a very long-term horizon.

Jack: Certainly, if someone didn't, as you say, get their threepennyworth in and contribute at all to the discussion there wouldn't have been any behaviour to observe. However, if the view that you had wanted to put forward had been a strategic one then that's where you would have chosen to, as it were, spend your threepennyworth.

Tim: Well, I can't deny the behaviour as you have presented it and I see how it could have been slanted differently though I must confess that I hadn't seen that at the time and I still would not have thought it was the exercise best calculated to produce that evidence.

Jack: Well, OK, on the basis of what we did see here, though, this performance would not have evidenced behaviour to the standard required of a senior manager in the company with regard to strategic vision and so this would show as a development need.

Tim: OK, well, I – yes, I can accept that for the moment.

Jack: If we move on to the individual analysis exercise you will remember one of the issues put to you was the marketing implications of a much more integrated relationship with suppliers.

Tim: Yes, I felt more comfortable with that because there were a number of echoes of work I'd done previously in total quality management and I pulled some of that experience out in what I wrote.

Jack: In fact, there was a lot of evidence of your thinking at a quite high level and you did refer to total quality. You suggested that there would be a need to see if that could potentially run counter to or alternatively be complementary to those initiatives – I'm quoting directly from your work here. This showed evidence of a clear approach to the analytical aspect of strategic vision. You actually took that further to work through some of the impact upon customers and followed up with the idea of putting yourselves and your suppliers in a further partnership relationship with the customer base.

There was also evidence later in the paper you prepared, when you looked at potential risks, that you had quite a grasp on the possibly changing business situation in terms of ultimate customer usage of the product. However, there was little acknowledgement of the impact of all this on people. There had been a clue to this in the briefing notes, but you really didn't do much more than acknowledge that there would be some people impact. You didn't talk further about the effects of changing work patterns and skill mixes.

Tim: Well, I'm not a personnel specialist and I suppose I would have been relying on someone of that sort to pick up that aspect for me.

Jack: In strategic vision, though, we would actually want to see a clearer intention of someone setting such an initiative in motion even if they did involve another individual or specialist group.

Tim: OK.

Jack: On that basis the picture of this exercise altogether is that this is a competency that was demonstrated to standard but it probably would have come out as a clear strength, that is above the standard basically required, if there had been some further work on the personnel side.

Sometimes the work with the participants goes on to a stage in which they produce detailed recommendations for their own further development action. This may then be the subject of a three-way interview involving their direct manager, who probably would not have been present at the development centre, and a representative of the training and personnel function. In such a follow-up interview it is likely there would be detailed discussion of their expectations and requirements for the future.

It may well be that first the assessors and then subsequently the reviewing management team will have at their disposal other information about the interviewee to inform their discussion, such as self-completion questionnaires on future career direction.

PRACTICAL ISSUES ABOUT USING ASSESSMENT CENTRES IN REORGANIZATION

Assessment centres have not uncommonly been used in connection with major reorganizations. Examples include BT and many government departments. On some occasions the assessment centre itself is seen as a distinct stepping stone to remaining in the organization under the general umbrella of 'applying for one's own job'. In other cases, the assessment centre can be seen as providing information about a pool of people who might be appropriate for consideration in future roles as these roles actually arise and become clarified. Yet in all these circumstances there is often a consideration that the competency model required for the organization as it is required to be will be different from the 'as is' organization.

There may also have been a perception by different parts of an organization that a general management competency model, possibly developed at the centre, will be 'OK for some parts, but not for our division/specialism/level'. This perception may or may not be justified in fact, but very often there is a degree of tinkering with the model with only limited system or justification. Sometimes this amounts to actual or virtual abandonment of the model and its replacement by something that may have been prepared on a less systematic basis. This obviously limits the degree of effective application of findings from a centre held in one part of an organization to another, thereby vitiating the role of local assessment centre data in making decisions about movements of staff or other aspects of reorganization.

In one large organization with which I once worked, a central HR team had devised a new management competency model. (Let us call it 'Model X' and the different competencies X1, X2 and so on.) Two divisions continued to use the competency labels, but stressed assessment against different behavioural elements in each competency. Thus when Division A talked about strength in X1 and indications of effectiveness in X2 they meant somewhat different things from the same evaluations presented by Division B.

Another division did not want to use the model directly at all, but claimed that at least effective levels across its entire scope could be assumed for all of those whom they wished to assess. They sought to undertake their assessments against a new model, with fewer elements than the original one.

Yet another division claimed that the model was outdated as far as they were concerned – this was about a year after it had been introduced. They wanted to introduce two further models, one of which was a list of labels only, with no supporting indicators of performance.

The central team did use the model, but in some applications tacked an extra competency on to the end of it!

Considerable care will also need to be taken with regard to the briefing given to participants. Among other things, it will be particularly important that questions such as who has access to the information and how it can be used are made explicit. The development of a structured Q & A format in this connection is likely to be valuable. It would generally be of value for the assessors in such programmes to be able to be seen as wholly independent from the organization itself. They will, though, need to demonstrate that their work in setting up and running the centres has been undertaken with sufficient care to ensure that they have reflected the scope to demonstrate the relevant behaviours well enough. The role of trial runs, debates with the internal bodies and ongoing review of data will be particularly important in this regard. As in most forms of design, specifying as much as possible in advance will be helpful in this connection. However, this will not necessarily prevent top management from coming along with their own questions requiring further investigation. The process can be weakened by any seeming air of the organization itself not being fully behind the process as it evolves. One way, partially, around this is to ensure reporting waypoints as the project develops and the establishment of a steering group with high-level representation internally and also from the body charged with delivering the work.

More is said about reorganization and other changes in Chapter 17.

VALUING DIVERSITY IN ASSESSMENT CENTRE OPERATIONS

This concept can operate in assessment centres in at least two senses. First is the question of equality so that the centre discriminates only on the basis of performance and not on other grounds. Second, there is the idea that when valuing diversity as such features within the requirements of the organization – as it does increasingly – then that should be reflected in the exercises themselves. The latter may be harder to achieve than might be supposed. Although many candidates will respond to some of the more blatant equal opportunity aspects of diversity when expressed in, say, an in-basket exercise, they may be slower to pick up on other cues if such values have not previously been paramount in the organization. It is, then, a question as to how far it is reasonable to expect internal participants to respond to issues expressed more subtly. It is by no means uncommon to find that people in an historically based interview – structured or otherwise – can talk clearly about championing diversity issues, but fail to pick up opportunities presented to them in an exercise to demonstrate that.

ASSESSMENT CENTRE ELEMENTS USED INDEPENDENTLY

The tools of the assessment centre are not uncommonly used outside the assessment centre itself. It is, perhaps, then that one should be more properly speaking of the use of job simulation exercises, for to describe the exercises in these other contexts as assessment centre exercises could be seen as implying that the full range of the assessment centre approach is being applied. Individual self-completion exercises such as in-baskets and written analyses are prime candidates for this type of use, followed by the one-to-one exercises, role-plays and fact-finds. Group discussions are less commonly used independently. Again the rigour of proper design, training and application of the assessment process should all be used in these applications.

SUMMARY

1. Assessors need to be selected with care if the power of the assessment centre process is not to be compromised.

2. Assessor training covers the observe, record, classify and evaluate process, as well as familiarization with the specifics of the exercises to be used, the assessor panel discussion and feedback. Report writing is also addressed, though often briefly.

3. Other roles for which training is required are role-playing, assessor panel discussion chair and centre facilitator.

4. Development centres take a variety of forms, ranging from those that closely resemble assessment centres to those in which participants assess one another and/or in which development begins to be addressed in the centre itself. In addition to the assessed exercises, a variety of other activities can be included to aid self-discovery.

5. Advance preparation and feedback require special attention in development centres and it is important to manage expectations carefully.

6. Special attention is required in using assessment centres in connection with major organizational change, including the challenges arising from the proliferation of competency model variants and positioning the centre appropriately vis-à-vis other aspects of decision making.

7. Diversity issues may need to be addressed in terms of fairness in the tasks set to participants and to see that competencies reflecting diversity concerns can be adequately represented in exercises.

8. Assessment centre exercises can be used outside assessment centres as such, but still need to be employed with care and rigour.

11

Structure in interviewing: the scope of structured interviews

Structured interviews run all the way from simply more organized approaches to conducting a conventional biographically based interview, to instruments that, in their form, lie very close to what would normally be regarded as psychometric measures. A major study of interviewing in selection (Wiesner and Cronshaw, 1988) found much higher levels of validity for structured versus unstructured methods. It is possible that the large differences they found still understated the situation with regard to interview practice. To be in a position even to be included in a study implies some degree of system, whereas many employment interviews are still practised along the lines of the horror stories shown in the box below. (Thus McDaniel *et al* (1994) in a meta-analytic study reported that 'even the unstructured interview was found to have a respectable level of validity'. However, their conclusions appear to have been based on public sector interviews with fairly clear criteria and often the use of rating forms, ie a degree of structure. Indeed, they state that 'the typical interview in the private sector is likely to be substantially less structured'.)

INTERVIEWING HORROR STORIES

▌ A candidate was interviewed by the personnel director for an internal post on a day on which major employee-relations trouble was anticipated and indeed broke. An hour's interview was interrupted no fewer than 13 times by phone calls or people coming in with messages. The interviewer did apologize for the disruption but did not offer to reschedule the meeting to an occasion when he could do a proper job of it!

▌ Two managers were interviewing a candidate who used a piece of jargon. 'At that time I was using the gobbledegook software system for project management,' she said. 'What is that?' asked one interviewer. 'Surely you know that,' asked the second interviewer of his colleague. The first interviewer glowered. 'Yes, I do, but I want to see if she does,' he said!

▌ It was the university milk round. A bored interviewer saw that his next candidate was studying music and French and he was cross with the sifting process for having produced someone so obviously unsuited for work in a technically oriented company. 'I see you study music and French,' he said. The candidate nodded enthusiastically. 'Then sing the Marseillaise,' the interviewer requested.

▌ Interviewers not being present themselves for the appointment arranged on their behalf is almost commonplace in some organizations. The next story unfortunately is a not atypical exchange that actually took place with a candidate and one of the world's leading firms of executive search consultants. A candidate presents himself (as requested by the sign at the office entrance) to the security officer on the front desk. 'I am John Bloggs to see Sue Smith.' The security officer looks through lists. 'Have you got an appointment? I'll phone through. What did you say your name was? Look, she ain't here. They're sending someone out. Do you want to leave a card or something? Are you sure you've got an appointment? What did you say your name was?'

▌ The two-person interviewing team had discussed the forthcoming day's interviews rather too enthusiastically the night before. One, rather the worse for wear, gulped some black coffee and then launched stoically into some questions. The other interviewer picked up a pen and made notes, wincing at the sound of shuffling paper. After a quarter of an hour the note-taker nudged the questioner and whispered in his ear, 'You've just repeated your first three questions.'

▌ In an interview on Wall Street one of two interviewers stood up and leant over the desk towards the candidate and said, 'If I picked you up by your collar and threw you against that wall over there, what would you do?' The candidate replied, 'Nothing.' When asked, 'Why not?', he said, 'Because you're bigger than me.' The candidate was later told that he didn't get the job because he didn't have the killer instinct.

▌ A woman interviewed for a job in an ice-cream factory was asked when her next menstrual period was due. (This story does date back to 1961: it couldn't happen today, or could it?)

Perhaps the earliest, but still used, form of structured interview is the approach advocated by Rodger and encapsulated in his Seven-Point Plan (NIIP, 1952) (see box). This was a way of planning an approach to an interview to ensure that a number of aspects of a person, seen as generally of relevance, were explored. A comparable scheme was the so-called five-fold grading system of Munro-Fraser (1954).

THE RODGER SEVEN-POINT PLAN

1. Physical make-up. Have the candidates any defects of health or physique that may be of occupational importance? How agreeable is their appearance, bearing and speech?

2. Attainments. What type of education have they had? How well have they done educationally? What occupational training and experience have they had already? How well have they done occupationally?

3. General intelligence. How much general intelligence can they display? How much general intelligence do they ordinarily display?

4. Special aptitudes. Have they any marked mechanical aptitude? Manual dexterity? Facility in the use of words or figures? Talent for drawing or music?

5. Interests. To what extent are their interests intellectual? Practical? Constructional? Physically active? Social? Artistic?

6. Disposition. How acceptable do they make themselves to other people? Do they influence others?

7. Circumstances. What are their domestic circumstances? What do other members of their family do for a living? Are there any special openings available for them?

THE FIVE-FOLD GRADING SYSTEM

1. Impact on others. Physical make-up, appearance, speech and manner.

2. Acquired qualifications. Education, vocational training, work experience.

3. Innate abilities. Natural quickness of comprehension and aptitude for learning.

4. Motivation. The kinds of goals set by the individual, his or her consistency and determination in following them up and success in achieving them.

5. Adjustment. Emotional stability, ability to stand up to stress and ability to get on with people.

Increasingly, with the legal requirement to avoid discrimination, and the emphasis on achieving 'political correctness', commenting on physical make-up as advocated by these schemes could be regarded as suspect. Armstrong (1995) refers to the use of schemes such as these as typically following the specification of requirements. Even so, their prescriptive nature in regard to areas likely to be irrelevant could operate against any careful requirement specification, in addition to being seen as intrusive or potentially discriminating. Today many employers will, in fact, proscribe questioning in areas relating to background where the specific relevance of these has not been confirmed. (Arvey (1979) reviewing legal cases involving discrimination in the United States found that one consistent theme was the questioning of women about marital status, childcare and related issues, areas of inquiry not put to their male counterparts.)

THE FOCUS ON BEHAVIOUR

With other forms of structured interview there is less emphasis on building up a general picture of a person and more on exploring specific behaviour. Thus in the interviews to be discussed under criterion-based and critical incident methods below it is evidence of relevant behaviour that is sought directly. Interestingly, though, in what can be regarded as the most advanced form of structure in interviewing and which is being called here the structured psychometric interview or SPI (explored in detail in the next chapter), the emphasis again may be in some cases away from specific behaviour and more towards tendencies to behave. These latter are established in a variety of ways including specific instances, and also by asking a range of questions aimed at tapping into attitudes of which a person may be only slightly or scarcely at all conscious.

Many psychologists writing on interview research seem to recognize the superiority afforded by structure in interviewing. As Boyle (1997) points out though, unstructured interviews conducted by untrained people who don't know what they are looking for are still 'too common'. Yet there are some who defend the unstructured position. Thus Oliveira (2000) discusses the view that there is a logic to unstructured interviewing with some managers able to apply implicit knowledge based on wide experience of their own organization when they opt for unstructured interviewing. (It may perhaps be questioned as to whether their 'opting' is in itself conscious or, more likely, the pursuit of an implicit and possibly institutionalized approach.)

These differing models have been labelled by Anderson (1992) as the objectivist-psychometric and the subjectivist-social perception perspectives. He sees the distinction as important in shaping the research that has been done on interviews. It is important, too, in shaping the practical approach taken to conducting interviews, even if not clearly acknowledged as such. Thus those with a strong objectivist-psychometric approach would see the subjectivist-social perception approach as woolly. Those who propound or practise the latter tend to see the objectivist-psychometric approach as overly remote or, as one recruiter put it to me on a structured interview course, 'something dreamt up by HR people and nothing to do with the real business of recruitment'. Given that these two different positions are not often clearly articulated – in these or equivalent terms – it is perhaps not surprising that the perception is more often just that others do it wrong.

Thus structured interviews would most generally be seen as lining up with the objective-psychometric model of interviewing of Anderson's distinction. However, the SPI may sometimes in effect break this distinction down by spanning the two sides of the divide.

The fact that structured interview techniques cover such a broad church is a complicating factor for those seeking to evaluate methods or decide on appropriate means to use in selection. Thus we have on the one hand methods where the specific content of the interview has been arrived at by careful and painstaking research and where those using the interview are required to go through rigorous training that can last up to a year. On the other hand we have the output of what might be a Friday afternoon huddle to discuss areas for questioning and not backed at all by any form of training or check on standards. Although it is contended here that structured interview methods may give considerable benefits and increments in accuracy that can make them, perhaps, the most cost-effective of all methods likely to be used in selection or performance management, their design and use requires considerable care. Certainly, as in fact with conventional selection interviews, the warning 'rubbish in, rubbish out' applies with some force here, so we turn next to a range of approaches to producing structured interviews. As the particular case of the structured psychometric interview is gone into in considerable depth in the next chapter, only brief further reference will be made to it in the following section.

DERIVING INTERVIEW MODELS

The repertory grid

One of the most powerful techniques established for determining relevant dimensions to explore in interviews is the repertory grid. This is by no means used exclusively for definitions to be fed into interviewing practice and it is a methodology that can be used in connection with assessment centres or counselling situations. It has been employed in a wide variety of settings with applications including those in the field of market research and even in areas such as the derivation of dimensions to describe the handling characteristics of military aircraft.

The repertory grid was developed by Kelly (1955) in connection with his Personal Construct Theory. Much has been written about it since, a lot of it highly technical in nature, but Bannister and Mair's (1968) book is still a good general text on the subject. A later volume (Jankowicz, 2004) provides a highly accessible introduction. The repertory grid (or rep grid as it is often abbreviated) is a way of sorting out the concepts or constructs a person uses to describe a particular area of interest. In the case of selection the area of interest would be the characteristic behaviours or attitudes relating to a particular job.

The method involves getting those who are knowledgeable about the particular area – the job, in this particular case – to go through a sorting process in which they can articulate the relevant dimensions. A variety of tasks may be used for this purpose but a simple and the most commonly used one is a card-sorting method. First of all the interviewee is asked to list a number of people currently performing the job or a similar one. Numbers from 8 to 12 are frequently used. The individuals are identified by the respondent to his or her satisfaction with a number being written down on a separate card to represent each individual. The interviewer then selects sets of three cards, usually initially at random. The interviewee is asked to group the cards in ways that indicate how two of the individuals represented are alike and different in some way from the third. The responses are noted. A second set of three cards is drawn and the process repeated. Further drawings are carried out either until all possible combinations are exhausted or until no new discriminating dimensions emerge. Thus very often part-way through, the interviewer is rapidly assessing which fresh combinations are likely to yield interesting distinctions.

Once the drawing of cards is complete, the interviewer goes on to request the interviewee to rank-order the individuals who are being discussed. This rank-ordering is in terms of their effectiveness in the job of relevance. The result of this is then explored further to resolve any ties given. Specific behaviours are then investigated, building upon the distinctions originally rendered and looking at why particular behaviour patterns are important. Repetition of this process with two or three people who are knowledgeable about the role concerned can fairly rapidly home in on the dimensions of relevance. An example of part of a repertory grid interview output is given below.

A REPERTORY GRID INTERVIEW

Interviewer: We are discussing the job of a level X manager in finance. Could you please identify for yourself eight level X managers whom you know. You should have a spread of capabilities among them. Write down their names or initials on a piece of paper for your own reference, and then just number them from one to eight. OK?

> *Interviewee:* OK.
>
> *Interviewer:* Now I have a set of cards also numbered one to eight to correspond to the people on your list. I am going to draw three cards at a time and show them to you. I want you to tell me a way in which two of them are alike but different from the third.
>
> *Interviewee:* OK.
>
> *Interviewer:* Here are the first three, numbers two, three and five. Can you tell me a way in which two of them are alike, but different from the third?
>
> *Interviewee:* Well, two and three are well organized with good attention to detail. Number five is, I guess, more entrepreneurial in style, and doesn't pay much attention to detail.
>
> *Interviewer:* And the next three are numbers four, six and eight?
>
> *Interviewee:* Four and six are strong people people, if you know what I mean, people managers I suppose, while number eight is much more focused on tasks.
>
> *Interviewer:* And what about numbers one, seven and five?
>
> *Interviewee:* One and five are quite strategic. Seven takes a much more short-term operational view.

From the questioning indicated in the box above it appears that being organized, managing people and thinking strategically are three of the dimensions that the interviewee uses in thinking about financial managers in the company. Further exploration will yield further dimensions and reveal which the interviewee sees as most important. Comparison with other interviewees will show the degree of agreement among them.

Critical incident techniques

In this method the emphasis is upon those incidents that have been significant or critical in determining the success or otherwise in the job. By exploring these important turning points one may build a picture of those behaviours that are required for effective performance in the role, and where lack of the capacity to cope with a particular type of incident would be especially disabling. These situations then form the basis for structuring the interview itself, as discussed later in this chapter.

The method was developed by Flanagan (1954) following earlier work (Flanagan, 1947) with Second World War US bomber crews. Then, in what today would probably be called business process re-engineering, attempts were made to study the various activities and processes that were critical to a bombing mission. In his 1954 paper Flanagan defined an incident as 'any observable human activity that is sufficiently complete in itself to permit inferences and predictions to be made about the person performing that act'. He also set out systematic protocols for exploring incidents. Those questioned clearly needed to have detailed acquaintance with the incidents and were labelled subject-matter experts (SMEs).

Job specification and job descriptions

A variety of methods is available for deriving job specifications and writing job descriptions. Some of these relate to scoping or sizing the job for remuneration purposes but these themselves will, of course, be of relevance in determining the types of behaviour that may be required. Thus someone with financial responsibility over a very large budget will require to have those skills that reflect the prudent handling of money. Someone required to undertake long-range resource planning is likely to need to be able to conceptualize strategically and comprehend the potential interaction of a variety of issues some time into the future.

Sometimes job descriptions are derived directly from an initial specification of organizational structure and a definition of areas of responsibility alone and do not give direct indications of behavioural requirements. Sometimes in a job description there is a rather long list of responsibilities and accountabilities. These may need to be considered carefully in terms of the required behaviours that they imply. There may need to be a process of grouping of areas of activity very specific to an organization before a clear enough picture of the behaviours can be gathered to construct an interview. Such a process is illustrated in the box below.

JOB DESCRIPTION: FLEET MANAGER (EXTRACT)

1. Good contacts in the motor trade and, preferably, the finance houses.

2. Familiarity with practical aspects of maintenance workshop management.

3. Ability to interact with colleagues at all levels.

---

4. As a major budget holder, financial planning experience is essential.

1 and 3 may imply communication skills.

2 and 4 may imply control and review skills.

1, 2 and 3 may imply negotiation skills.

2 may imply staff motivation skills.

It may be difficult to produce an effective structured interview if the number of areas indicated in the job description is large. Similarly, whether or not a job description is produced, if a checklist of behavioural descriptions is presented to a recruiting manager it is not uncommon for nearly every area to be endorsed as relevant to the job. Clearly this complicates rather than helps the task of identifying relevant behaviours.

The essential simplifying process that techniques for studying and analysing jobs are meant to provide is neatly captured by Algera and Greuter (1988). They see this role as one of interconnecting between criteria of job performance and predictors of that performance, including interviews.

The output of the above approaches can all be expressed in terms of competencies, as discussed earlier in this book.

CRITERION-BASED, COMPETENCY-BASED AND CRITICAL INCIDENT INTERVIEWS

There is a class of interviews where evidence is sought related to particular competencies or criteria. Criterion-based interviews actually have their origins in the field of assessment centre technology, discussed in Chapters 9 and 10. It is from that field that the term 'criterion' comes, a usage that pre-dates 'competency', though no practical distinction is made here between criterion-based and competency-based interviewing. The criterion-based interview is discussed briefly below, but other aspects of interviewing in the context of assessment centres are addressed in Chapter 10. The idea of exploring critical incidents as a way of establishing areas of relevance was discussed earlier in this chapter. The critical incident framework can also be used, in effect, as the script for an interview.

The criterion-based interview

Typically the questions themselves in criterion-based interviews are only partially predetermined, giving scope for individual follow-up. The degree of licence that this might imply is not necessarily extreme. To begin with, part of the proper use of the criterion method involves the careful training of interviewers. This again helps with standardization.

An illustrative sequence of questions is shown below.

CRITERION-BASED QUESTIONS – DIRECT INFLUENCING

1. Tell me about a time when you resolved a disagreement between two people.

   (If necessary)

   What was the source of the disagreement?

   Did the problem arise again?

2. How do you get other people to do things?

   (If necessary)

   Can you give me an example?

   Was that something that they did not originally want to do?

   How do you know that?

3. Think of something fairly technical or complex in your work; how would you explain it to a layperson?

   Can you explain it to me now?

The critical incident technique as an interviewing method

As noted above the idea behind the critical incident approach is that the response to some incidents may be critical in determining the success or otherwise of a job. The publican shouting time to a rowdy group of revellers and how the consequent strongly expressed desire to remain in the pub drinking was handled would be one example. Another might be pushing through a capital expenditure budget in the face of opposition in order to make a department viable.

The use of the critical incident technique to structure an interview is based on the idea of exploring the candidate's capacity to respond appropriately to the incident. There are variations on the style of the question used. In the so-called situational interview (Latham *et al*, 1980), candidates are asked how they would behave in a given situation. Responses are rated using behavioural statements developed by experts in the job concerned (the subject-matter experts or SMEs again) as benchmarks. Thus the immediate focus is on hypothetical behaviour. In the Patterned Behavioural Description Interview – PBDI or sometimes just BDI (Janz, 1982) – candidates are asked about specific critical incidents again, but now in terms of actual experience. These two types are illustrated below.

CRITICAL INCIDENT INTERVIEWING

A situational question

'You have been working on a product advertising campaign with a client for several weeks and have finally agreed the whole plan including all the copy. You have media space booked for three weeks ahead and have a photographer and studio lined up for product shots next week. Your client contact phones you and says that her boss's boss has just seen the copy and is not happy about some of the messages. What would you do?'

A patterned behavioural description question

'Have you ever managed to get to the nub of a resource allocation problem when others seemed to be floundering or casting about? Tell me about an occasion when you experienced this.'

The distinction between these two types of critical incident interview is superficially that between the hypothetical and the actual. Taylor and O'Driscoll (1995) have emphasized this distinction in their book on structured interviewing, but the distinction is not absolute. In many cases one would expect respondents to the situational interview to draw upon what they had actually done. The two techniques can, in fact, be merged by the simple follow-up of 'Have you ever experienced anything like that?' to a situational question. Rather similarly, either of these types of question might be used in competency-based interviewing. Indeed, the first example in the box showing direct influencing questions could be regarded as a PBDI question.

Limitations

As with all interview methods there are some limitations in these approaches. Using the criterion-based interview technique in the context of assessment centre work requires a detailed understanding of that methodology. Using it outside an assessment centre may be to do so without the rigour implied by having a facilitator chairing a discussion and without the interplay of comment from a group of others.

With critical incident interviews an unskilled interviewer may give too many clues as to the area of exploration, may rephrase or paraphrase acceptable questions and in effect cue the interviewee to the right answer. Of course, this happens with conventional interviews but there is an added danger that perversely because of the very specificity of the criterion-based approach it may be more open to cueing than otherwise, because the situation is clearly defined.

Integrated interviewing

In this approach the principles of historic interviewing, situational interviews and competency-based techniques are combined. The idea is to focus on a series of circumstances in which the interviewee has been involved (as in conventional or classic criterion-based interviewing) or those that can be envisaged (as in situational interviewing) and to explore them in accordance with a competency model. The techniques of evidence elicitation as used in good practice in conventional interviewing and the specificity of focus as provided for in competency-based methods are combined. The historic (past performance is the best guide to future performance) aspect is a prevailing one, but complemented by the attitudinal (tendency to behave in a particular way) evidence that can be gleaned from situational questions. The latter are extended, as in turning PBDI questions into situational and vice versa by exploring circumstances in which the otherwise hypothetical situation has been experienced or could be envisaged.

Convergence on structure

There are perhaps a number of forces, some operating in specific fields and some more generally, that suggest structured approaches are here to stay. Although they may not wholly supplant conventional interviews across the board, they may supplement the conventional approach or actually replace it in certain instances. First, there is an increasing recognition of the very existence of structured interviews. As a consultant I have found clients increasingly aware of and familiar with such approaches. Thus discussions once characterized by questions such as 'Structured interviews: what are they?' are now typified by 'Structured interviews: what sort do you use?' Search and selection firms who would once have wholly anathematized a structured approach have more recently sought to include it as part of their unique selling proposition. The subsequent stage is its recognition as something routinely expected by clients and of commodity status.

Next is an increasing awareness, albeit varying in its specificity and intensity, of the ills attendant upon prejudice plus its pervasive nature as encapsulated in relation to one particular type in the term 'institutionalized racism'. This has prompted moves towards enhancing manifest objectivity in many aspects of employment. It has been a point of emphasis in recent literature on interviewing (eg Awosunle and Doyle, 2001; Anderson, 1997; Wood, 1997a, b; Ramsay, Gallois and Callan, 1997).

Last but not least is the move to call centre operations. These currently employ some 400,000 people in the United Kingdom, with a substantial subset working in the recruitment field. Working over the telephone to assess potential recruits for clients, these people tend to follow prescribed patterns of questioning for each of their recruitment campaigns. Thus at any one time a dozen or more interviewers may be responding to incoming calls and screening to a common-structured interview pattern. The screening may be on the basis of a number of 'status' variables, reflected in questions such as, 'Do you hold a clean UK driving licence?' Alternatively, they may deal directly with competencies such as interpersonal sensitivity, or planning and organizing. Sometimes this screening process is followed by more extensive questioning, also conducted by telephone but this time on an 'outbound call' basis. The initial screening interviewer will often have set the appointments for the follow-up interview for those successfully screened. The degree of system necessary in conducting high-volume recruitment in this way lends itself very readily to structured interview approaches. There is, in fact, nothing new about the use of screening interviews in high-volume situations. Miles *et al* (1946) describe a study in which US Marine Corps recruits were effectively screened for 'neuropsychiatric disability' at a rate of three per minute (*sic*).

SUMMARY

1. Structured interviews vary in form, from simple planning aids to precise prescriptions of questions and admissible responses.

2. A number of forms of structured interview are aimed at gathering clear evidence of behaviour.

3. A variety of methods is available for deriving the dimensions for a structured interview. One of these methods is the repertory grid in which expert judges reveal the dimensions relevant to their judgements through a simple card-sorting task. Another is the critical incident technique in which subject-matter experts (SMEs) are questioned about significant processes. Various other job analysis techniques also lead to the specification of relevant behaviour.

4. Competencies are used as the basis for many interviews. A competency is defined as: an underlying characteristic of a person that is causally related to effective or superior performance in a job or role.

5. Criterion-based interviewing is derived from assessment centre technology and involves the systematic exploration of evidence in relation to practically discrete areas of behaviour. 'Competency-based interviewing' is used interchangeably as a term with 'criterion-based interviewing'.

6. Critical incident technique has given rise to the situational interview, in which candidates indicate their responses to hypothetical situations and to the Patterned Behavioural Description Interview (PBDI) in which they are asked about their actual experiences.

7. In integrated interviewing, a variety of different questioning techniques is used in combination with a focus on a range of different and quite extensive real-life situations.

8. Research generally shows the predictive superiority of structured over unstructured interviews.

9. Currently a number of forces can be identified that support the increased use of structured interviews.

12

More on structured interviews

STRUCTURED PSYCHOMETRIC INTERVIEWS (SPI)

Origins

The origins of the SPI approach go back to the 1950s in the United States. The SPI is predicated upon the notion that those who are the most effective exponents of a role – the most competent – actually talk about their work in ways that are different – perhaps qualitatively as well as quantitatively – from those who are not. There are some conceptual links, of course, between this idea and the illustrative behaviours that can be brought out in the criterion-based or critical incident interviews. Some links can also be seen with those areas relating to the idea of expression in speech being a fairly direct reflection of personality, as referred to in Chapter 1 (Wrenn, 1949). It is this latter notion that, of course, is arguably at the basis of all interview methods but it is also arguably only with the SPI that its exploration is systematized.

The idea of speech as an indication of consistent patterns of behaviour is, of course, not by any means new. As indicated in Chapter 2, the whole matter of Freud's 'The psychopathology of everyday life' is full of links between what we say and our underlying attitudes and behavioural tendencies.

It is also noteworthy that methods aimed at modifying behaviour, even on an enduring basis and so arguably involving some modification of personality, concentrate on manipulating speech patterns. This is most graphically illustrated in George Orwell's novel *Nineteen Eighty-Four*. There two particularly powerful principles are applied in the controlled language 'Newspeak'. One is the explicit use of labels opposite in meaning from what they actually denote; the other is the contraction and so limitation in thought underlying the language. These concepts are both illustrated particularly in the abbreviations to 'Minipax' and 'Miniluve' of the War Ministry and Secret Police respectively. Arguably, also, the use of repetitions in religious ceremony and the chanting of slogans by political or sporting groups can be seen as tending to comparable ends. It is against this relatively complex background that the SPI should be seen.

Excellence modelling

As indicated, a key to developing an SPI is the modelling of excellence among the current exponents of a relevant role. This does, of course, assume that who is excellent can be known in advance but arguably in any form of modelling of effective performance the same requirement applies. It is likely to be somewhat easier, though not *particularly* easy, to discover in those fields where there are hard data. Thus in areas such as selling or other jobs involving measurable performance, for example control of materials wastage, there will be some objective measures. These measures may be complicated by a variety of other factors and usually it is as well to check the apparently hard data with more subjective information. For instance, a salesperson working with a product group towards the end of its natural cycle will be disadvantaged in relation to colleagues already in a position to sell the latest types or models.

Once such excellently performing individuals have been identified it is usual to undergo detailed discussions with them, typically in focus-group mode. The focus group is a semi-structured means of gathering views from a number of people, all of whom can be expected to have something to contribute. Its use in relation to the SPI involves exploring attitudes, behaviours, situations and circumstances relating to the role, and how problems are overcome, what would be factors making for success and what would be likely to lead to difficulty.

The focus-group participants are asked to reflect on their own attitudes, behaviours and experiences and those of others, to characterize truly effective behaviour and contrast it with that exhibited by the mediocre or wholly ineffective. Usually such discussions are recorded for detailed transcription. In analysing this material, in addition to the various pieces of information gathered on the circumstances, situations and behaviours of relevance, such as would apply to the critical incident and criterion-based techniques, one notes the particular use of words. Thus if a particular situation is spoken of with intensity or vividness, this may give a clue to attitudes supporting success, which can then be reflected in the interview itself.

One-to-one meetings may supplement the focus group or groups but one does then lose the opportunity for the most effective practitioners themselves to thrash out differences in views expressed. Typical of an issue that might arise is consideration of whether the most successful salespeople in a particular field insist only on meeting the top person in an organization, or whether success is related to having one's foot inside any door!

A number of questions are then derived from the information gathered. They are likely to be related to a tentative competency or dimension model. This question set and the model may be further fleshed out by additional one-to-one discussions, possibly with those in charge of the target group. More information may be added, too, from the study of relevant documentation such as mission statements, policies or business plans for extended periods of time ahead. From the questions generated on the basis of this material one would then trial a first version of the interview on another group of clearly expert exponents of the role, using their responses to refine further the questions and define the interpretative framework for them and the competency model. Sometimes this stage may be skipped as a specific step and collapsed with the following one, in which two contrasted groups are studied. One group will, again, consist of excellent exponents of the role. The other will be made up of those who are seen as less effective. By applying the interpretative framework to the responses of these two different groups, one may see if the instrument is overall capable of discriminating between them and so if it is an effective tool in selection. As part of this process it is sometimes necessary and appropriate to discard quite a large number of question items. Once the interview has been developed in this way it is necessary to train those who are going to use it.

The amount of effort required in training will depend not only on the capabilities of those trained, particularly their degree of comfort in handling the complexities of language that may be involved, but also on the complexity and clarity of the coding frame used. There will be some cases where a fairly broad framework can apply to questions and others where the framework is narrower. For instance, it is possible that a high-performing sales group will have distinguished themselves from their average colleagues by giving, say, three rather than just two examples of selling a new product in its first week on the market. This difference will need to have been captured in the interpretative framework and then reinforced in the training. ('Two examples may sound good so why not give the interviewee the benefit of the doubt?' Answer, 'Because if you do then you will tend to be selecting more like your mediocre, rather than more like your best.') Sometimes the questions show up relatively unusual responses that are characteristic of some of the expert group but not of all of them, so it is necessary to ensure that these are also captured in the interpretative framework.

Types of question and interpretation

The range of questions used in an SPI may be quite broad, corresponding to the PBDI and situational questions discussed earlier, as well as exploring attitudes and feelings or intentions: 'How would you feel if...?' 'How would you endeavour to go about...?' Some questions will explore simple matters of fact, while others will pose hypothetical situations. Some ask very open-ended questions – 'Tell me about...' – while others are closed – 'Would you prefer X or Y?' The touchstone in deciding whether to include a question in the final format is always whether or not it produces different responses between the higher- and lower-performing groups that it is intended to distinguish.

In all cases an important tenet of the approach is that interpretation of the question is not given to the respondent. Although this may be thought of as an aspect generally applying to interviewing, for otherwise the interviewer might well be at least halfway to supplying the answer, it is particularly important in the SPI. Here respondents are required to operate from their own frame of reference and it is recognized that this is likely to give the strongest clue to their typical or consistent behaviour. Adding to that frame of reference, for instance by illustrating an unfamiliar word, will tend to change the picture. For example, the term 'equity' can refer to fairness and justice or to the shares of a limited company. The question, 'Tell me about the equity in your present company' might produce a response in terms of, say, equal opportunities consciousness or financial ownership. To elaborate the question by specifying which use is meant is to supply the frame of reference for the candidate – virtually to give the answer – rather than to tap into his or her natural frame of reference, which forms the basis of each person's natural behaviour. Elaboration is tempting when the interviewee seeks clarification, but this at least distorts, if it does not wholly destroy, the value of the SPI approach.

Use and delivery of the SPI

As with a variety of other advanced techniques, such as personality questionnaires, there is little doubt that the SPI method is likely to fare best in the hands of specialists, either external consultants or a more or less dedicated group within an organization. The former are often likely to be more comfortable in fulfilling a requirement to prepare narrative reports on candidates. Such reports can, in fact, be as detailed as those written on the basis of a standardized psychometric battery (see box below). They may be particularly useful when the SPI is applied in development rather than selection, giving as they can scope to suggest development options that are likely to be effective.

SAMPLE SPI REPORT

Name: Allson Somebody

Overview

Alison Somebody is focused on end results and directed in her approach. She has a strong tendency to work to produce definite outcomes. She will be straightforward in her dealings with others and will generally carry them along with her. Along the way, though, she may not do all that is necessary to build rapport for the longer term. She appears to be interested in change and will seek to use it effectively to help gain objectives. She may be uncomfortable in situations in which she is not able to be in the driving seat herself and is likely, in fact, to seek a substantial degree of independence in her work.

Personal drives and motivations

Ms Somebody likes to have distinct goals and objectives, in the sense of having particular things to aim for. When she has achieved her objectives she will feel a sense of success. It will be important for her to have the opportunity of experiencing successes on a short-term as well as a continuing basis. To this end she is likely to break activities down into a series of sub-projects, each with their own clear goals, and to work towards these. She will also, though, have her sights clearly set on the longer term and will have quite substantial ambitions. It will be important for her management to recognize that she is personally ambitious and would wish to know that there is continued scope for growth within the organization. This may be afforded either by prospects of promotion or by her having the opportunity to

---

feel that she will continue to be challenged and given scope for personal development along the way.

Goals and targets are also important for Ms Somebody because they provide her with the structure for her work. She will be diligent herself in directing and controlling her activities in an orderly way and will probably wish to impose her sense of structure on others. Thus, a little paradoxically, it is not clear that she would necessarily fit in with the systems, procedures or even structures determined by her organization. It may be important for her to be helped to recognize the degree of balance that the company will be prepared to accept in this regard and where they would insist that their predetermined ways of doing things are to be followed.

Perhaps not surprisingly, Ms Somebody is quite positive about change. Although not wishing to involve herself in chaotic situations she will see orderly and systematic change, in which she has a driving and central part to play, as being critical for her success and that of the organization. She will respond flexibly, we believe, and would be likely to produce new ways of doing things as she seeks to harness the possibilities afforded by change. She gave very clear evidence of a range of situations in which changes that others had perceived as overly challenging and, indeed, potentially disastrous afforded her with the opportunity for finding new growth potential personally and in terms of the part of the business that she was directing.

Interacting with people

Ms Somebody has an awareness that she can sometimes be rather overpowering with others. On the positive side of this she has sometimes used her tendency to be lively and combative with her staff and colleagues in order to spur them on to greater endeavours and successes. Thus she likes challenge and, to some degree, expects others to respond to challenges as well as challenging her on occasions. She is less comfortable, in fact, in working with and through those staff who require support. She sees this herself as an area of some deficit in her approach and has sometimes taken some steps to alter her behaviour. This having been said, though, it seems likely that she will continue to be rather forceful and, by the same token, not typically empathetic at times. Continuing to surround herself with effective others who respond positively to challenge is likely to be a more appropriate tactic than expecting her to shift her natural behaviour through 180 degrees. Indeed the awareness that she already has of tendencies to be overly forceful, challenging and hard driving may be as far as she will go in this direction and at least do a little to mitigate the adverse impact that her naturally forceful behaviour will have on some people.

Although independent, success-minded and tending to define successes herself, Ms Somebody will also appreciate recognition from others. These others will need to be significant and she may, in fact, not react well if what she sees as minor accomplishments are recognized by those whom she would not perceive as of particularly high status or very effective themselves. Thus to some degree she sees herself as operating in a masterclass environment in which praise for business success is hard won but where, too, due recognition is appropriately given. Although material rewards appear to have some importance for her, these really seem to stand as symbols for recognition and have not, in fact, featured strongly in the motivational picture that we have seen.

Handling information

Ms Somebody appears to be systematic and also rapid in her approach to handling information. In gathering information from others she would tend to ask them about significant points or heads of issues. Then she will function in one of two ways, depending on the circumstances. To begin with she will be likely to form an overview, dismissing from further consideration those aspects of the situation that are not critical but seeing links between the main flows and direction of issues. For example, she was clear about the balance between handling short-term change while still maintaining the company's core business strengths, which in fact appear to lie in a relatively stable area of business. Having made her general overview of an issue or set of issues she is then likely to delve down into considerable depth to follow through further on specific topics. She is, perhaps, more comfortable in handling complexity when it is expressed verbally rather than in terms of numbers. However, she does not appear to be without facility in the latter area, although she would tend, where possible, to get others to do the donkey work in this regard.

Part of her orientation to change appears to be to build pictures of possible future scenarios. When she is doing this she will be likely to consider a very wide range of options and, in working with a team of others, will want to go through processes of brainstorming and speculation about ideas. She sees this work as particularly important for handling a changing environment. She sees her mental preparation at this time as putting her in a good position to cope with a variety of eventualities that might come up and, indeed, appears to have done this quite effectively on a number of occasions in the past.

In the SPI it is not necessary for interviewer and interpreter to be one and the same. Just as two or three paper-and-pencil psychometric instruments might be administered by one person and interpreted by another, the same can apply to the SPI. This will often involve the use of a tape-recorder and the services of a transcriber, so that the person making the interpretation will work from a printed text of the interview. This also provides scope for further checks on standardization in interpretation.

The standardization of the process also means that a part of it can be clearly separated out and used as a shorter screening device, with the remainder of the questions being delivered only to those who pass this first stage. In this way time and money can be saved while still preserving the objectivity derived from the use of a common and highly specified process. Also questions in the SPI are frequently arranged so that competencies are addressed successively question by question. Thus if eight competencies are to be covered, the first of which is direct influence, questions 1, 9, 17, 25, 33 and 41 of a 48-question interview would seek to tap into this competency. This obviates the problem of cueing referred to above in connection with other forms of competency-based interviews.

The structured psychometric interview is often delivered by telephone, an approach that appears to work well. It has the advantage of saving a large amount of time and money. It can sometimes appear unfamiliar as a method to candidates and appropriate briefing is necessary. This will often be done initially when an appointment for a telephone interview is booked, when expectations, for instance as to the time that might be required, will be set. The use of a standard introduction at the time of the interview is also important. This should cover, among other things, the important point discussed above that no interpretation of questions will be offered. It will also include gaining permission to make a tape-recording of the interview.

Reservations and caution about SPI

The training to work effectively with the method can be quite daunting and without it the technique rapidly defaults to a loose semi-structured interview. Training focuses on the delivery of questions as illustrated above, and also upon their interpretation. It is the latter that after initial difficulties with delivery are likely to pose the most problems. It is sometimes difficult to refer back to the original source of the interpretative framework and it is not uncommon to find manuals of SPI interpretation littered with year after year of amendments without any necessary basis in fact.

Caution by the uninitiated about the use of the SPI is typically based on particular assumptions of what an interview should be. Armchair critics are also much inclined to view any form of highly structured interview as overly mechanistic. For example, Harris (1989) reviewed the so-called comprehensive structured interview (CSI), which comprised a mix of questions covering situational and job knowledge, job simulation and worker requirements. He concluded that this might be viewed as an 'oral version of a written test'. To retort 'And why not add the rigour of testing to the comfortable medium of the spoken word?' might seem to line up too firmly on the objectivist-psychometric side of the debate between that philosophy and the subjectivist-psychometric one.

The SPI is such a broad technique that it is sometimes seen as universal in its application. No real limitations have yet been found as to the types of role that can be explored. My experience in the last 10 years alone has covered sales reps in a new insurance company, hybrids linking IT and business, middle and senior managers in the NHS, and North Sea oil-rig engineering supervisors. But of course the SPI does not directly assess current level of skill in a particular field any more than do other interviews or, say, personality questionnaires.

It is also sometimes assumed that it is just another interview and there is therefore a temptation to see it as only applicable at an early and crude stage of the selection process, whereas in fact it can yield data comparable to, say, a battery of psychometric methods. Again it has sometimes suffered by being put together with far less effective methods such as ill-thought-out presentations or poorly conducted conventional interviews.

Last but not least is the question of costs. Although when established the method is likely to be as cheap as other one-to-one methods and far less expensive than, say, full assessment centres, thorough bespoke research is required for it to realize its full potential. The training required if it is to be done properly is likely to be on a par with that needed for the interpretation of psychometrics (But if training seems expensive, what price ignorance?) One may also need to consider the cost of having tapes typed up. All that having been said, both published studies such as that of Wiesner and Cronshaw (1988), Wright, Lichterfels and Pursell (1989) or Robertson and Smith (1988) and, from my own professional experience, bespoke research typically show structured interviews in general to have substantial validity.

THE EXTENDED INTERVIEW

Degrees of structure

One aspect of selection processes is the idea of taking people through an extended procedure. Such procedures seem often to be based on the idea of making an exacting scrutiny of the candidate and/or the notion of giving a number of interested parties the opportunity for involvement in that scrutiny. Regardless of the degree to which the procedures used are actually made up of interviews as such, a number of organizations refer to them as the 'extended interview'. The term 'second interview' is sometimes used similarly. While a second interview is sometimes simply an interview undergone by those who survived a first interview, and its methods are not defined, in some organizations second interview denotes a different and generally extended process.

As well as assessment centres, as discussed in Chapters 9 and 10, the processes considered here include somewhat less structured but still quite extensive methods. There are sometimes whole days in which groups of interviewers are gathered together to take candidates through a series of separate interviews, each to cover at least broadly predetermined areas. Thus candidates for an engineering post might experience a technical interview from a specialist, a personnel interview from a human resources manager and then an overall interview from a senior manager. How far the content of such processes is prescribed in advance will vary, but it would be unusual for this to extend to the detailed level of specification set out in the more advanced forms of structured interview such as the SPI. However, because there is some structuring and very often some degree of final discussion about what has gone on, these processes are likely to be somewhat more rigorous than those usually used in conventional selection interviewing.

Relatively little research has been carried out on this class of interview outside the area of assessment centres. I have sat in on some of the discussions following these processes, and often the view of one of the interviewing team prevails, and evidence is adduced that was not covered in any form of initial job specification. Again, though, at least this evidence is out in the open when there is such a discussion.

Quite often, additional information such as that provided from psychometric instruments will be considered in discussion together with the interview information. Even so the procedures together are unlikely to represent the levels of rigour and accuracy attained either by structured interviewing or by assessment centres. Having a number of interviewers involved, having them explore more or less prescribed areas and having at least semi-formalized discussion of all the information gathered may help reduce the level of subjectivity somewhat.

THE BOARD OR PANEL INTERVIEW

In the board interview, interviewing is carried out by a group of people, typically acting under the chairpersonship of one of their number. (The term 'board' is sometimes used in the sense referred to here, but also in the sense of a body responsible for a recruitment process as a whole, as in the erstwhile Civil Service Selection Board (CSSB). This has sometimes led to confusion.) As with other forms of extended interview process there may be a division of labour, with different people exploring different aspects of the candidate's suitability. This type of interview should be distinguished from a two-person interview, where two interviewers each take on the role of questioner or note-taker. In fact in many panel interviews there may be some degree of control in terms of the chairperson allocating time to different interviewers and inviting them in turn to put forward their questions. However, there is typically little or no control over note-taking and there may be little control over the deliberative processes or discussion used to formulate the evaluation of the candidates.

Usually when a board interview has been decided upon there is a strong representational element in those making it up. Thus such processes are frequently used in local government situations where the panel may comprise a mixture of voluntary elected members and salaried officers and where there is a requirement for concerned stakeholders to have a say in the interview process.

In certain medical appointments, a variety of parties is common; doctors, managers, nurses all have their say in the appointment process by sitting on a board or panel. Sometimes these panels are preceded or followed by an informal meeting, the 'trial by sherry' discussed earlier in this book. In every situation the degree of control varies. It cannot be assumed that those interviewing will have had any relevant training and they may only gather together as a body for the purposes of making a particular appointment, with the next appointment to be made requiring in its turn a different group of representatives. Panel members may also turn up or not in a relatively arbitrary way, so that the panel chairperson may not know in advance who will be present.

Panel interviews are also used internally in organizations in connection with determining suitability for promotion to the next level rather than for a particular job. Sometimes the promotion may be effectively immediate, while in others it may be a matter of entering a pool, from which the actual promotion may become substantive only upon a specific post becoming available. In yet others the short-term outcome of the panel will be to determine acceptance on to a programme of development, with considerable resources being applied to those who 'pass'. Such arrangements are more commonly applied in large organizations and form a part of the whole process of management and utilization of the human resource, in effect part of performance management. In these cases the panel may have access to a portfolio of information provided by the candidate, his or her line management and probably drawing too on records of appraisals and career path to date in the organization concerned. This information may include a number of ratings specifically made against an organization-wide competency model, with the panel outputs often including assessments in terms of the same model, as well as an overall recommendation. Again, the degree of structure actually applied by the panel and the amount of training received by the panel members will vary.

Despite a certain haphazardness on occasions in the application of panel interviews, in some measure such processes can be seen to be fair. They may have the important advantage of gauging whether the candidate in potentially politically sensitive roles can be seen as sufficiently 'one of us' to be able to be acceptable to the stakeholders present and those whom they may represent. This carries with it the notion that changing the status quo may be hard with such methods, almost regardless of what may be in a job description or competency model. It may, by the same token, promote or preserve the exercise of prejudice. Notwithstanding these difficulties, Wiesner and Cronshaw's (1988) study showed higher levels of validity even for unstructured board than for unstructured individual interviews. Structured board interviews produced validities only slightly lower on average than structured individual interviews.

FEEDBACK AND FOLLOW-UP INTERVIEWING

When candidates have gone through various forms of extended procedures there is scope to give them feedback on their performance to date. As indicated in Chapter 1, this is quite commonly done in conjunction with psychometric procedures and, indeed, with regard to psychometric instruments it is a principle enshrined in the recommendations of the Chartered Institute of Personnel and Development on psychometric use. Giving feedback can also provide an opportunity to gather further information, which may in itself be used to refine the initial interpretation of the candidate's psychometric results. Thus the feedback then incorporates an interview process within it. One commonly asked question during follow-up discussions is whether the results just fed back were in line with expectations and common experience. Where there are discrepancies these may be a matter for further exploration or comment. The box below shows an example of a feedback interview following the administration of a standard psychometric procedure and the relevant passage from a subsequent write-up.

Interviewer: There are several indications from your 16PF results that you are quite independent-minded.

   Candidate: Yes, I'd go along with that.

   Interviewer: You will probably have some pretty clear views yourself in advance on an issue or problem and you may actually come to conclusions quite quickly.

   Candidate: Yes.

   Interviewer: Can you think of a time when you have done that?

   Candidate: Yes. We had a major refinancing job to do last year on a line of credit required for expansion. I felt we should work with XYZ Bank and I approached them and just one other source, as a sort of benchmark, and then I drove through the choice of XYZ.

   Interviewer: Like many people who are independent and quick in their summing up, you may not always see the need to take others along with you. You do not seem to feel a strong need for the support of a group.

   Candidate: I'm not so sure about that. I think you have to carry the team along, and I always make a point of consulting with other people.

The candidate shows evidence of elevated independence and also a high level of enthusiasm. She appears quite dominant and will probably seek to impose her position upon others. During feedback she recognized aspects of this style, but felt she adopted a more consultative approach than indicated here. It may be worth exploring further the way in which she has worked with her current subordinates and peers, in terms of team building.

Reports of feedback interviews can be used to indicate yet further issues for interviewers to explore later on. However, there is a note of caution to be sounded here. While helping the next stage interviewer, they may also cue the interviewee in advance. It is necessary, if such approaches are not just to produce contrary evidence at the later stage (ie the interviewee denying or explaining away the difficult behavioural area opened up), for the interviewer to have training in probing in sufficient depth. In the example given above, the follow-up interviewer would need to elicit evidence vis-à-vis the candidate's team behaviour, not just seek affirmation or denial of support to the team.

   Another approach is to reserve feedback until after all processes are complete. This obviates the difficulty just outlined of cueing the candidate, but it does also mean that the maximum value may not have been extracted from the interviewing process. One potential solution to this is to give very strong guidance to interviewers as to specific questions to ask. Such an approach was developed by the test publishers ASE in relation to follow-up interviewing after applications of the 16 Personality Factor Questionnaire (16PF). Questions were provided for a range of different combinations of scores on the various 16PF scales.

CONCLUSION

There are many strands in the so-called extended interview process. One common thread is a degree of structure. This may at the very least be implied even if there are multiple interviewers, in that each is to some degree given an area to pursue. The scope for pursuit of different areas and the balance of different viewpoints in interpretation may be a reason for the apparent superiority of the unstructured board over the unstructured individual interview. Thus the board interview can scarcely avoid some structure. Certainly, without structure there is little chance that the extended time will be used profitably.

SUMMARY

1. The structured psychometric interview (SPI) involves the development of questions, the responses to which distinguish between superior and ineffective exponents of a role. The dependence of the technique on precise patterns of language implies that both questions and interpretative frameworks for responses are tightly specified, with implications for training.

2. Extended or second interview procedures may include a number of activities not necessarily in interview format as such. Assessment centres are sometimes referred to in this way.

3. Board or panel interviews, where a candidate is interviewed by a number of people, may involve a significant element of representation among board members. Research suggests higher validity for these interviews than for unstructured individual interviews.

4. Giving feedback on a procedure such as a psychometric test may provide an opportunity for a follow-up interview on that procedure.

13

Performance management – background and approaches to measurement

THE MEANING OF PERFORMANCE MANAGEMENT

A definition of performance management was given in Chapter 1, with stress on both elements: the performance and the management part. For performance to be understood in any practical sense there is an implication that it must be assessed, ie measured.

THE PERFORMANCE CONTEXT – BUSINESS PLANS AND MANAGEMENT OF PEOPLE TO REALIZE THEM

In fully integrated business operations there would be a clear continuity and 'joined-upness' between business plans and the management of people to address them. I say 'would be' because in practice this rarely seems to be the case. In Chapter 17 we shall look more at situations involving major change, but for the moment it is worth noting that amongst the reasons cited for mergers and acquisitions to fail the most significant typically appears to be the lack of attention to people aspects (see eg KPMG, 1999). This can be seen as one aspect of a failure to follow through from high-level ideas to their practical realization at the 'coal face', where people are actually required to deliver them. Sometimes there can just be seen to be a bewildering array of measures that can be used to define business success, both day to day and medium term.

Of course in a well-ordered world each person's performance goals – with the attendant scope for measuring them and the related and regular direction of individual performance that would ensue – would be very closely coupled. In practice this is often not the case. One often hears of 'silo mentality', ie different parts of an organization each pursuing their narrow field of interest without reference to other parts of the business or to an overarching set of *business* performance requirements. In fact many organizations seem prone to this lack of connectedness and to general discontinuities in thinking and practice about performance requirements. (Assemblages of occupational psychologists – my own profession – are by no means immune. I recall working in a government department where the head psychologist suddenly announced that the team's performance over the past two years had been disappointing as only a couple of papers had been published by team members in the peer-reviewed psychological literature. To the best knowledge of the entire team that was the first time that such publications had been set as a performance criterion.)

We are faced today with substantial fragmentation with regard to defining what performance is actually required of each role or set of roles. To put the case starkly – if with some degree of emphasis – we have on the one hand a picture of top management defining overall objectives and key performance indicators for the business and some of the workers being encouraged to improve the modern equivalent of Taylor's shovel strokes (as described in Chapter 2).

Even at the topmost level, the definition of what is really required may not always be clear. An example from my own experience concerned the life insurance industry. In one case a research study I was leading required the identification of top performers in the ranks of middle to senior management. I gathered together the company's top executive and led them through a discussion of who was to be included in the sample of outstanding performers. Although there was clear and more or less universal agreement on a handful of 'really good guys', there were diametrically opposed views around the table as to who else should be included. This might be seen as surprising from a company that routinely bombarded actual and potential investors and policyholders with statistics on the performance of its *products* and where the actuarial underpinning of the business can be seen as amongst the more sophisticated applications of numerical techniques in business. It was, perhaps, surprising not only that there were no agreed measures of management performance, but that the executive had not been aware of that fact and had not evidently seen it as a matter of importance. (There had arguably been plenty of time to sort it out as the company traced its origins back nearly a hundred years.)

Another case from the insurance industry involved, rather unusually, a company start-up, representing a joint venture between two major players with complementary strengths who were seeking to capitalize on these in their new subsidiary. My role was to help the top team – the managing director, sales director and a non-executive director – clarify the performance requirements of their sales force. Again diametrically opposed views were expressed and a very extended period of debate was necessary to produce the model of required performance. (I am, though, glad to report that the model was able to be translated into a specification for use in recruitment that proved highly successful, and the company has now, some 15 years on, joined much longer-established enterprises as one of the bastions of the industry.) What was surprising in this case was that although addressed relatively early in the life of the company the question of required performance was not defined *right* at the outset and, again, that the top team had not been aware of one another's very differing views until the meeting specifically to discuss it.

What causes the apparent discontinuity of thinking between overall direction and the performance necessary to achieve it? There are probably several answers. One is almost undoubtedly that HR heads often do not have an equal say amongst the counsels of the mighty. Associated with this is an implicit view that we are 'all experts on people'. Of course, tacit assumptions, implicit models and intuitive views can take an enterprise so far. However, it is my contention that better results can be achieved by pursuing a more actively joined-up approach. Much of the rest of this chapter and some of the ensuing one are concerned with some of the practicalities in this connection.

PRACTICAL ISSUES IN COMPETENCY MODELLING

Scope for confusion

Working with the definition of competency given in Chapter 1, it is self-evident that competencies must underpin performance. In practice, this may work varyingly well. The systematic understanding and development of competencies is in fact rarely followed through and there is considerable scope for confusion. This can stem from several sources. The examples given in the box below show how, on the one hand, differing competencies in the same model may include **common** elements and, on the other, how very contrary elements may sometimes be juxtaposed. In the first case, this can lead to elements of double-counting in considering performance according to what are labelled as **different** competencies. In the second case, it can lead to confusion in the sense of averaging over the different elements, which are in effect pulling in different directions.

A MODEL WITH CONTRARY ELEMENTS

▮ Ability to identify and deliver a creative and imaginative approach to service delivery.

▮ Ability to **inspire**, lead, motivate and develop employees and teams in a performance-led organization.

▮ Excellent **interpersonal**, presentational, communication and **analytical** skills.

▮ Ability to deal with complex, delicate and wide-ranging issues with sensitivity, taking a robust line where appropriate.

▮ To operate in a complex, political, multidisciplinary, multicultural environment with credibility and trust.

▮ Highly developed oral, written, numeracy and presentation skills.

▮ To work across boundaries and **inspire** employees, members, schools, agencies and other partners to deliver the highest level of achievement and care for the vulnerable.

Over-elaboration in competencies can show itself in other ways. To begin with, there may just be too much verbiage for the user of competencies in a performance context to 'see the wood for the trees'. Next, there is the possibility of assuming that, because one element of the competency is met, then the whole of the competency is actually demonstrated.

Yet another complication is the idea of measuring **levels** of competency and hence of performance to a degree that may not actually be justified. Thus, it can sometimes be assumed that, because one has a grading structure covering the workforce from relatively low to relatively high, this must automatically be able to be reflected in the measure given. In other words this implies a degree of resolution or 'granularity' in the model that may not have been established in practice.

Yet another issue in this muddled world of the use of competencies is the possible existence of multiple competency models at the same time. Sometimes this arises as different waves of management arrive with different ideas of competencies required, but without necessarily seeking to change all that has gone before. Sometimes it is reflected, too, in differences of nomenclature so that an organization may talk about competencies and simultaneously have other terms in play such as ' themes' or 'skills', which are in essence used in the same way. I have found it personally not uncommon to come across two or even three models seeking to be used simultaneously and, in one case, worked with an organization that had no fewer than six models on the go at the same time and, not surprisingly, little or no effective handle on performance.

Bringing clarity

What is the way out of this morass? It is obviously an issue not amenable to a single solution but in general there seems to be a need for a more systematic approach in the actual application of disciplines that are by no means new. One may see as something of a culprit in this the HR departments that do not actually exercise any degree of control over management's use of modelling and even in parallel with systematic procedures will allow idiosyncratic additions or amendments to be made. However, in such cases, the use of the systematic approach in the first place may, in turn, permit the survival of more than a thread of coherent thought. One aspect of this is to ensure that when the whole of the competency definition is set up research is undertaken to see what elements do actually hang together.

Part of the systematic approach, too, is to consider at the outset just how a competency model is to be applied; is it just meant for use in a selection context, for instance, or is it intended for development or performance management purposes? Among other things this will determine the level of detail in which the model is expressed.

It is also important to consider who is to be involved in the development of the model and how. If the relevant people in the sense of those who are knowledgeable about the role concerned are not involved, then it is quite apparent that the model is likely to be flawed. However, subject-matter experts may not be entirely the same group as those with an interest in the role. Without the involvement of the latter it is likely that the model will suffer from the tinkering already described or be subject to the neglect or pooh-poohing inherent in the 'not invented here' syndrome. These interested parties, who would not normally be regarded as subject-matter experts as such, may also have a proper part to play in shaping the competencies so as better to reflect the organization's present or future needs. I can recall clearly a number of discussions with chief executives concerned to add new dimensions to the behaviours typical of their companies better to support their current intentions. In several of these, ethics, integrity and honesty were thought to be somewhat lacking. In another case it was staff development – often a neglected area.

Other future requirements that I have come across include **strategic thinking** and **commercial sensitivity**. Grafting such concepts on to the competency model can, perhaps, be seen as a step towards producing a 'designer organization'. However, care must be taken to involve these other stakeholders in a way that does not just reflect a passing whim. Quite often, too, a senior executive's pet behaviour or his or her *bête noire* will already have been captured in another part of the competency model. Challenge and checking any newly minted competencies against the business plans and experience elsewhere are important in ensuring that such contributions are meaningful and helpful.

Where a competency model is in existence but the organization takes initiatives to introduce a new one, sometimes calling it by another name, then, at the very least, this should be questioned. Otherwise confusion will often reign accompanied by wasteful attempts to translate between the two models.

There is also sometimes debate as to whether a particular label can properly be seen as referring to a competency or not. My view is that, according to the definition of competency being used here, if the label can be seen to refer to an underlying characteristic making for successful performance then it is properly designated a competency. However, there still seems to be scope for ambiguity and reference, for example, to 'competencies and skills', when the latter are, in fact, a subset of the former.

Perhaps the overall guidance here with regard to competencies is 'gang warily'.

STAKEHOLDER VIEWS – CUSTOMER MEASURES AND 360 DEGREE ASSESSMENTS

Increasingly, performance management is turning to sources of information beyond those provided by a person's immediate line manager. This is very patently so in the case of 360 degree, where views from peers and subordinates, as well as superiors, are typically included. There is also, here, the possibility of using customer measures in the form of ratings of satisfaction. Both of these approaches hold out promise of better measurement, and so management, of performance, but neither is entirely straightforward to implement.

Customer satisfaction

In order to measure customer satisfaction one needs the ongoing cooperation of and input from a sufficiently representative sample of the customer base. This may be hard enough to gather internally, but may be more difficult with an organization's external customers. There the tendency to respond at all may well itself be a function of the level of satisfaction felt, but in a way that is, perforce, difficult to gauge.

To the extent that the customer satisfaction information can be gathered it can be used as a tool in managing performance. Most commonly applied to the functioning of groupings of individuals, even up to the level of whole companies, customer satisfaction measures *can* be applied at an individual level, too, giving qualitative information about one or more staff members supplying services to a customer.

The findings from customer satisfaction research can be used to identify significant trends that could have major impacts upon customer behaviour. This is particularly applicable to situations with multiple customers, as in a retail environment. There externally supplied customer satisfaction studies may have a part to play in gathering information.

Of course relevant customer behaviour, such as purchasing, does not always follow satisfaction in accordance with a smooth curve, but can be subject to step function changes. This becomes particularly important for the organization dealing with a relatively small customer base. Knowing the point at which such change is likely to happen can be absolutely vital with regard to the input of effort on remedial work or, for instance, on continued research, marketing or product improvement. Thus a highly satisfied corporate customer might afford our supplier preferred provider status and/or give it the next really big order. Conversely a highly dissatisfied customer may refuse to pay or haggle endlessly over a bill or switch supply to another source. It would be great for the supplying organization to manage the performance of its people with particular attention to these points, so that the 'last straw' resulting in a switch is avoided and that the extra effort is put in to raise the satisfaction level to the point of gaining the award of long-term supply (see Figure 13.1).

This understanding of customer behaviour is extremely difficult to obtain and requires close monitoring of their intentions. This is, in fact,

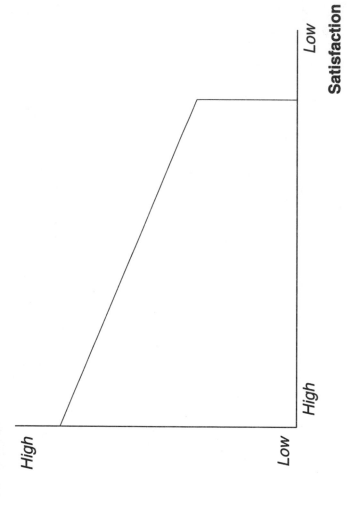

Figure 13.1 Individual customer behaviour

part of the objective of those suppliers who locate one or more of their staff with a corporate customer, generally to manage relationships and be an ear to the ground with regard to intentions. Even in a retail environment, although the trend information may be relevant, there is greater value to the organization if the customer satisfaction ratings can be linked back to an individual or, failing that, to a relatively small team. Then there is real scope for individual managers to use this information actually to manage the performance of their teams.

In some areas there are further compounding difficulties. Although there have also been some sound intentions with regard to performance indicators in the healthcare field, these themselves have often been resented and blocked by those being measured. In addition, although in principle it is particularly helpful to have measures of customer, ie patient, satisfaction, this may be clouded by the overwhelming effect of outcomes, either positive or negative. Much of this will be beyond the scope of the medical team to influence. This then raises the question as to whether and, if so, how far measures of customer satisfaction should be regarded as proper measures of individual performance and, potentially, as proper drivers of reward.

Sometimes, though, even in the tricky medical field, there is quite a close coupling between customer satisfaction and reward and I have come across some hospitals in the United States whose doctors had quite a substantial element of their total pay determined in this way. More generally the use of complaints indices relating to whole groups of workers in a range of service industries also fits in with this type of thinking. So, too, does the collection of customer comments in the hospitality and catering industry and their use in connection with recognition programmes such as 'employee of the month'. Undoubtedly, though, a considerable amount more remains to be done before customer comment and satisfaction ratings are used systematically and directly, as opposed to being employed as a rather broad-brush indication of whether things are going well or not so well.

360 degree as psychometric

The production of ratings of strength by self, bosses, peers and subordinates, and the comparison of the self-ratings with those of others are characteristics of 360 degree assessment. The comparisons indicate agreement or disagreement on each of a number of competency scales and may show the spread amongst the other people's ratings. The output is then discussed, typically with a line manager or an HR specialist, depending on the context. In the case of performance management it is usually with the former. Refinements to the process can include rating the different competencies for their importance in the role. In this way a discussion on the performance implications of the ratings and the importance of differences amongst the different sources can help shape a discussion on performance.

There is an interesting statistical conundrum in putting together 360 degree assessments. It has been argued (eg McHenry, 1996) that 360 degree assessments should be subject to psychometric properties as discussed in earlier chapters. In order for necessary statistical tests to be undertaken, however, there is a principle that numbers of observations, on which the judgements are based, should not be too small. (There is a key principle in statistics called the Law of Large Numbers and conversely the Law of Small Numbers by which small samples are more likely to come up with unusual events than larger ones – see box below.)

Consider the following situations. A bag contains nine red balls and one white ball. A ball is picked at random. The chances of it being white are 1 in 10 or 10 per cent. If an inference is made on the basis of this single sample then the wrong inference will be made on 10 per cent of occasions on which such an experiment is undertaken. Supposing, however, that the first ball is replaced and the second one drawn before any conclusion is made. The chance of two successive drawings being white and so giving the wrong impression is 1 per cent. Thus, as the sample size increases the chances for a misleading picture to arise diminishes. It is this simple fact of sampling that is the basis of most currently applied statistical methods.

For many people acquiring 360 degree feedback from subordinates and peers the numbers involved will be too small for statistical significance testing 'legitimately' to be carried out. Hence one is left with simply recording the numbers without any view of their psychometric properties as such. However, there is another view of the 360 degree approach which is that it is a *census* not a *sampling* approach. (In fact, it would be a complete census if all possible peers and subordinates were to be covered, but it is not quite to the point, as in practice the majority of relevant people will often have been used.) Put more simply, the results tell us just what other people – relevant people – think about us.

Quite commonly 360 degree reporting includes narrative comment as well as numbers, and the use of these in 360 degree work tends in the direction of treating them as specific views, rather than simply numerical ratings.

Pros and cons of 360 degree

The popularity and importance of 360 degree assessment is well attested to by a claim that US companies spent $152 million on this form of feedback for development purposes as long ago as 1992 (Garavan, Morley and Flynn, 1997).

Amongst the advantages claimed for 360 degree methods are that they are quite cost-effective. Certainly when compared with, say, an assessment centre this is so. There is also a point that, although an assessment centre is based on objective behaviour and the views of a number of people, their conclusions, being derived from a 'special occasion', may still have less credence with some participants than formalized views gathered over a period of time. The fact that participants' own views of themselves are required to be made explicit also means that any contrast between self and others' ratings can be made absolutely explicit. This gives scope, among other things, for self-awareness and impact on others to be explored and addressed directly. It also allows measurement to be made more clearly in terms of the organization's specific requirements than a standardized method such as a personality questionnaire. This flexibility is well served, too, by the increasing availability of shell software systems, permitting ready adjustment of content.

Having embarked on 360 degree processes, many organizations tend to use them on a continuing basis so as to provide year-on-year measurement to track areas of improvement and areas of slippage. Because the areas to be judged are made very explicit to a large number of people, these processes can also be seen as reinforcing messages about what the organization sees as important.

Although rather rarely used on their own for the purpose, 360 degree systems can also feed in to decision making about promotion or succession.

Next in this list of plus points, it is often found that people are rated notably higher by others than themselves in certain areas. This may give them the confidence to try new roles and/or an understanding of those strengths that will be capable of making the maximum contribution to their performance.

It is also claimed that the process provides an opportunity or platform for the discussion of performance issues and opens up better two-way communication.

Not all is necessarily plain sailing, however. For 360 degree to work, those undertaking the ratings need to have knowledge of the relevant behaviours, and the opportunities to make the necessary observations to supply such knowledge are likely to differ from one rater to the next. This may result in either inflated ratings, on the basis of 'no evidence to the contrary', or a relatively large number of holes in the data, ie 'cannot say' returns. Another point here is that, although organizations will typically prepare quite careful instructions for the completion of ratings, they rarely provide any training in this connection. The importance of this point can, of course, be debated and some would argue that it is unvarnished views that are sought. This does mean, though, that various biases such as halo effects are likely to enter into the ratings given. Nor is there necessarily much support given in interpreting findings. I have found that when provided in workshop mode, say as part of a management development event, there is quite an insatiable appetite for understanding. Such an appetite will scarcely be satisfied by an e-mail with attached results and/or a perfunctory discussion with a line manager.

The view has sometimes been expressed that the process could undermine a manager's authority if, as it were, a *vox populi* assessment from peers conflicted with the manager's own perceptions and hence the representations he or she might wish to make to the staff member. There is a logic to this, but in practice it is not something commonly encountered. Of more concern is a tendency for someone receiving what he or she regards as adverse and unfair ratings from peers to embark on something of a witch-hunt to track down the culprits. I have heard such intentions expressed and, indeed, it is not difficult of execution, given the relatively small number of people making the ratings. If supporting comments are made it may be a ready matter either from the style of expression or from the specific content to effect the identification. Whether or not the person rated is likely to engage in such behaviour the view that he or she *may* do so can affect the ratings made.

There is also a considerable danger that the process can be seen as 'yet another' piece of bureaucratic administrivia, given scant attention and got out of the way as quickly as possible. If such is the case the ratings may well be impressionistic and made without due consideration of the particular competencies being described or the examples of relevant behaviour on the part of the person being rated.

Yet another point is that people do not have an equal balance all round, owing to the fact that most report to one or, more rarely, two bosses and hardly ever more. If the boss category is separated out as one of three groups, apart from 'self', that is identified, then this may have the effect of relatively over-weighting his or her opinion. (In practice, this may be relevant, given the likely significance of the boss/subordinate relationship.)

Like much else in the assessment and performance management field, the use of 360 degree needs to be thoroughly thought through and planned.

REWARDS AS DRIVERS OF PERFORMANCE

The idea of rewards as drivers of performance is, of course, nothing new but does require fairly close coupling of the two. This was established initially by psychologists such as Thorndike writing in the 1920s and speaking of the 'Law of Effect'. A rather similar idea was neatly captured by an experimentalist, Ward Edwards (1961), in a paper entitled 'Costs and pay-offs are instructions'. In the workplace, though, there is often a less-than-close coupling between the reward and the behaviour that it is intended to reinforce.

I have frequently come across managers in what had professed to be performance-driven companies who could not identify a direct link between, say, bonuses and results. I also had the experience recently of a company considering extending the range of flexible benefits that they offered their staff. When I asked if they had considered using this scope for tailoring to fine-tune reward to match performance and the specific motivation of the individual concerned – perhaps the most obvious point to an occupational psychologist like myself – it was clear that I was suggesting a complete novelty to those involved. Relativities in pay, guaranteed annual increments with seniority (ie time in grade) and recognition of contributions to longer-term performance as in developing other staff all have a part to play in complicating the performance–reward link. Even in sales environments the relationship is not always clear cut, as illustrated in the box below.

LIFE INSURANCE SUCCESS: THE MOVING TARGET

Life insurance has large numbers of people, lots of data and some history of using psychometric methods. The volume of business written by an agent would seem to be an obvious and objective criterion of success and a basis for performance-related reward.

However, all is not plain sailing! Here are just a few of the complicating factors:

▪ within the overall criterion of business volume, the need for refinement of the criterion measure to reflect business cancelled at different times during the originally intended life of a policy;

▪ differential ease of business by geographic area – city versus rural, affluent versus non-affluent, age of population;

▪ changes of company organization such as mergers;

- very high staff turnover;

- varying competitor activity;

- varying effectiveness of agents' managers;

- the practice of dividing up successful 'patches', giving part to new entrants;

- new products constantly coming on to the market;

- changes in regulation – legal and industry imposed – affecting, for example, what can and cannot be said to clients, potentially impacting ease of sale.

ROLE OF THE DEVELOPMENT CENTRE IN MANAGING PERFORMANCE

Chapter 12 described the variations for development, the content and the form of centres used for development purposes. At the level of the individual the output from a centre provides an opportunity to consider how performance can be better managed. Thus when a participant and his or her line manager – the critical part of the 'front line' in performance management – meet to review the findings there is often a better understanding of the behavioural causes underlying either good or poor performance and hence how the one can be harnessed and the other addressed directly or managed around.

Consideration of development centre outputs on a grouped basis, say the management of a division or for a whole company, can suggest how performance might be improved by centrally driven or supported initiatives. For example, if a number of participants are found relatively wanting as internal networkers it may be worth putting mechanisms in place ranging from open-plan offices to the establishment of contact groups or secondments. Such moves can be a way of ameliorating the limitations found.

Another approach to performance improvement is the 'action learning set'. Although this may be born out of a variety of initiatives the development centre quite often provides a spark. Pioneered by Revans (1971) the approach involves a group of managers who meet regularly, providing support to one another in their development and/or consideration of day-to-day issues. The groups are essentially self-managing, but often make use of an external facilitator at the outset or on a more continuing basis. Other outsiders may be invited in, too, to provide input on a specialist topic. When a development centre is the starting point it may be that the managers have different needs, but have established a sufficient degree of trust and rapport to feel that their fellow-participants provide a safe environment for the free exchange of ideas and exploration of different approaches. In other cases common interests and issues of concern are identified across a number of development centres, and those charged with running the centres may have a part to play in identifying this community of interest to the different participants. One of the strengths of this approach is the opportunity to bring together people from different parts of an organization on a relatively sustained basis, with meetings taking place over periods ranging from several months to a year.

Central to Revans's philosophy is the idea of learning (L) arising as a result of programmed learning opportunities (P) together with questioning and insight (Q). Thus:

$$L = P + Q$$

For the process to work there needs to be a motivation and willingness to learn. A lack of this may be demonstrated if there is unequal commitment amongst the members, which may show itself in variations in attendance at the set's meetings.

PERFORMANCE MANAGEMENT DAY TO DAY – CONTROLS AND FEEDBACK

For performance management to work, both the elements **performance** and **management** need to be in place. The former implies some careful measurement, as we have already discussed above. The latter implies, particularly, that there should be a close link between the measurement and the performance it is intended to support. For **feedback** to be effective it needs to be timely and specific. If the lag between the feedback being given and the performance to which it relates is too long then there will be no appreciable effect or, potentially, destabilization of the effect. Another principle worth noting is that feedback can be either positive or negative. Negative feedback seeks to change a direction, whilst positive seeks to support an existing direction. (The terms have historically been used in a number of engineering contexts. Thus in sound engineering feedback from a microphone to itself, making it produce a loud and high-pitched sound, is properly called positive feedback. In tracking, such as in controlling a missile from the ground, feedback typically means negative feedback and one is seeking to 'null' an error.)

The time aspect is well illustrated, again, in connection with appraisals, which are discussed at greater length in the next chapter. If this is done on an annual basis and that is the only time feedback is given, then the scope for fine adjustment, as opposed to major shifts in behaviour and hence performance, will inevitably be limited. In many fields where there are daily debriefs, eg in high-level catering and in some manufacturing environments, there is much closer coupling of the feedback to the performance to which it relates. A monthly competitive cycle with attendant bonuses is common in many sales environments, for instance.

OTHER CONSIDERATIONS

Although the thrust of this book is in terms of the link between **assessment** and performance, it should be noted that there are many other factors that will come into play. For example, performance management can also be seen as an extension of quality-management ideas. Indeed, there is much to suggest that, without taking the human element into account, quality initiatives almost invariably fail.

Perhaps the coming of age of a movement can be signalled by the publication of a review indicating its progress. This was the case for performance management in 1992 with the production of a research report by what was then the Institute of Personnel Management. Today it can be seen as a broadly based, well-founded concept with activities reflected in the various strands briefly commented on here, some of which, together with further links to assessment, will be discussed further in the next chapter.

SUMMARY

1. Performance management would ideally be integrated with other aspects of business management, but in practice this is done with varying levels of effectiveness. It can be regarded as having close connections, among other things, with total quality management.

2. Competencies should underpin performance management. However, the research into and application of competencies is, again, variable in practice. The systematic procedures that are at the heart of competencies need to be followed more routinely to optimize the contribution of the competencies movement.

3. Customer satisfaction measures have the scope to fine-tune understanding of group and individual performance and so help optimize the contribution that performance management can make.

4. The feeding of views from a constituency of relevant colleagues into the overall picture with regard to the performance management of individuals is enabled by 360 degree assessments.

5. The management of reward offers tremendous scope to influence performance, but these opportunities are rarely fully grasped.

6. Development centre outputs can be used as a lead in to performance management. Follow-up activities such as action learning sets have much to offer in this connection.

7. Feedback, properly used, is another vital ingredient in performance management.

14

A variety of one-to-one interactions in performance management

INTRODUCTION

The one-to-one interactions considered in this chapter differ in several ways from those discussed in the earlier chapters dealing with psychometrics, assessment centres and structured interviews. First, they are related to the performance of existing staff as opposed to the selection of new staff. They can involve day-to-day aspects as exemplified in the disciplinary interview. They may also reflect a more forward-looking stance as shown in interviews related to the future development of staff. Sometimes these interviews are well integrated with other aspects of performance management. Sometimes, though, they stand apart from other management processes with little or no integration. This may well limit their effectiveness.

A second difference between the interactions discussed in this chapter and those considered earlier is to do with the intended flow of information. As we saw in connection with all of the forms of assessment for selection, the main emphasis there is typically upon gaining information from the interviewee by use of the interview process. This was the case, too, in the interviews used as one form of assessment in the assessment centre.

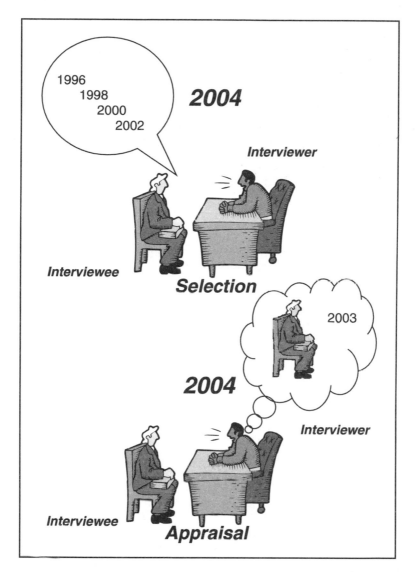

Figure 14.1   Performance management and enhancement

Interviewees clearly draw upon their personal history in making their responses. In the appraisal interviews considered here the interviewer gathers and reflects upon information available in advance of the interview and then presents this to the interviewee, albeit for discussion and possible elaboration or amendment (see Figure 14.1). (One variant upon this concept is when the person being interviewed provides his or her own evaluation of his or her performance, which may then be compared with ratings and other information produced by or available to the interviewer. This of course takes a clear form in the 360 degree processes discussed in the previous chapter. Elsewhere, and far less systematically, it may be that the interviewer simply asks for the interviewee's feelings as to how he or she has performed in the project or assignment in question.)

In the coaching and counselling interactions the coach or counsellor will be getting the other party to reflect on the information he or she is presenting and may offer different interpretations of it. Of course, in feedback after an assessment intervention the primary flow of information is from the assessing party to the assessed and, in that sense, selection processes begin to bridge over into performance management.

One-to-one interactions of different sorts and at different stages are an integral part of any system of performance management, but they are not the whole of it. The formulation and communication of the overall vision and direction of the organization is another critical, underpinning, part. So too is the actual provision of the development opportunities identified.

APPRAISALS

Who conducts?

These interviews are usually conducted directly by the manager of the person concerned. In other cases they are conducted by a manager two levels up, though quite often in such cases the immediate manager is involved in some form of follow-up discussion.

A survey conducted a few years ago now (SHL, 1995) found appraisal by peers being used in 7 per cent of respondent companies but suggested a substantial interest in extending the range of appraisers. It is common for all such interview processes to be subject themselves to further sign-off by another authority. The most common example is when an appraisal conducted by a manager is endorsed and/or annotated by that person's own manager (the 'grandparent'). Sometimes the sign-off process may use a body such as a career management review panel. In such cases information about the person being reported upon may be presented by the appraising manager, who in effect is interviewed by the panel on the appraisee's behalf (a situation comparable to that extent to the questioning of an assessor in the assessment centre wash-up discussion, as described in Chapter 9).

Appraisals and pay

Appraisals have commonly been used with the purpose of reviewing performance over the previous period and setting some standards and objectives for the future. Typically the previous period is a year and very often the appraisals are, accordingly, conducted around the period of the year end.

One of the complications to which this gives rise is that the process inevitably gets bound up with the question of determining pay rises. Much has been said and written on this subject. There is a school of thought (eg Maier, 1958) that says that pay discussions should be entirely separate from appraisal, as the former can sometimes take the shape of a negotiating exercise, whereas the latter is intended to be an objective review of what has gone before. In some organizations there is an effective separation of the two, perhaps by a time period as long as a quarter of a year. In other organizations the nettle is firmly grasped and the two are linked together.

Variations in practice

Some of the ups and downs in the practice of appraisal over the years were traced in Chapter 2. Armstrong (1995) attributes much of the failure of traditional appraisal schemes to the tendency to make them form-filling exercises, with an emphasis on centrally held records, rather than as notation relating to a worthwhile interview process and something to be used to support continued interaction and discussion throughout the year. In similar vein I have recently come across one public body in the UK that has made a point of indicating that its performance management system is separate from its appraisal system, but exactly to what end was not clear.

Fletcher (2004) has stated that there are few more persistent topics of dissatisfaction in the workplace, but goes on to point out that an appraisal process is, in fact, simply a way of formalizing what the organization is intending to do anyway, noting that 'there is no real alternative to appraisal'. He goes on to say that organizations that try to manage without formal appraisals will find informal, uncontrolled, subjective ones springing up in their place. He also indicates one of the strengths of the process as a way of lining up the organization's and the individual's expectations. He is very clear, too, about appraisal and performance management, seeing the former as one significant element in the latter.

One approach possible in appraisal interviewing, though one not apparently widely employed, is that of rank-ordering strengths on the various competencies covered. Thus the appraisee is not faced with ratings on an absolute scale or one fixed by reference to a peer group, but rather is provided with information reflecting the relative performance one to another of the different areas rated. This does, of course, have a disadvantage where the appraisal is to be linked to reward. Its advantage would seem to be its 'non-destructive' nature (compare a similar argument by Fox (1996), with respect to psychometric measures of ability). Thus the appraisee is not distracted by the potentially emotional connotations of negative-seeming evaluations, which can make him or her defensive. Rather the appraisee is helped to consider relative degrees of strength in his or her own profile. In practice this approach seems little used, probably because of the imperative to indicate performance vis-à-vis others, either in connection with pay or in terms of overall standards defining expectations.

As noted, many organizations provide appraisal training for their managers, and an outline of a training programme is set out in the box below. The box after that indicates the stages in the application of an appraisal scheme.

APPRAISAL TRAINING

A typical programme

Input – introduction to appraisal;
   – purpose of appraisal;
   – use of appraisals in context of performance management;
   – personal performance impact on business results.
Exercise – what is behaviour?
   – what are competencies?
   – review behavioural descriptions and competency definitions.
Input and exercise on setting behavioural targets.
Input on behaviourally anchored rating scales.
Exercises – appraisal practice – role-plays, observation and videos.
Exercise – appraisal write-up practice.

A MODEL APPRAISAL PROCESS

Beginning of year – objectives set and clarified in discussions between appraiser and appraisee.
Ongoing through year:
– gathering of performance data;
– routine feedback on performance.
One month before appraisal meeting – date set.
Appraisal interview:
– review of work including successes and areas for improvement;

– consideration of special circumstances or constraints placing limitations on performance;
– review of job description/responsibilities as appropriate;
– discussion of professional or managerial development needs;
– identification of targets for development;
– setting of objectives.
Appraisal write-up:
– within two weeks of meeting;
– space for comment by appraisee.
Review by appraiser's boss (grandparent).

PERFORMANCE IMPROVEMENT AND DISCIPLINARY INTERVIEWS

Underperformance

Interviews relating to underperformance mix two strands. One is the exploration of information and, associated with that, the setting of standards for the future. The other is the need to maintain a legitimate disciplinary line with the individual concerned. The first of these purposes is something that could be regarded as comparable to the appraisal process. The second, though, can conflict with this, and the 'stating of problems' part of the interview may in itself make either party ill placed to consider a positive way forward. Thus, conflict between the two parties involved may arise as a result of the discussion unless it is handled with extreme care. As the interviewer may feel him/herself on the same occasion to be an aggrieved party this may be problematic. If the person being interviewed feels that this is the first time that the expectations now being aired as unfulfilled are being made clear, he or she too is likely to feel upset.

There will also be pressure on the interviewer to make the discussion as short as possible, both to reduce discomfort and to ensure that what has been said can clearly be noted for the record. In some cases it may be an effective tactic to split the interview in two: the 'what is wrong' part and the 'way forward' part. Both may then be addressed in a calmer atmosphere.

Of course, prevention is better than cure. In an atmosphere in which feedback is given and accepted on a continuing basis in a series of interactions throughout the year the need for the disciplinary interview as such is far less likely to arise. Thus in environments characterized by ongoing performance management, positive and negative aspects of performance are routinely discussed.

Gross misconduct

Disciplinary interviews relating to gross misconduct are, for the moment, separated out from other forms of performance-improvement interviews. However, note that the differences are not absolute. In some cases, such as theft, the interview is seen merely as a formal necessity prior to dismissal, but in others there is a potential continuum with other aspects of perform-ance-improvement interviewing. Thus issues of poor timekeeping or apparent incapacity to deliver work effectively will in some cases result in the type of performance-improvement interactions discussed above. Some of these may be entirely supportive, but others may fall in effect into the gross misconduct category. What judgement is made of the starting point may depend on the views of the manager or, indeed, the impact upon a third party. A minor error that results in the loss to an organization of a mil-lion-pound order is likely to be seen as more serious than the same error picked up before it issues in such a disaster. A disciplinary interview is likely to concentrate on procedures and facts. In some cases the interviewee will have the right to have a trade union or other representative present.

STAFF DEVELOPMENT

Development centres

As discussed in Chapter 10, in development centres feedback is usually more detailed than in the related field of assessment centres. Preparation for the feedback and its conduct were also discussed there. A point to be made here is that the feedback can be set clearly in the context of the requirements of the organization and, among other things, the potential for development there, if the same competency model is used as for other aspects of performance management. In fact this is one good reason for using a common model, rather than permitting the type of proliferation of models described in Chapter 10.

Other staff development interactions

In some cases interviews are designed specifically to explore the future inter-ests of staff members and how they see their careers as developing. This may also give an opportunity to look at areas where there may be performance issues requiring resolution. However, the main aim of such interviews is meant to be forward looking rather than having the largely backward-looking focus of the appraisal system. Such interviews may be conducted by staff other than those routinely involved in appraisal interviewing. Thus they may include personnel or HR staff with a special responsibility for development or career planning. Sometimes, again, such interviews are supported by documentation with a variety of questionnaires often being used in advance.

They may also merge into the field of counselling, which is discussed further below. Such interviews may also take as a starting point the output from development centres or other processes that include assessment. A sample staff development interview programme is set out below.

STAFF DEVELOPMENT INTERVIEW PROGRAMME

Before interview

Interviewer reviews outputs from other sources (eg development centre, appraisal, career influences questionnaire, psychometric battery).

Interview

Interviewer asks pre-set questions and probes for further understanding.

Interview concludes with summary of understanding and action plans for interviewee and interviewer.

After interview

Action plans written up by interviewee.

Ongoing

Interviewer and interviewee check on actions involving other parties (eg opportunities for job shadowing, course availability).

After interval

Follow-up meeting – status of plans reviewed.

MENTORING, COACHING AND COUNSELLING IN PERFORMANCE MANAGEMENT

Use of terms

In large measure these forms of interaction have in common the idea of a third party being involved in interactions with a staff member. In the case of mentoring, this third party is likely to be someone in the same organization but not in the same 'command structure' as the employee or his or her immediate manager. In the case of coaching it may be someone internally but if so he or she is likely to be placed at a considerable distance organizationally from the person being coached and may sit in a central function. More commonly he or she will be in an outside organization, very often these days operating as a freelance consultant. For counselling, the third party may again be an outside person or an internal person specializing in this work.

The picture with regard to all of these interventions does, however, become complicated by matters of definition. Probably the greatest difficulty here stems from the fact that there is no agreed overarching category for these activities, although 'coaching' is more commonly used in this way than the others. However, that term is applied not only to third-party interventions but also to instructional interactions between a manager and a staff member on specific skills. In similar vein it is also used quite widely to refer to instruction by a more experienced but essentially peer-level colleague. (The practice of 'sitting by Nellie' as a traditional method of instruction in factory operations is essentially the same.)

This usage, referring to more or less direct instruction, is about as common in general management parlance as its use when an 'external' party is involved. The former features widely, for example, in job descriptions where 'coach junior staff' might well appear amongst a list of job responsibilities, positioning it as a routine part of day-to-day management. It is, however, coaching as a specialized activity involving another person that is something of a burgeoning industry. It is this that people refer to when they talk of being assigned a coach and it is this about which an increasing number of books are being written. (It is of some note that people do increasingly make reference to their coaches, in a way that they were far more reluctant to do some years ago. Management had not then really taken on board the analogy with sport, where having a coach was certainly seen as a 'good thing' and where coaching of the best people clearly helped them to perform even better. That this reserve about coaching has diminished over the years is, perhaps, due to some increasing awareness of its substantial potential as a strand in performance management.)

Coaching as an activity involving external support is also increasingly the subject of study and professional interest. One sign of this current at the time of writing is the setting up in the UK of a special interest group by the British Psychological Society.

'Counselling' as a term is sometimes reserved for 'problem' situations. However, it is more broadly defined by the British Association for Counselling (BAC), with its overall aim being positioned as 'to provide an opportunity for the client to work towards living in a more satisfying and resourceful way'. (That counselling as a practice is well established can be seen from the fact that there is such a professional body.) However, it is often a problem that is the trigger for a *coaching* intervention. For example, as O'Neill (2000) says, 'Coaches show up in the executive's office when the leader is most likely to act from an automatic, less-effective response.'

Mentoring as a role may be somewhat easier to identify, although mentors may certainly use coaching techniques. The mentor is often someone in the same organization as the person being mentored, but with considerably more experience of that organization and in a more senior role. The mentor may help the other person understand how his or her role fits in, what he or she might do to progress and generally provide a sounding board. The two parties may not interact very frequently, with the highest level of interaction typically arising around times of transition. The mentor may, for instance, encourage the mentee in connection with a promotion or, after a promotion, help him or her to understand likely expectations in the new role.

The mentor may also function as a sounding board, say on a risk issue or one that is otherwise sensitive, providing an impartial view independent of the line management structure. The interactions may be less structured and formal than those in coaching or counselling. For example, it would not be uncommon for a meeting with a mentor to be held over lunch or dinner, which would not be the norm for either coaching or counselling.

In both coaching and counselling, third parties may not have the organizational knowledge of a mentor. Their role will rather be to use their skills in relation to issues raised by the person concerned. Thus if interpersonal concerns are raised, a range of approaches may be discussed in which coaches or counsellors will draw on their experience to help the other party develop an approach in line with his or her capabilities and with the particular issue concerned. The box below gives an example of a coaching intervention and its outcome.

A manager who had been established in an organization for a long time was having difficulty interacting with a group of new colleagues following a major reorganization. His personality profile showed coolness rather than warmth and a tendency to favour abstract rather than concrete ideas.

Under coaching he learnt some active listening techniques, helping him to tune in better to others. Although he never became effusive, his colleagues began to understand that he was interested in them and their ideas, and that he was, in fact, quite keen to help them. Improved listening helped him in his presentation of ideas: he captured the language of his colleagues better and so spoke at what appeared a much more practical level.

So how do third-party coaching and counselling interventions differ? Counselling is sometimes seen as handling more deep-seated issues than those addressed by coaching. It may also be pursued with a greater degree of structure than used in coaching, progressing through stages variously identified as pre-counselling, counselling proper, guidance and post-counselling or follow-up review. Counselling is also more likely to involve some use of psychometric measures. When a personality questionnaire is used it can have the result of accelerating the process, moving it on to a level of understanding that would otherwise only be reached after a fairly lengthy series of interactions.

At the core of the counselling process is the use of one-to-one discussions, which can be quite intense for either or both parties. (I recall one single session that I held that went on for eight hours, though that was an exception.) Much of the time initially is likely to be spent by the parties exploring what the real issues are, as those that are presented may be merely the occasion for the counselling, not its underlying cause. This intensity of the activity is also suggested by the fact that those who work in counselling will typically have another one or more counsellors with whom they share their counselling experiences.

In coaching, the interventions also take the form of one-to-one interactions to explore issues of importance. There is, though, likely to be more of an emphasis on the development or utilization of skills and often on seeing these in the context of career management. The emphasis on skills here is akin to the role of the coach in the sporting arena, very much to do with building on specific strengths and eliminating behaviours that interfere with these. This was very much the case in the example shown in the last box. Altogether the emphasis in coaching is on learning. In counselling, learning is likely to be secondary to aspects of self-discovery and personal decision making.

Choosing and using third-party interventions

Many organizations that make use of third parties take considerable trouble to see that the coach, counsellor or mentor and the person with whom he or she is interacting are matched so that useful outcomes are likely to emerge. There will be some common criteria applied in all cases such as listening and other communication skills. The effectiveness of the match may be checked early on by the person with overall responsibility for the use of the third parties, to see that both sides feel the working relationship will be effective. Typically there will be no direct intervention and it is usual for the interactions to be kept confidential. This will usually be agreed by all those concerned at the outset.

This is one factor making the link between such interactions and performance indirect. Another is that although the starting point, particularly for coaching, may be a development centre or appraisal, with the emphasis on the organization's criteria, the specific agenda will be determined by the two parties directly concerned. Thus although within the overall framework of performance management, these interventions all represent situations where the commissioning management is unlikely to have its hands directly on the levers of control. The investment is long-term, not a quick fix.

SUMMARY

1. Interviews used in managing and enhancing performance are directed at existing staff. They typically utilize information already gathered rather than using the interview primarily as an information-gathering exercise.

2. Appraisals involve a retrospective examination of performance. They often become bound up with pay reviews. Training in appraisal processes can underpin more objective use of appraisal systems.

3. An ongoing focus on performance with continuing reviews may preclude the need for disciplinary interviews as such. Disciplinary interviews can be seen as one extreme of performance management interviews.

4. In development centres, the feedback interview is seen as pivotal in setting performance enhancement in train.

5. Staff development interviews may be conducted by specialized staff with particular responsibility for development and/or career planning. Such interviews will seek to link individual development to specific business goals and outcomes.

6. Although coaching, mentoring and counselling can be seen as distinct activities, the use of these terms and exactly what work is entailed by them often overlap. Coaching in the sense of skills transfer may be performed by an immediate superior, but other forms of coaching, as well as mentoring and counselling, typically involve a third party.

15

Supplier and client relationships in assessment and performance management

In seeking to optimize the contribution of specialist or expert input to an assessment situation, whether for selection or for performance management purposes, it is worth paying some attention – on both sides – to a range of aspects of the relationship. To begin with there is the question of how different parties will actually get on and be able to cooperate together. Related to this in some ways, but also having substance in its own right, is the question of the **information** available to the two different parties. The points set out below explore that aspect of the relationship using a model loosely based on Johari's Window (Figure 15.1) in which a person can consider information available to him or her and to others about him/herself. (Rather intriguingly, the name 'Johari' is composed of the parts of the first names of its two developers: Joseph Luft and Harry Ingham, who came up with this formulation in the 1950s.) It is suggested that there will be things that we know and things we don't know. There will also be things that others know about us and things that they

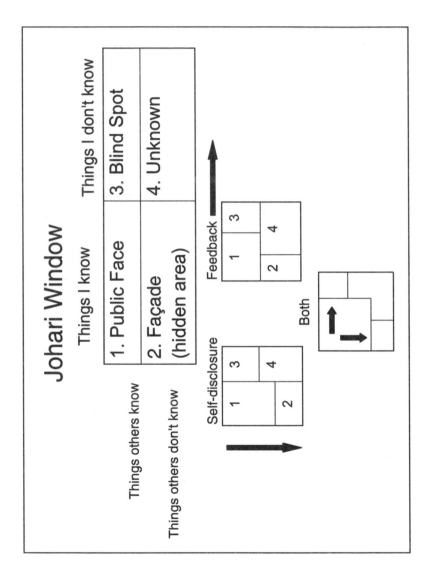

Figure 15.1 Johari window

don't know. Where there is agreement about the things that 'I' know and things others know, we are talking about the public self. If there are things that others know but that 'I' don't then we have a blind spot. Things 'I' know about myself that are unknown to others constitute a façade, and things unknown to both parties are in the unknown area. Feedback can lead to elimination of the blind spots, while self-disclosure can lead to revelation of what is behind the façade. If both of these processes are utilized together, then there is an incursion into the whole of the unknown area.

A similar situation can be said to arise in relation to the specialist supplier and the client in our assessment and performance management situation. A redundancy programme may be in hand and it may be evident to both the supplier and the client that outplacement counselling is the intervention required. In another situation, the symptom presenting itself may be a dysfunctional team. If it is known to the client but not to the specialist that the cause for this is an aggressive boss, then the client will be in the position of **briefing** the specialist accordingly (see Figure 15.2).

In another situation a client may be puzzling over what appear to be poor-quality staff, while it may rapidly become evident to the specialist supplier that the real problem is a poor selection method. Solutions relating to this particular aspect of the problem will be what the specialist will then endeavour to sell to the client. High staff turnover, for instance in the catering industry, may be the issue of concern in the next case. The exact cause may be unknown to either the client or the specialist with 'it's that sort of business', poor selection methods, poor rewards and poor management all being possibilities. Before offering solutions, client and specialist may agree that further research is required by one or both of them.

A complication to this simple model may arise where one or other party *think* they know what is happening whilst actually being on the wrong track (see Figure 15.3). For example, I came across a case some years ago in which I was called in to advise a major supermarket that was unhappy with its assessment centre and thought it had been supplied with poor job simulation exercises. I was asked to make a preliminary appraisal. Brief examination of a rather comprehensive manual of instruments and instructions for their use suggested that there was unlikely to be anything much wrong there. I then asked about assessor training, to be answered with the response that 'we simply hand them the manual'. The client thought it knew what the problem was and hence the solution lay in the replacement or redesign of the exercises being used, while in fact the issue was otherwise: a complete absence of training. In other cases the specialist may not know what the causes are of the problems presenting themselves, while the client thinks it knows but is in fact none the wiser than its potential supplier. For example, poor performance might be attributed to a motivational gap, and the client may brief the specialist accordingly. If the

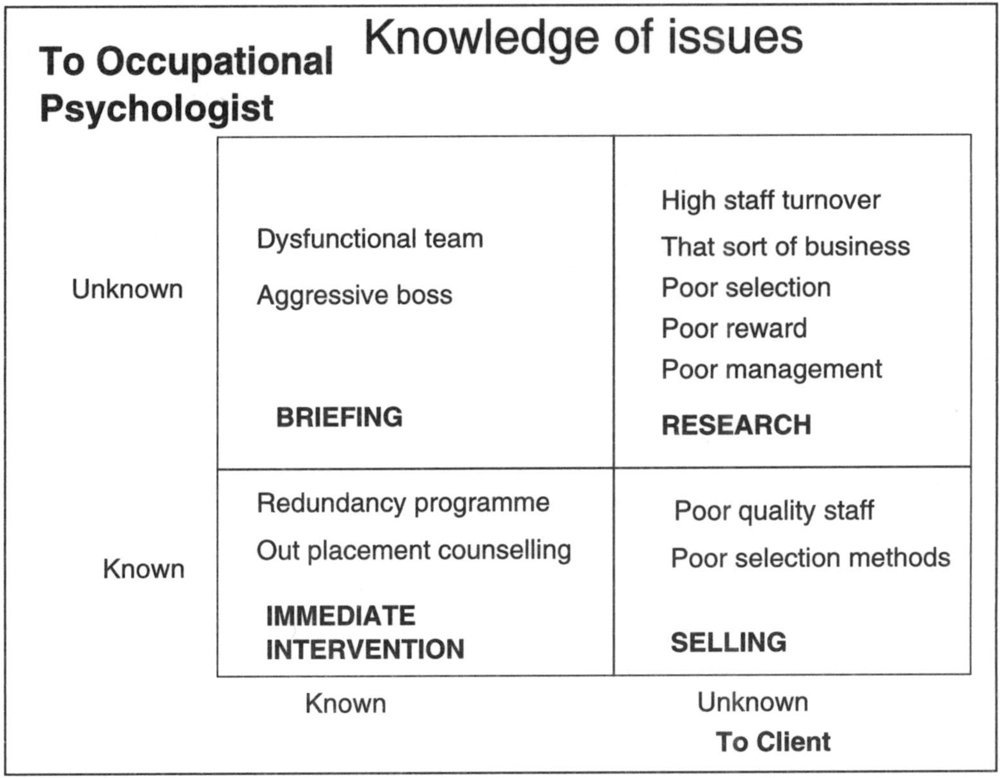

Figure 15.2 Mix of known and unknown information 1

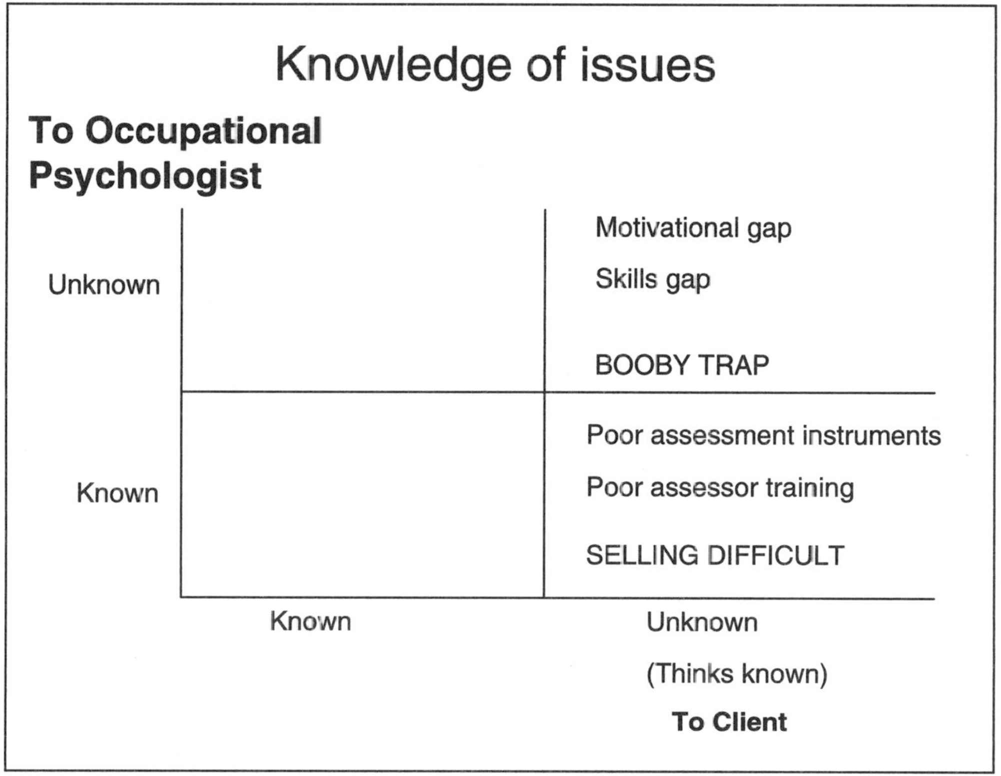

Knowledge of issues

To Occupational Psychologist

	Motivational gap
Unknown	Skills gap
	BOOBY TRAP
	Poor assessment instruments
Known	Poor assessor training
	SELLING DIFFICULT
	Unknown
	(Thinks known)
	To Client

Known

Figure 15.3 Mix of known and unknown information 2

problem is, in fact, not that but a **skills** gap then the 'booby trap' situation arises as wrong solutions are pursued, with problems not being correctly identified and likely to escalate.

In the next phase of the model we have the situation where the specialist thinks he or she knows the solution but is in fact mistaken (see Figure 15.4). An example might be absenteeism, which a specialist could be inclined to put down to a lack of variety in the range of work experiences offered. If the client knows that in fact the organization has been highly unstable and that people have, as a consequence, had a lot of variety in their work, the client may quickly be able to disabuse the supplier and, as like as not, dispense with his or her services. In yet another situation, the client will admit to ignorance and the supplier will again think he or she knows the solution. Consider a case where the presenting problem in the organization is poor communication. This can be put down to a variety of reasons. If the supplier has as a pet answer that communication is hindered if people work in individual offices, he or she may be inclined to advocate open-plan working. In some situations this could exacerbate the problem, for example by disturbance from noise or issues of confidentiality, not to mention matters of status. In its ignorance, the client may be inclined to accept this situation and both parties may only realize the mistake after, for example, costly adjustments to office layouts have been set in train.

Finally, we have the situation where both parties think they know what is amiss, but in fact both are wrong (see Figure 15.5). In these cases they will not see the need for research, the correct approach where things are unknown. They may agree on an approach and a solution if their diagnoses actually coincide or they may fail to see eye to eye. For example, limited use of IT in an organization might in fact be due to the poor quality of the software or hardware, of the communication links or of the support available. If a client is convinced that the real cause is technophobia and the supplier that it is boredom then they are unlikely to progress with implementing any solution. On the other hand, if they are both in agreement that it is one of these then they will proceed down a path to address the matter according to their common diagnosis. For example, if they think it is technophobia then they may agree to embark on a desensitizing programme, getting those who are reluctant users to experience IT in small increments. If the IT itself is still at fault then there can be something of a 'time bomb' here.

There are also other aspects of the use of particular expertise. One may say why use an expert at all? Very often it is because there will be parts of diagnosis or formulation of a solution that will be known or, through research, knowable to the specialist. There could also be value in having an independent view. This may be for objectivity, pure and simple, or

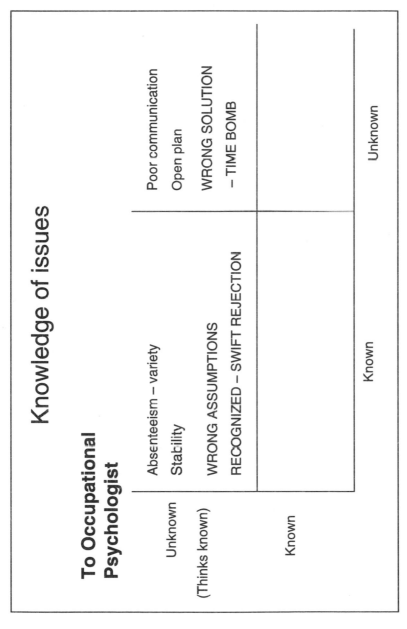

Figure 15.4 Mix of known and unknown information 3

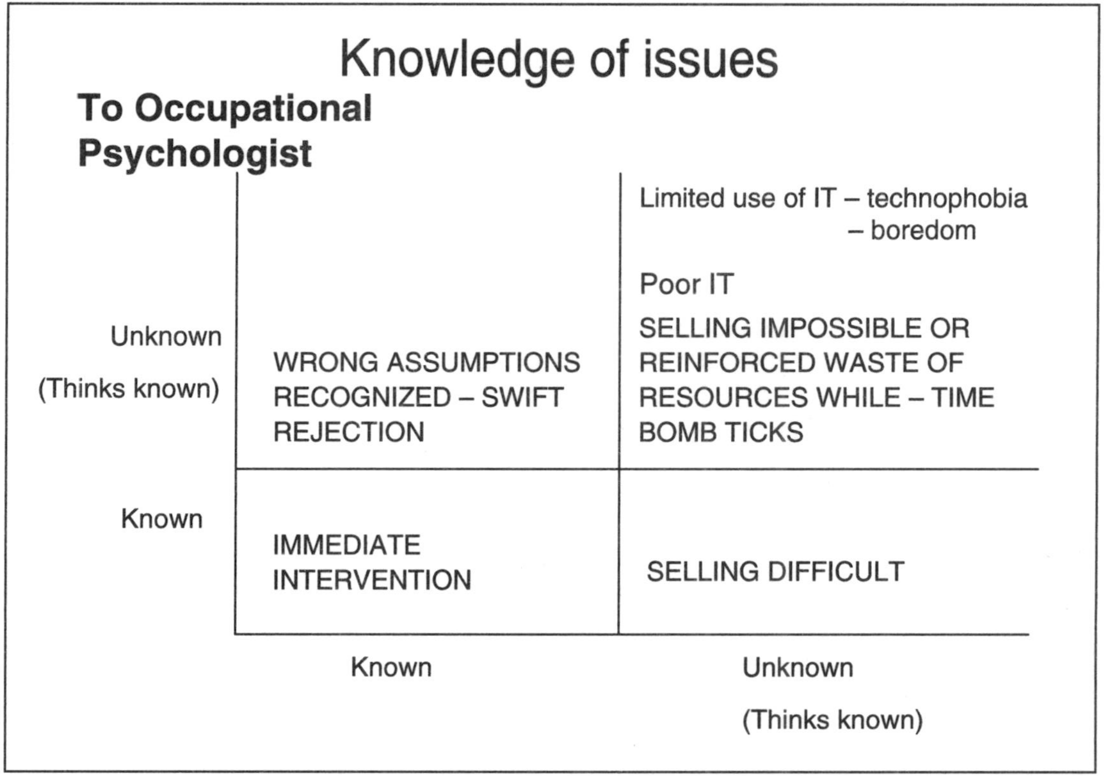

Figure 15.5 Mix of known and unknown information 4

because of a perception that a fair approach may be given in this way. There may also be the question of time available for appropriate assessment or performance management interventions to be carried out. The specialist, whether from a wholly external organization or, say, from a central pool, may be best positioned to offer such services. In considering the use of such support it is always worthwhile asking oneself what will be gained, what the consequences of not going down this path will be and what problems will be associated with it. Among the latter, apart from aspects of misdiagnosis discussed above, there can be questions of misunderstanding of expertise and particularly the speed with which a solution may actually be offered. Again referring to IT, interventions there are littered with good intentions and delayed projects. There may also be the issue that, because the specialist is from an external contracting company, any desire to extend or 'tweak' the services offered may require further contractual referral. This may involve irritating delays and further cost to the client or, on the other hand, be perceived as 'scope creep' by the supplier. In sum, the relationship between supplier and client in the assessment field is not altogether straightforward and is worthy of careful consideration.

16

The use of information and communication technology in assessment and performance management

NUMBER CRUNCHING TO NORMS

The early use of computers in connection with psychometric testing was to do with the analysis of research data. Previously, laborious hand calculation methods had been employed to work through the extensive correlations involved in large-scale validity studies. It might take a researcher up to a year to complete a complex analysis of data (such as a factor analysis) from a single study in this way. Subsequently, computers have come to be used increasingly for the administration and the scoring of tests and such use is now commonplace. However, notwithstanding the value of this there are some pitfalls.

A note of caution certainly should be sounded in relation to the norming of test procedures. Norms developed on a paper-and-pencil basis may not necessarily apply to tests administered by computer. Visual scanning patterns should not be assumed to be the same for material presented on-screen as for the printed page. Moving forward and backward in the material may not be allowed with some computer presentations and correction of errors using a keyboard cannot be assumed to take the same time as with a pen. Such differences will be particularly important in timed ability tests. Best practice involves norming or re-norming with the computer administration so that appropriate comparisons can be made.

Some of the difficulties of translating from one medium to another, in this case from paper and pencil to film, were reviewed in a study by Ridgway (1977). He concluded that in effect a different test had been produced with the change to the new medium. At present it is by no means clear that test publishers have always taken sufficient trouble to examine the effects of different media of presentation and produce appropriate sets of norms. (I first became aware of some of the effects of different presentations of tasks that were formally equivalent in a series of experimental studies that I conducted in the late 1960s and early 1970s (Edenborough, 1975). How the information was displayed on the computer screen had profound effects on the responses made.)

Because of the issues of norming and of control, caution needs to be exercised in any applications involving different media of presentation to different candidates. One would certainly not plan for such differences. However, it is by no means uncommon in selection applications to find that having planned for all candidates to attend a testing session to undertake paper-and-pencil testing one of them is prevented from being present, say by travel delays. Amidst the exigencies of a tight recruitment reporting schedule the natural recourse is to provide an online facility to the missing person. However, this may mean a different experience for him or her and so compromise the level playing field that should be available to all. Even if those attending at a central point experience computer, as opposed to pencil-and-paper, administration, cutting out the norming issue, that of differences in control in the two situations still remains.

SELECTION AND GENERATION OF ITEMS

Another development that has taken place is the use of computers in item selection. As mentioned in Chapter 3, in some cases items are generated in relation to an adaptive model, so that difficulty is adjusted depending on the performance of the person undertaking the tests. This same end is also served by an approach in which a large bank of items is developed and their difficulty levels established through research. Software is used to select amongst the items, giving scope for a very large number of tests with equivalent overall levels of difficulty to be produced. Both of these approaches diminish the risks of tests being compromised through the heightened exposure to which the proliferation of information technology can lead. It is not clear why this movement, which seemed to hold promise some years ago, does not seem to have been taken very much further in recent years. Another development is, though, the use of computers not only to deliver and select items but actually to generate them. Among other things this solves the problem of repeated exposure to the same tests. The work of Irvine, Dann and Anderson (1990) was significant in this connection and, although not universal, the use of algorithms for item generation is on the increase. Item response theory, a related field, also discussed in Chapter 3, also requires the extensive use of computers.

GUIDELINES

In recent years the internet has provided an increasingly important medium for information on tests, as with much else. Ensuring adequate security in terms of copyright and personal confidentiality is clearly an issue here. So, too, is the question of limiting use to those appropriately qualified. In general, though, the increase in computer-based assessment (CBA) has prompted professional consideration of the special concerns that arise. A set of guidelines produced by the BPS (1999) distinguishes between the following four components:

▌ assessment generation – including the algorithm-based methods just referred to;

▌ assessment delivery – presenting the items on-screen;

▌ assessment scoring and interpretation – including the production of expert system reports;

▌ storage, retrieval and transmission – use of electronic media for storage of assessment information and its transmission to recipients.

Recommendations are made for each of these components in the guidelines, with different points being made in each case for the developers and the users of the assessments.

REMOTE DELIVERY

Although the largest boost to CBA has been the internet, with its scope for remote delivery and scoring of tests and other assessment procedures, the remote application of assessment pre-dated that development by several decades. Thus in the 1970s systems began to be developed for sending test material electronically from one site to another. (Use of computers to generate tasks in experimental psychology settings, without the remote delivery aspect, became common in the 1960s.) A typical sort of application would involve candidates attending a central location to go through a series of tests presented on-screen and piped in from a psychological consultancy. Responses would be piped back and, after scoring, results and interpretation sent to the client organization. The advantage of this was that the provider consultancy could serve a number of clients at the same time and without extensive travelling. The requirement for candidates to attend at a central location meant that there was scope for adequate controls to be exercised. The disadvantage was that there was a requirement for the client organization to have the requisite equipment, which was necessarily highly specialized and expensive in those early days.

Another development is the use of the telephone to deliver questionnaires by recorded voice, with multiple choice responses entered via a telephone keypad. This approach can be seen in part as a development of the application of structured interviews by telephone (as discussed in Chapter 11) and, as such, represents a blending of the interview and psychometric testing philosophies.

ASSESSMENT CENTRES

Assessment centres, too, have scope for using electronic support and, in fact, the number of ways in which this can come into play is quite broad. A number of aspects of this have been covered in the BPS guidelines referred to in Chapter 9.

One of the aids much vaunted by those who supply them has been a means of constructing assessment centre timetables. My personal view is that this is not much of a time-saver and that, in practice, for any one application there are not too many variations of the timetable to be made in the initial design. I also find that last-minute adjustments, eg following a late arrival, are best made by human intervention. (I recall turning up on a Sunday evening prior to an assessment centre due to start on the following day. My colleagues proudly showed me what the computer had produced with variations in colour and hatching and, altogether, quite a work of art. However, I noticed that one of the assessors was doublebooked. Three hours later my colleagues, and the software, had produced a new timetable that actually worked!)

Software can be employed for computing assessment centre evaluations, which may help the assessor wash-up discussion a little. However, the power of the computer will be more evident in connection with the research and review aspects of centres, such as accumulating results and summarizing findings across several centres. The BPS guidelines refer to this aspect as well as to the scope for using computers to help activities ranging from job analysis through scoring assistance to assessors and report writing. However, caveats are expressed in connection with all of these activities, for example not thinking that assessors' prompts can be substituted for proper assessor training.

The use of computer-generated in-basket materials was referred to briefly in Chapter 9. Clearly this is an emergent and still controversial area. There is, however, a simpler issue to consider, namely providing computers as an option for the completion of any form of written exercise. When first considering this in centres my colleagues and I were designing and running, I had some serious misgivings. Although it is not uncommon to experience practical difficulties in this connection, including matters such as incompatibility of laptops and printers at an off-site location, my concerns rather stemmed from the fact of what I had anticipated to be wide differences in typing speed, as between those who touch-type and people reliant on the use of just two fingers. This seemed likely to be of importance in a timed exercise to an extent that might not show itself in the more 'diluted' activities of real life. I was then involved in running a long series of centres at which candidates were given the choice of completing an analysis exercise in handwriting or using a laptop computer. About half chose each option. There appeared to be no systematic differences in performance related to the medium of response used. Care does, though, need to be taken if there is to be a choice to see that this really is a free choice. In another application that I came across where candidates were, again, given the option of handwriting or using a laptop, one of them who had chosen the laptop produced a very sketchy and limited output. He said on his participant report form, and confirmed during subsequent feedback, that he had mistakenly responded to what he had perceived as peer pressure as all the other candidates on his particular centre were evidently comfortable with the laptop option. He had realized, too late, that his computer skills were far too elementary for this to work for him. This type of issue is, again, noted in the BPS guidelines referring to the use of computers to attain a 'better replication of the 21st century work environment'. However, they warn against requiring candidates to have knowledge of the functioning of a particular piece of software.

FEEDBACK

Remote delivery methods can, of course, also be used for feedback, with both telephone and videoconferencing potentially coming into play here.

Telephone

Telephone feedback is, not surprisingly, popular with participants in assessment activities who are located at a distance from the person providing the feedback. As with conducting interviews over the telephone, which as discussed in Chapter 11 appears to work perfectly well, there can be resistance at times. This, in my experience, is more likely to be a concern on the part of a potential or present employer than of the participants themselves, with a view from the former that the participants might somehow be getting 'short-changed'. Worries expressed include the shorter time typically spent using the phone and the importance of visual cues, such as those provided by the facial expression of the recipient of the feedback, the absence of which is seen as detrimental to the sensitivity of the proceedings. Certainly it is the experience of those giving feedback by telephone versus face to face that the former is usually much quicker. However, I have not experienced any concerns after the event on the part of the recipients of feedback that their experience from the telephone delivery has been anything but comprehensive.

It may be that there is a tacit understanding on the part of recipient and feedback provider that neither party wants to have his or her ear glued to the phone for an hour and a half. And speakerphones are not necessarily the answer, as sound quality is often compromised. It may be too that, having taken the trouble to travel, albeit often a short distance, to the feedback venue for a face-to-face session, both parties feel it incumbent upon themselves to expend at least an hour on the activity. I suspect that this point and the offering of tea or coffee and the social interaction nature of the exchange are all reasons for a perception that a face-to-face feedback session is somehow more proper and deserving of a 'decent' allocation of time.

The significance of 'acquaintance formation' in interviewing and, indeed, the need to see that this was allowed for in the dynamics of the situation was a point made by Herriot (1987).The importance of the social element in a variety of work interactions was something that I commented on originally some eight years before embarking on the present volume (Edenborough, 1996). I noted then that, despite technological advances and possibilities, tele-commuting was still very much a minority activity. In the intervening years the fact that further improvements in telecommunications and the more widespread access to e-technology, heightened terrorist threats, increased traffic congestion and a larger awareness of traffic-related pollution have made little impact on the tendency to 'turn up' at the workplace are all testimony to the power of that social imperative.

Videoconferencing

As a feedback mechanism, videoconferencing can be seen as a halfway house between live face-to-face feedback and the use of the telephone. I have come across it as a favoured mechanism by those who find the telephone uncongenial for this purpose, but who are reluctant to undertake a journey of perhaps 200 miles to the metropolis! The quality of the technology available does, though, vary. Methods commonly used have effectively instantaneous sound transmission, but there is typically a slight lag and a certain amount of jerkiness in the pictures. Nevertheless this seems well enough for feedback purposes and, interestingly, the time taken to give feedback appears intermediate between that for telephonic and that for live face-to-face media. However, to conduct an exercise such as a group discussion or role-play by video appears to require a higher-quality transmission and reception. With this in place and with comparable furnishings and settings at either end of the video link it is relatively easy to suspend disbelief with regard to the location of the other party or parties. Thus it appears perfectly feasible, with the right equipment, to have three people at one end of a table and three at the end of a similar table in another location and for a group discussion to proceed as if they were in the same room. As yet, however, such applications are the exception rather than the norm. Both the idea of being 'on camera' and coping with the technology could be a cause of concern for those who are unfamiliar with video methods. These concerns suggest the need for particular care in administrative arrangements.

There are also technologies that allow for the presentation of holographic images, so that a person at one location can appear to be in the same room as those in a different location and to interact with them largely as if that were the case. Not yet (2004) in anything like widespread use in any context this is not even really emergent in the assessment field. Its time will, though, surely come!

Expert systems

The use of computers to generate reports is noted in the BPS guidelines for both psychometric testing and assessment centres. In each case skilled interpreters of the instruments are used to produce a library of descriptions covering different levels on each of the scales or dimensions concerned. They also capture the most common combinations of these under groups of scales and define a logic for selecting the appropriate mix of descriptors. Descriptions and logic are captured in software, so that any combination of scores can yield a computer-generated narrative.

Early attempts at this met with mixed success, with reports that were often clumsily worded and sometimes self-contradictory. Nowadays the results are far more polished and presentable. The approach offers the scope for a quick – in effect instant – turnaround of findings in narrative form. This removes the burden of report writing from whoever would otherwise be tasked with it. The people thus relieved of a responsibility could include line management assessors, HR staff or occupational psychologists acting as consultants. In working with each of these groups I have often found reluctance and a considerable degree of difficulty in putting pen to paper, or fingers to keyboard. The output of sometimes strenuous efforts have been distinctly variable in quality, even amongst the ranks of the 'professionals', ie the occupational psychologists. (Amongst my acquaintance in the latter group I have found the speed of writing reports varying in a ratio of 5:1 from the fastest to the slowest, a point that I have taken due note of in assembling project teams!)

The downside of the expert system approach is the relative lack of flexibility. Standard reports tend to reflect a single instrument or standardized configuration of instruments. Development of bespoke expert systems is costly and not feasible for any but large-scale and/or repeat applications. This constraint means that the expert system report will not be geared to the competency model for a particular role. Thus either a further stage of 'manual' interpretation will have to be undertaken, partly negating the saving of effort, or the expert system report will be left as a separate, unintegrated source of information, potentially limiting its relevance. In addition to 'manual' intervention to interpret such a report in terms of particular competencies, there will be a need to do so where the report covers part only of an assessment battery. This will generally be the case with bespoke applications and sometimes the editorial effort involved can be equivalent to preparing an overall report from scratch in the first place. There is also the point that a hand-crafted report has the scope to reflect input from a validation or feedback interview, as discussed in Chapter 7.

In addition to reflecting both the competency model and this further source of information, the personally written report also gives scope for the patterns and nuances, the interplay amongst the different competencies, to be more fully revealed. Of course, realizing the last benefit, or indeed any of the benefits of the personally written report, is dependent on the skill of the author. It is perhaps a truism that a fluent and comprehensible expert system report will be more useful than an inarticulate one written without computer support.

In this connection the absence of very fine nuances in the expert system report can be likened to the use of Krug's simplification of the outputs from the 16PF, as described in Chapter 4.

Yet another point to consider is the general form of the report. With broadly comparable input material, eg a personality measure, two reasoning tests and a structured interview, I have found my clients' requirements to vary enormously. They range from 'Short sentences and bullet points, please; our management has a brief attention span' to 'All the evidence must be set out or we will be open to challenge.' This is a further aspect of flexibility with which the expert system will be unlikely to deal readily and/or which again might imply the need for substantial editing. Generally if clients are paying for a specialist input, they will expect it to be tailored in content and form to their particular needs, rather than being machine generated, even if an expert has determined how the machine will tell its story.

In summary, whether or not to use an expert system requires 'horses for courses' considerations, in which timescale, final outputs required and the skill of people available to originate reports all have their part to play.

USE OF THE INTERNET

Writing of the internet a few years ago, Fox (2000) described its advent as like that of the atom bomb in that it 'preceded the expertise to deal with the problems it creates'. Certainly there are cons, as well as pros, in its use in connection with assessment.

At the simplest level the internet offers scope to send an exercise, say a written analysis, by e-mail to a candidate for him or her to complete and send back a response. Thus here the technology is used in a way that is highly analogous to the postal system. There is a question here of the identity of the participant, a problem shared with other aspects of remote delivery – or the use of the post as such for that matter. However, the chances of impersonation or substitution appear diminished the more specialized the application. (If you were a candidate for the position of finance director for a FTSE 350 company, would you really trust somebody else to do a better job of completing an exercise than you would yourself?) Perhaps of more concern is the question of timing. With simple 'postal'-type delivery, with no automated time constraints or lock-outs, even with strict admonitions as to the time to be spent on the exercise there can be no guarantee of adherence to the time-frame set out. The position is, perhaps, similar to another one obtaining in selection where, outside an assessment centre process as such, candidates are invited to prepare a presentation to a final panel and are given the required topic in advance. It may be that relatively little harm is done with this relatively uncontrolled administration, provided that all candidates are, in fact, treated alike. Thus, what could not be seen as fair or acceptable would be for some candidates to have whatever leisure they could contrive to complete an exercise delivered to them by remote electronic means, while others were constrained by the limits of a traditional assessment environment. Also what would be lost by uncontrolled timing for all candidates would be any sense of performance to be expected with a time limit. This implies and requires that piloting and trialling should take place under the same conditions of lack of close time constraints as would be provided for the remote administration.

Of course the internet offers scope for more than just a postal style of delivery. Administration and scoring can both readily be accomplished by this means, and timing controls and constraints can be incorporated. (Further developments here include timing of individual items, with reports on any extra-long response times, which can be indicative of excessive deliberation in a personality questionnaire.) Yet the identity issue remains as do other aspects of administrative control. What is to stop someone asked to complete an ability test from conferring with a friend or substituting that friend for him/herself?

Amongst the measures mooted here has been the use of web-cams so that a remote administrator can see what is going on. However, whilst adding to the element of control, this adds, too, to the administrative burden, in effect requiring the administrator's presence throughout the testing session or, if a recording is used, for an equivalent period of time. This increased time adds to the cost, as does the additional equipment required. Another linked approach is that of corneal imprint registration to confirm identity, but this is hardly in widespread use as yet.

A rather different tack is to emphasize the importance of an honest approach by setting up an 'honesty contract', whereby the intended recipient of the assessment is advised that if cheating is detected it will make any employment arrangements null and void. This may be underpinned by set-ups in which the remote assessment functions as, and is represented as, one of a number of steps along the selection path. Advising candidates in particular that they may be subject to further testing and that any marked discrepancies with the results of the remotely delivered tests will be viewed with suspicion is likely to have some practical effect.

The position with regard to personality measures is somewhat different. The identity question remains although, rather like the case of our friend the FD, one may ask whose personality would you rather present, yours or someone else's? Control, though, is still limited. I arranged for the remote administration of the 16PF5 to some 30 people in a management development context in a private sector organization. During feedback several of them volunteered that their completion had been interrupted, either by colleagues or, if completed at home, by 'having to go to the school to pick up the kids' or the like. Just how much 'noise' this put into the system for the personality aspects of the measure as such is hard to say. However, the 16PF5 concludes with a series of reasoning items. Amongst the group of 30, several performed below expectation in the resultant ability scale. All of these confessed to having been rushed or having suffered one of the aforementioned interruptions during the completion of this part of the instrument.

360 DEGREE

The use of electronic media facilitates 360 degree assessments, as these media provide a ready way for gathering information in such a way that the different inputs can be summated and presented. Most of the organizations that make regular use of e-mail will gather, process and disseminate the information by this means. The graphic capability that computers afford can also be turned to advantage here in presenting the findings at the press of a button in a vivid and comprehensible way.

The ease, most of the time, with which information and communication technology can now be bent to the purposes of assessment is of great potential benefit. However, as will have been evident from the points made above there are many practical issues to deal with if these benefits are to be fully realized. It is also evident that the skill of software specialists in putting a test on to a computer may often outstrip their expertise in the area of testing as such and it would appear that there may well be some enthusiastic computerization where the necessary background work has not in fact been done! However, albeit haltingly, as with many endeavours, this field is clearly progressing. Looking back at my own and others' early work in the human–computer field (eg Green and Edenborough, 1971) and considering today's offering, I perceive there have been great strides. Earlier concerns were very much about the mechanisms of displays as much in hardware as software terms. Clearly the progress will continue. To mix a metaphor, it would be a Luddite who would play Canute here!

SUMMARY

1. Analysis of research data was one of the earliest uses of computers in assessment.

2. Tests and other procedures developed for paper-and-pencil administration need to be re-normed carefully when delivered by computer.

3. Item generation, both from banks and using algorithms, by computer enables multiple forms of tests to be produced as well as the ready application of adaptive testing and associated methods.

4. Remote methods pre-dated the internet and include the use of the telephone with automatic administration and recording of responses and video methods.

5. Published guidelines for both psychometrics and assessment centres address the use of information and communication technology.

6. The use of computers in assessment centre technology includes data management, generation of exercises and a medium of response for written exercises.

7. Expert system reports can provide a quick solution to the generation of narrative results, particularly from psychometrics. However, their use entails lack of precision and flexibility.

8. The internet offers great advantages in terms of administrative convenience for psychometric and assessment centre applications, but diminishes control over processes including even over the identity of the participant.

9. Computer-based methods are routinely used by 360 degree assessments.

17

Current issues and future trends

CONSTRUCTING TEAMS FOR MAJOR CHANGE

It was many years ago now that Peter Drucker articulated the view that the only certainty was that of change. Where change is substantial, as it seems to be increasingly in many organizations, both private and public, then there is often a need to review models of competency, selection and performance. Looking at all these in combination may sometimes create fairly dramatic requirements for new approaches, new directions and, often, new people. Change itself is often likely to be resisted, and so part of the consideration of new models may be to weigh up carefully who actually have the capacity and appetite for change and who can act as change agents themselves, either catalytically or more likely being trans-formed as individuals to some extent as the change is in progress.

One major set of changes current at the time of writing is that in the British Civil Service. These have been reinforced by reviews of efficiency and procurement practices. These Whitehall-wide initiatives have been echoed in departmental and interdepartmental ones such as the merger of the Inland Revenue with Her Majesty's Customs and Excise and the Agenda for Change (AfC) pay reforms in the Department of Health.

Private organizations change direction, too. Sometimes the effect of change may apply to part of an organization only and within that to certain categories of staff. For those categories, though, the changes required can be quite dramatic and, not surprisingly, difficult for many. Given what has been said earlier (eg in Chapter 3) about the problems of altering one's characteristic behaviour, personality, then those who fit the model of the old organization will not necessarily fit the new. (With hindsight, of course, the ideal approach would have been at least to have anticipated some change, albeit not necessarily exactly what, by having in place those who were personally adaptable and sound change managers.) Combined with downsizing (or, as it is sometimes currently more euphemistically called, 'right-sizing') the threats can appear immense and this in itself can throw obstacles in the way of gaining an effective handle on the relevant characteristics.

I have recent experience of a company undergoing change where, out of a group of some 80 top managers and directors, two absolutely refused to undertake an assessment process intended to be used as input to decision making about future roles and individual development. Five others, who have undertaken the process, judged it to be irrelevant to them, several of them insisting that their specialist roles could not possibly change and so seeking to reject the outcomes. Fortunately top management have been more inclined to accept the findings. What weighed with most of the parties involved was the stress laid by my team on the fact that we were entirely independent, with no axe to grind about any of the findings. The impact of the failure to plan and implement assessments to support change is illustrated in the two boxes below.

I worked some years ago with a large British utility company, shortly after it had become privatized. It had previously enjoyed a near-monopoly position, but the privatization represented a step on the road to operating in a more competitive environment. This involved creating a sales force for the first time, which in one part of the business was attempted by moving people about internally. I was asked to look at the sales talent of the newly created team. As there was no history of active selling and no internal models to serve as guides it was agreed to use a structured interview designed for selection to sales positions in utilities in the United States. Although not providing a perfect comparison, there was a degree of benchmarking in this approach. Early into the process my colleagues and I were struck by the lack of evident sales talent amongst the group being studied. Among other things there was little or no interest in prospecting for or winning business, nor in customer service as such. There was, however, a pride in the 'product' and in technical know-how. Altogether it was evident that this so-called sales group more closely resembled a group of engineers. In fact this was hardly surprising since this is what they had been before their abrupt and largely enforced transition. After a few months' perseverance with this group, the company took a different tack and moved to hiring people with more evident sales talent.

Perhaps nowhere has the pace of change and associated reorganiza-tion and redirection been more dramatic than in the field of informa-tion and communication technology, with profiles of products and services to support them changing unrecognizably over the years. I was at one time dealing with a medium-sized software house, then part of a large and diversified technology group. The post of manag-ing director of the subsidiary became vacant and I ran an assessment centre on the shortlisted candidates, who included a couple of inter-nal people. One of these was a divisional director who, in a break in the process, told a story about one of his salespeople. This man was about to complete a deal with the vivid and entrepreneurial owner-manager of a car dealership to supply him with software; the final contract was on the table and champagne on ice was waiting to be uncorked. 'Before I sign,' said the entrepreneur, 'let's talk about another deal: I'd like to supply your company's car fleet.' The sales-man turned pale, stammered something about group policy, pur-chasing not being his part of ship, and finally trailed off hopelessly. 'Take away the champagne,' boomed the OM. 'There will be no con-tract signed today!'

Returning to his boss, my candidate, the salesman poured out the sorry tale. 'Well,' mused the divisional director, 'he wouldn't really have expected a group-wide deal at all and certainly not just like that. Maybe he's angling for our own [the subsidiary's business], but that's not really negotiable either, certainly not quickly, but we do want to supply them with software. I tell you what, we'll take two cars from him; I can just about swing that on my own authority.' 'But surely that won't be enough to sway him, will it?' the anxious salesman asked. 'It might be if you take cash along; I'll arrange it,' said the boss. Cash was duly handed over, the contract was signed and toasted in champagne and two cars were delivered.

My candidate was appointed, not on the basis of the anecdote, but on a range of proactive commercial characteristics that the story reflected. 'Sailing close to the wind', 'having street smarts' and 'a nose for a deal' were among the terms used about him and which he recognized himself.

Six months later, new top management decided the software house was unhelpfully competing with an applications department that directly supported one of the group's own hardware divisions. That department was positioned very much as a back-room operation, with a strong emphasis on structure and compliance. The subsidiary and the supporting department were merged. The MD of the former was only briefly considered to lead the new entity. He and many of his colleagues left in the ensuing months, after some fruitless efforts to bend them to the new realities and the, to them, uncongenial way of working, with considerable disruption all round. The group might have prevented some of the turmoil during the transition phase had it taken the trouble to profile the behavioural requirements for the merged operation and assessed the subsidiary's staff against these.

ASSESSMENTS LINKED TO PRIVATE EQUITY INITIATIVES

Another area of application of assessment methods is in the major changes in which private equity houses become involved. These include mergers and acquisitions, joint ventures or moves into new lines of business. In each case there is a group of managers actually or potentially in place whose capabilities and attitudes can critically affect the success of the changed or new operation. Looking at them individually, as a whole and in relation to other groups with which they will have to interact can give the private equity house leading the change a greater understanding of the management capability in its potential investment. Variations on this theme include assessing candidates for top jobs in an organization newly acquired, when the acquisition has involved the departure of the previous owner-manager. Ideally such assessments would be complemented by those on existing (or remaining!) management teams to understand the fit between the old and the new, the possible management challenges facing the new top person and how he or she is likely to manage them. Yet other possibilities here include the assessment of larger management teams after a merger or acquisition, to provide, in effect, an audit of overall management capability.

Figure 17.1 shows the distribution of ratings on a number of areas studied in a division of an international services company after a merger. One of the parties to the merger had a strong brand based on a sound historic reputation. However, they were seen as complacent and it was not clear that they were sufficiently commercially minded. The other party was relatively new. They had made some breakthroughs with the way their services were delivered. However, although this had brought some commercial benefits, they were generally seen as focused on technical possibilities at least as much as on their commercial exploitation. The new top management of the company also wanted to place emphasis on staff development. They reckoned there was a lot of untapped potential and were worried that little might be done to realize it.

The study of this particular division confirmed some, but not all, of the fears. In fact representatives of both the heritage companies appeared to be adequately prepared to entertain change. This was not surprising in the case of the younger company and, indeed, they were somewhat ahead of their colleagues in the older entity. The details of the assessment study showed that members of the older company were aware that their reputation had been founded on a philosophy of continuous service improvement, and generally senior management there had fitted into the appropriate mould in that respect. Also commercial awareness altogether was fairly strong, but there were some wide variations, with a number of individuals in high-level posts being relatively lacking in this respect. Also, as anticipated, in common with many other organizations, staff development was not something to which the managers on the whole took naturally. Combined with this, with direction setting coming out as relatively low, there were concerns about the division's scope to plan for the growth of its business, potentially hindering the exit plans of the private equity house.

So what did top management do with this information? (One might also ask why, given their suspicions, they did not have the assessments undertaken *before* rather than *after* the merger had proceeded. The answer to that was that both parties saw marketplace advantages, including working with, rather than against, a competitor. These advantages were perceived as outweighing risks represented by possible limitations in senior management attitudes or capacities.) What they did, in fact, was to manage around some of the limitations. The few people who were in fact quite weak on commercial awareness were replaced by external recruitment and internal moves. The unexpected adequate, albeit not outstanding, indication on change management meant that these and other moves

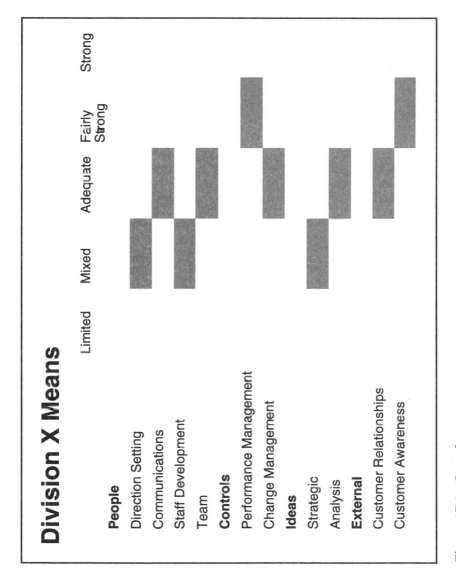

Figure 17.1 Sample management team

tended to be accepted rather than leading to entrenched positions or rear-guard actions. The existing divisional head was replaced by a new person with an outstanding profile in terms of strategy and direction setting and the top management also worked closely with him in these areas. Staff development was tackled differently. The company was quite widely spread geographically and detailed central initiatives on development did not appear feasible. Instead regional managers were given specific overall responsibilities in this field and quite senior HR support was put in place, also on a regional basis, to manage the implementation of development initiatives. The company progressed and the private equity house made its exit on time, having profited adequately from its investment.

Among the difficulties often cited in undertaking assessments in the private equity-related field are those of access to the relevant people and problems of using what can be seen as intrusive methods. The former is certainly something of an issue in hostile takeover situations. Intrusiveness may still remain a problem for some forms of assessment; for instance, psychometrics could often well be contraindicated. This points to the use of interview methods as representing an approach most likely to be effective and generally acceptable. Structured interviews are most commonly used in these cases and will often address issues of motivation as well as competency. Sometimes it does prove feasible to apply standard psychometrics too, which can aid benchmarking through the use of norms.

References can also come into play in the merger and acquisition scene and related fields. The referencing process may well involve clients, suppliers and previous employers of the key individuals in a target company. It will often be appropriate, here, to delve beyond the first range of names volunteered by the subjects of the referencing, obtaining from them details of other people with relevant experience to contribute. In one case that I recall, one of these 'second-tier' referees commented, 'John is a good salesman, but personally I would not feel comfortable buying anything from him.' Such remarks can give some fairly distinct indications of the likely difficulties that may be encountered in the company moving forward and the chance of an investor 'losing his shirt'.

Another very powerful source of references in situations involving mergers, takeovers and other major changes is other people involved in aspects of the process. Those concerned with various facets of financial due diligence will of course find themselves interacting with the relevant people, and often at much greater length than the psychologist consultant whose time may be confined to a couple of hours with each of the relevant managers or directors in a potential investee company. Their insights are likely to be particularly valuable, with the value being further enhanced if they are subjected to a formalized debriefing process comparable to that applied to external company referees.

Where an assessment process using structured interviews or psycho-metrics has been undertaken, the output of that can be used to inform some of the questions asked of the referees, to gather confirmatory or illustrative evidence.

Limitations and risks associated with failure to undertake assessments in such circumstances have been attested to in a number of studies (eg Smart, 1998; KPMG, 1999). The need for such formal assessments was also some-thing that I first raised in print some 10 years ago (Edenborough, 1994). Their use, though, is still emergent rather than really well established, but seems likely to grow as the level of merger and acquisition activity, which has been slow for some time now, begins to increase and as the private equity world seeks ways of optimizing its investment decisions.

FUTURE DIRECTIONS: INTEGRATING AND OPTIMIZING CONTRIBUTIONS

Armstrong (2003) describes an aim of human resource management (HRM) as 'to achieve strategic integration and coherence in the develop-ment and operation of HRM policies and employment practices'. One might hope that this would include pulling together assessment methods and performance management, but in practice this has not always been the case, with much fragmentation. I know of one organization where no fewer than four different competency models were in place at the same time in relation to exactly the same range of jobs and others where assess-ments of external candidates were never required to be presented in relation to either a general competency model or the specifics of a job description.

Yet many organizations have progressed at least some way down the path of integration. One approach has been the application of the bal-anced scorecard approach to measuring performance and capability. Originally developed in connection with setting and assessing progress towards overall business targets, this approach sought the simultaneous utilization of a number of measures covering financial and operational aspects of a business. Applied to the measurement of people the approach has scope for the simultaneous consideration of, again, hard financial measures and other indicators, such as acquisition of skills or the ratings of co-workers, eg from 360 degree assessment.

There are other, broadly based models used in business that either implicitly or explicitly encompass aspects of the assessment of people and their performance. Not all of these have borne fruit, for instance the human resource accounting movement of some 20 years ago took a rela-tively narrow and non-behavioural approach and is not now in common use in HR management, although it has some currency in economic circles. More promise of an integrated approach stems from the European Foundation for Quality Management (EFQM). Their model takes account of leadership, the people and other resources deployed in combination with business processes to drive employee and customer satisfaction as well as the impact on society, all of which issue in business results. This type of approach is gaining ground and can be seen as a step on the way to dismantling silos.

Yet the silos do remain. Some years ago, working with colleagues designing reward systems in a multinational, there was initially no recognition of the power of **flexibility** of reward in shaping **behaviour** to desired ends by offering inducements tailored to individual motivations. Exploiting individual differences in such a way to optimize performance is, I would argue, a potentially potent tool for performance management. The failure to think in terms of individuals but to make general provisions, whether for reward or development, has the advantage of simplicity in arrangements, but the distinct disadvantage that behaviour is unlikely to be optimized. (The question of whether to work to the average or to tailor matters for individuals is something that I considered some 30 years ago in relation to workplace layout (Edenborough, 1974).)

There are also many other factors to be taken into account if one is to optimize the various contributions of systematic assessment methods to the management of performance. I have already made the point in this book about competency models being often half-baked or where fully baked having been picked at and perhaps unnecessarily cut or iced by the impact of top managerial input – I hesitate to say 'whim'.

More optimistically it appears that there is, despite all the difficulties, a continuing and probably irreversible drive to understand motivations and capabilities and certainly to drive down forever harder on those factors that make for improvements in performance. Within this the role of self-development and a self-driven desire for personal growth will undoubtedly play a part. Increasingly I find such aspects gaining in prominence in nearly all of the occupational groups that I study, whether in the public or the private sector and across a range of specializations. This desire for personal growth is one of the linking factors between assessment and the effective management of performance. I have known a number of people who have kept a copy of an assessment report immediately to hand in a desk drawer and have referred to it over a period of years as they have sought to sharpen their performance and track the course of their development. In similar vein are those who carry an abbreviated form of the results of a personality measure in their heads – the most common form of this being the four initial summary of the Myers

Briggs Type Indicator – and who quote from it in connection with a range of work situations as they reflect on their own performance.

Amongst the gaps that will need to be filled, though, if assessment is to be more clearly lined up with performance management are better-established and relevant norm groups, the joining up of systems and descriptors, so avoiding the proliferation of competency models or the development of performance management separately from considerations of assessed capability. As the physical and motor component of work continues to diminish along with more routine aspects of information handling then it will be a confirmation of those characteristics that tend to be motivational, that tend to relate to long-term strategic thinking and, perhaps most importantly, that relate specifically to the management of other people that will come to the fore in the workplace.

Coda

I have attempted a degree of integration in this book. The extent to which that attempt has been achieved will be for the reader to judge. In doing this I have taken as 'anchor points' the three types of assessment: psychometrics, structured interviews and assessment centres, together with performance management. Each of these fields is in itself huge, with its own substantial literature both in terms of research and represented in practical tests. I have referred to some of this material along the way, as well as that in other large fields, such as quality management, which I see as having links to the topics addressed here. Particularly to the reader coming to any of these topics afresh, I suggest the pursuit of some of these other sources will be rewarding.

Glossary and technical notes

GLOSSARY

ability test A test in which the ability to perform certain types of task is assessed.

achievement test A test in which the level acquired in a particular area of skill is assessed (see also 'attainment test').

aptitude test A test measuring the aptitude or capacity to master a particular skill area.

assessment centre An event in which a group of individuals undertake set work-like simulations, which are typically assessed by a group of trained assessors who pool their findings before finalizing their conclusions.

attainment test An alternative name for achievement test.

big five theory of personality A theory that says there are five fundamental aspects of personality, viz extroversion, agreeableness, conscientiousness, neuroticism and intellect.

chartered psychologist A person qualified to practise psychology according to the requirements of the British Psychological Society (BPS), as laid down in its Royal Charter and associated statutes, and who is registered with the BPS as chartered and who is bound by a code of professional conduct.

coaching A process of specific guidance involving giving feedback on performance and advising on methods of improvement.

cognitive test A test of thinking or mental ability.

competency An underlying characteristic of an individual, causally related to effective performance.

concurrent validity The extent to which a test is found to distinguish between two groups, themselves differentiated according to the attribute intended to be measured by the test.

construct validity The degree to which a test measures the psychological construct or attribute that it is intended to measure.

content analysis The systematic analysis of the detail of verbal material in either a written or spoken form.

correlation coefficient A statistic showing the degree of relation between two measures, eg a test score of persistence and sales figures (see also 'Technical notes').

counselling A process of helping an individual to understand him/herself and his or her preferences, needs and capabilities through detailed and usually one-to-one discussion.

cut-off score The level on a test used as a decision point for final or provisional acceptance.

development centre An assessment centre held particularly for purposes of aiding staff development, often used as an entry point to a development programme.

direct discrimination Using race, gender or religion as a criterion for selection or promotion.

domain mapping A self-analysis technique for an individual to explore the current status of life and work domains relevant to him or her, and to begin to map a transition path to the desired status.

face validity The way in which a test appears to be measuring the attribute that it is supposed to measure and/or the degree to which it appears to be a credible process.

factor An underlying behavioural attribute or characteristic whose existence is established or inferred through factor analysis (see also 'Technical notes').

factor analysis A statistical process by which factors are identified through correlational methods.

indirect discrimination Using a means of determining selection or promotion decisions that is linked to membership of a particular racial, gender or religious group, rather than ability or potential to perform the job concerned.

intelligence quotient (IQ) Originally the ratio of mental age to chronological age. Now used as a generally standardized way of reporting intelligence measures (see also 'Technical notes').

interest inventory A questionnaire comprising items requiring ratings or rankings of preference for different types of task or role or job.

ipsative A test item in which comparisons are made between two different attributes, also applied to a test comprising such items.

item In a test a question, statement or other stimulus requiring its own separate response.

multiple regression The prediction of performance on one variable, such as speed of mastering a software syllabus, from scores on a number of other variables, such as scores on the tests in a programmer battery (see also 'Technical notes').

negative skew A condition in which a large number of respondents produce high scores on a test.

norm A standard of test scores related to a population or group.

normal curve The Gaussian or bell-shaped curve that is applied to the distribution of many attributes (see also 'Technical notes').

normative A term applied to a test item in which a statement is rated directly rather than in comparison with other statements. Also applied to a test made up of such items.

percentile The position of a score indicated in relation to the percentage of values in the norm group falling at or below that score (see also 'Technical notes').

personality questionnaire A psychometric instrument, made up of items for self-report, designed to reveal typical aspects of behaviour.

positive skew A condition in which a large number of respondents produce low scores on a test.

predictive validity The degree to which a test predicts future performance, eg in a job or role or in training.

selection ratio The proportion of those tested who are selected.

semantic differential A rating scale in which responses are made in relation to a series of bipolar statements, eg friendly–reserved.

standard deviation A statistic describing the spread of scores about a mean value (see also 'Technical notes').

standard error The standard deviation of a sampling distribution, used to calibrate the expected variability in a set of scores and so to indicate the range in which the true score might lie (see also 'Technical notes').

standardization The process of producing a set of norms.

team role A term usually applied to the characteristic behaviours in a team originally described by Meredith Belbin.

trainability test A test designed to measure the candidates' suitability for undergoing a course of training.

trait A personality characteristic.

type A personality description usually based on the work of Carl Gustav Jung.

TECHNICAL NOTES

Correlation coefficient

The correlation coefficient is a fundamental statistic in psychometrics. It is the way in which predictive, content and concurrent validity are expressed. Reliability is also indicated by a correlation coefficient, but termed then the reliability coefficient. It may be determined in that case in several different ways, the most common by using repetitions of the same test or by making comparisons of performance on two halves of the same test – the split half method.

Correlation is also the cornerstone of factor analytic and other multivariate methods.

Very often in conducting validity studies the measure of success will be less detailed than the test score. It may only be possible to regard people as falling into a rank order of performance, or divided into effective or ineffective performers. Fortunately, different forms of correlation coefficient are available to cover such cases.

Factor analysis

Factor analysis is the name given to one set of multivariate techniques, that is methods for studying the interplay among groups of variables. By looking at patterns of correlation among test items they show how the items group together to form factors. To the extent that these factors are comprehensible they may be used as descriptors of abilities or of dimensions of personality.

Other multivariate methods are used in market research to see, for example, how different groups of consumers may be clustered together.

Factor analysis is used to reduce the number of dimensions in a range of tests by examining the correlations among the test scores. Groups of tests with high correlations would be described as reflecting a general factor, while those with low intercorrelations would represent a specific factor. Although starting with the fairly simple idea of correlation, the statistical methods used are complex and varied. The wider field of multivariate analysis of which factor analysis is a part also includes regression analysis.

IQ

The use of a standard score basis for interpreting intelligence tests – sometimes termed deviation IQ – represents a development some time after the origins of intelligence testing. The term 'IQ' stands for 'intelligence quotient', originally referring to the ratio or quotient of mental age to chronological age multiplied by 100. Thus if a child of 11 has a mental age of 11 he or she is of average mental age and his or her IQ is 100:

$$\text{Here IQ} = 100 \times \frac{\text{Mental Age} \left(11\right)}{\text{Chronological Age } (11)}$$

An 11-year-old with a mental age of 15 is evidently superior intellectually, while an 11-year-old with a mental age of only 7 is inferior intellectually and these differences are reflected in the IQ computed in this way. However, there are difficulties in interpreting IQ in this way as age increases, particularly beyond the age range of normal intellectual development. Thus, a mental age of 11 as opposed to 7 makes sense, in a way that a mental age of 40 versus 30 does not. Thus the deviation IQ provides a more common basis for comparison among intelligence test scores and, indeed, between them and other psychometrics.

Item response theory

This is a technique for examining responses to individual items in a test, as opposed to looking at total scores. It involves item characteristic curves showing the probability of a test item being responded to correctly by people with different levels of ability.

Multiple regression

In calculating a multiple regression equation one needs to know the separate correlations of each test with performance on the behavioural variable of interest and the correlations among each of the tests. If the correlations between two tests were particularly high then the second of them to be considered would add little to the ability to predict behaviour given by the first of them.

Multiple regression equations are of the form: Performance W1 = T1 + W2 T2 + W3 T3 +... WN TN + C, where W1–WN are the weights to be applied to standardized test scores T1–TN and C is a constant.

For example, suppose sales performance was predicted from a battery of three tests for which we had sten scores, the multiple regression equation might be as follows: sales (£,000) = 3.3(4) + 2.8(5) + 6(8) + 5. Here the third test indicated has the highest correlation with sales, as reflected in the higher weight for that test (6).

Normal curve

The normal curve is sometimes referred to as the Gaussian distribution after the 19th-century mathematician Gauss, although it was actually discovered in the 18th century by Demoivre. As it is strictly a continuous distribution, the representation of the y-axis or ordinate as 'number of cases' is inappropriate. Numbers of cases lying between two points on the x-axis or altogether below a single point on that axis would be found by mathematical integration of the function describing the normal curve between the two points or below the single point respectively. However, in practice it is common, and often appears helpful, to label the y-axis in terms of number of cases.

Percentiles

When raw scores are clustered around the mean, one or two raw score points' difference on a test represents a relatively large percentile difference. At the extremes of the scoring range, however, several raw score points' difference may be required for a single percentile point's difference. This inequality of percentile scaling means that percentile scores cannot wholly meaningfully be averaged or otherwise manipulated.

Standard deviation

The standard deviation of a set of numbers is defined as:

$$\sigma \text{ or SD} = \frac{\sqrt{\left(\Sigma x^2\right)}}{(N)}$$

where x represents the individual variations from the mean and N is the number of cases. The square of this, namely $\dfrac{\left(\Sigma x^2\right)}{(N)}$ is known as the variance. This is not to be confused with the same term used in accountancy to refer to the absolute difference from a budgeted figure.

Standard error

The standard error of measurement (SEM) is given by:

$$\text{SEM} = \text{SD}\sqrt{\left(1 - r_{11}\right)}$$

where SD is the standard deviation of scores on a test and r_{11} the reliability coefficient – a correlation between some form of repeat measure of the same test. Note that with perfect reliability the standard error becomes zero.

Bartram (1994) has pointed to the value of considering standard error rather than reliability alone. Among other things he reminds us that a test with the same item repeated over and over would have high reliability, but little practical value.

The standard error of difference (SE diff) enables one to establish how far apart the scores for two individuals on any one test need to be for them to be regarded as representing significantly different levels of performance. It is given by:

$$\text{SE diff} = \sqrt{\left(\text{SEM}_x^{\,2} + \text{SEM}_y^{\,2}\right)}$$

where SEM_x = SEM for first individual
SEM_y = SEM for second individual

The standard error of estimate is used when a test has been correlated with some criterion score of performance in order to estimate the band of error around the criterion score as predicted from the test. The formula is:

$$\text{SE}_{est} = \text{SD}_c \sqrt{1 - r^2_{tc}}$$

where SD_c is the standard deviation of the criterion scores and r^2_{tc} the square of validity coefficient for the test and criterion scores.

References

Abrams, B, Edenborough, R and Harley, P A (1998) *A School's Guide to Recruitment*, NFER-Nelson, Windsor

Algera, J A and Greuter, M A M (1988) Job analysis for personnel selection, in *Advances in Selection and Assessment*, ed I Robertson and M Smith, John Wiley, Chichester

Allnutt, M F (1970) Performance under environmental stress, PhD thesis, University of Nottingham

American Psychological Association (APA) (1954) Technical recommendations for psychological tests and diagnostic techniques, *Psychological Bulletin*, **51** (2), Pt 2

APA, American Educational Research Association and National Council on Measurement in Education (1974) *Standards for Educational and Psychological Tests*, American Psychological Association, Washington, DC

Anastasi, A (1961) *Psychological Testing*, Macmillan, New York

Anderson, N (1997) The validity and adverse impact of selection interviews, *Selection and Development Review*, **13** (5), pp 13–16

Anderson, N and Shackleton, V (1993) _Successful Selection Interviewing_, Blackwell, Oxford

Anderson, N R (1992) Eight decades of employment interview research: a retrospective meta review and prospective commentary, _European Work and Organisational Psychologist_, **2** (1), pp 1–32

Anstey, E (1977) A 30-year follow-up of the CSSB Procedure, with lessons for the future, _Journal of Occupational Psychology_, **50**, pp 149–59

Armes, J and Greenaway, A (1998) _Future Education and Training Services (FEATS)_, NFER-Nelson, Windsor

Armstrong, M (1995) _A Handbook of Personnel Management Practice_, Kogan Page, London

Armstrong, M (2003) _A Handbook of Human Resource Management Practice_, 9th edn, Kogan Page, London

Armstrong, M and Baron, A (1998) _Performance Management: The new realities_, CIPD, London

Arvey, R D (1979) _Fairness in Selecting Employees_, Addison-Wesley, Reading, MA

ASE (1998) _Testing People with Disabilities_, NFER-Nelson, Windsor

Awosunle, S and Doyle, C (2001) Same-race bias in the selection interview, _Selection and Development Review_, **17** (3), pp 3–6

Ballantyne, I and Povah, N (2004) _Assessment and Development Centres_, 2nd edn, Gower, Hampshire

Banking Information Service (1993) _Psychometric Testing: Getting a better picture_, Banking Information Service, London

Bannister, D and Mair, J M (1968) _The Evaluation of Personal Constructs_, Academic Press, London and New York

Bartram, D (1992) The personality of UK managers: 16PF norms for shortlisted applicants, _Journal of Occupational Psychology_, **65**, pp 159–72

Bartram, D (1994) What is so important about reliability? The need to consider the standard error of measurement, _Selection and Development Review_, **10** (1), pp 1–3

Bartram, D (1997) Distance assessment: psychological assessment through the Internet, _Selection and Development Review_, **13** (3), pp 15–19

Bennett, G K, Seashore, H G and Wesman, A G (1947) _Differential Aptitude Tests_, Psychological Corporation, New York

Bevan, S and Fryatt, J (1988) _Employee Selection in the UK_, Institute of Manpower Studies, Brighton

Binet, A and Henri, V (1895) La psychologie individuelle, _Annie psychologie_, **2**, pp 411–63

Binet, A and Simon, T (1905) Methodes nouvelles pour le diagnostic du niveau des anormaux, *Annie psychologie*, **11**, pp 191–244

Boyatzis, R F (1982) *The Competent Manager: A model for effective performance*, Wiley Interscience, New York

Boyle, S (1997) Researching the selection interview, *Selection and Development Review*, **13** (4), pp 15–17

Bray, D W (1985) Fifty years of assessment centres: a retrospective and prospective view, *Journal of Management Development*, **4** (4), pp 4–12

British Psychological Society (BPS) (1999) *Guidelines for the Development and Use of Computer-based Assessments*, BPS, Leicester

BPS (2001) *Review of Personality Instruments (Level B) for Use in Occupational Settings*, BPS, Leicester

BPS (2003) *Design, Implementation and Evaluation of Assessment and Development Centres: Best practice guidelines*, BPS, Leicester

Bryon, M and Modha, S (1991) *How To Master Selection Tests*, Kogan Page, London

Buros, O (ed) (1941) *The 1940 Mental Measurements Yearbook*, Mental Measurements Yearbook, New York

Burt, C (1922) Tests for clerical occupations, *JL NIIP*, **1**, pp 23–27, 79–81

Carroll, J B (1980) *Individual Difference Relations in Psychometric and Experimental Cognitive Tasks*, Report no 163, Thurstone Psychometric Laboratory, University of North Carolina, Chapel Hill, NC

Castle, P F C and Garforth, F I de la P (1951) Selection training and status of supervisors: I selection, *Occupational Psychology*, **25**, pp 109–23

Cattell, H B (1989) *The 16PF: Personality in depth*, Institute for Personality and Ability Testing, Champaign, IL

Cattell, J McK (1890) Mental tests and measurement, *Mind*, **15**, pp 373–80

Cattell, R B, Eber, H W and Tatsuoka, M (1970) *Handbook for the Sixteen Personality Factor Questionnaire*, Institute for Personality and Ability Testing, Champaign, IL

Clark, R and Baron, H (1992) *Guidelines for Testing People with Disabilities*, Saville & Holdsworth Ltd, Thames Ditton

Clifton, D O and Nelson, P (1992) *Soar with Your Strengths*, Delacorte, New York

Clifton, D O, Hollingsworth, F L and Hall, E (1952) A projective technique to determine positive and negative attitudes towards people in a real-life situation, *Journal of Educational Psychology*, May, pp 273–83

Cook, M (1992) An evaluation of the DISC/Personal Profile Analysis, *Selection and Development Review*, **8**, pp 3–6

Cooper, C (2002) *Individual Differences*, Arnold, London

Cox, J and Tapsell, J (1991) Graphology and its validity in personnel assessment, *Proceedings of BPS Occupational Psychology Conference*, Cardiff

Cronbach, L J (1966) *Essentials of Psychological Testing*, 2nd edn, Harper & Row, New York

Doppelt, J E, Hartman, A D and Krawchik, F B (1984) *Typing Test for Business*, Psychological Corporation, Sidcup

Downs, S (1973) *Trainability Assessment: Sewing machinists*, Industrial Training Research Unit, Cambridge

Edenborough, R A (1974) Flexibility or optimality in design? A human factors dilemma, *Controller*, **13** (3), pp 42–44

Edenborough, R A (1975) Order effects and display persistence in probabilistic opinion revision, *Bulletin of the Psychonomic Society*, **5** (1), pp 39–40

Edenborough, R A (1994) Psychometrics and discrimination – using tests fairly, *Employment Law and Practice*, **2** (1), pp 7–10

Edenborough, R A (1996) *Effective Interviewing*, Kogan Page, London

Edenborough, R A (1999) Many mansions: a review of the status of psychometric tests, assessment centres, structured interviews and all that jazz, *Proceedings, The Fourth Test User Conference*, BPS, Leicester

Edwards, W (1961) Costs and payoffs are instructions, *Psychology Review*, **68**, pp 109–35

Evarts, M (1987) The competency programme of the AMA, *Journal of Industrial and Commercial Training*, January/February

Eysenck, H J (1957) *Sense and Nonsense in Psychology*, Penguin, Harmondsworth

Feltham, R, Baron, H and Smith, P (1994) Developing fair tests, *Psychologist*, January, pp 23–25

Flanagan, J C (1947) Army air force aviation psychology program, *Research Report No 1*, US Government Printing Office, Washington, DC

Flanagan, J C (1954) The critical incident technique, *Psychological Bulletin*, **51** (4), pp 327–58

Fletcher, C (1986) *How to Face Interviews*, Thorsons, London

Fletcher, C (2004) *Appraisal and Feedback: Making performance review work*, CIPD, London

Fox, G (1996) Nondestructive use of assessment in guidance and career development, *Proceedings Division of Occupational Psychology Test User Conference*, British Psychology Society, Leicester

Fox, G (2000) Putting tests on the Internet – problems and pitfalls, *Selection and Development Review*, **16** (5)

Freud, S (1901) The psychopathology of everyday life, *Monatsschrift für Psychiatrie und Neurologie*, July, pp 1–32, and August, pp 95–145; modern edn, Penguin Freud Library (1975), Penguin, London

Garavan, T N, Morley, M and Flynn, M (1997) 360 degree feedback: its role in employee development, *Journal of Management Development*, **16** (2), pp 134–47

Goodge, P (2004) Twenty great development centre ideas, *Selection and Development Review*, **20**, pp 13–18

Green, B F (1981) A primer of testing, *American Psychologist*, **36**, pp 1001–11

Green, R G and Edenborough, R A (1971) Incidence and effects at the man–computer interface of failure to optimise the display, *Displays*, Conference Publication no 80, IEE, London

Haney, W (1981) Validity, vaudeville and values: a short history of social concerns over standardized testing, *American Psychologist*, **36** (10), pp 1021–34

Harley, P A (1995) A window on an alien world: development centres in the context of director competences, *Executive Development*, **8** (6), pp 28–31

Harris, M H (1989) Reconsidering the employment interview: a review of recent literature and suggestions for future research, *Personnel Psychology*, **42**, pp 691–726

Hartshorne, H and May, M (1930) *Studies in Deceit*, Macmillan, New York

Hartshorne, H, May, M and Shuttleworth, F (1929) *Studies in Service and Self-Control*, Macmillan, New York

Herriot, P (1987) The selection interview, in *Psychology at Work*, ed P B Warr, Penguin, Harmondsworth

Holt, R R (1958) Clinical and statistical prediction: a reformulation and some new data, *Journal of Abnormal and Social Psychology*, **56**, pp 1–12

Humble, J (1972) *Management by Objectives in Action*, McGraw-Hill, Maidenhead

Institute of Personnel and Development (IPD) (1997) *The IPD Guide on Psychological Testing*, IPD, London

Institute of Personnel Management (IPM) (1992) *Performance Management in the UK: An analysis of the issues*, IPM, London

IPM (1993) *IPM Code on Psychological Testing*, IPM, London

International Test Commission (ITC) (1999) *International Guidelines for Test Use*, ITC, Amsterdam

Irvine, S H, Dann, P L and Anderson, J D (1990) Towards a theory of algorithm-determined cognitive test construction, *British Journal of Psychology*, **81**, pp 173–95

Jankowicz, D (2004) _The Easy Guide to Repertory Grids_, John Wiley, Chichester

Janz, T (1982) Initial comparisons of patterned behavioural description interviews versus unstructured interviews, _Journal of Applied Psychology_, **67** (5), pp 577–80

Jenkins, C D, Zyzanski, J and Roseman, J (1979) _Jenkins Activity Survey_, Psychological Corporation, Sidcup

Johnson, C E, Wood, R and Blinkhorn, S F (1988) Spurioser and spurioser: the use of ipsative personality tests, _Journal of Occupational Psychology_, **61**, pp 153–62

Jones, J W (1994) _Personnel Testing_, Crisp, Menlo Park, CA

Jones, J W (1995) _Personnel Testing_, UK edn, Kogan Page, London

Kellett, D _et al_ (1994) Fair testing: the case of British Rail, _Psychologist_, January, pp 26–29

Kelly, G A (1955) _The Psychology of Personal Constructs_, Norton, New York

Klopfer, B and Davidson, H H (1962) _The Rorschach Technique: An introductory manual_, Harcourt Brace Jovanovich, San Diego, CA

KPMG (1999) _Unlocking Shareholder Value: The keys to success_, KPMG, London

Krug, S E (1981) _Interpreting 16 PF Profile Patterns_, Institute for Personality and Aptitude Testing, Champaign, IL

Ladurie, E L R (1978) _Montaillou_, Penguin, Harmondsworth

Latham, G P _et al_ (1980) The situational interview, _Journal of Applied Psychology_, **65** (4), pp 422–27

Lee, G (2004) Fact find exercise, _Selection and Development Review_, **20**, pp 10–13

Lee, G and Beard, D (1994) _Development Centres_, McGraw-Hill, London

Lindley, P C (snr ed) (1993) _Review of Level B Instruments for Use in Occupational Settings_, BPS, Leicester

Mackenzie Davey, D (1989) _How To Be a Good Judge of Character_, Kogan Page, London

Mackinnon, D W (1980) _How Assessment Centres Were Started in the United States: The OSS Assessment Program_, Development Dimensions International, Pittsburgh, PA

Maier, N (1958) _The Appraisal Interview_, Wiley, New York

McDaniel, M A _et al_ (1994) The validity of employment interviews: a comprehensive review and meta-analysis, _Journal of Applied Psychology_, **79**, pp 599–616

McGregor, D (1957) An uneasy look at performance appraisal, _Harvard Business Review_, May–June, pp 89–94

McGregor, D (1960) *The Human Side of Enterprise*, McGraw-Hill, New York

McHenry, R (1996) Should instruments for 360 degree feedback have psychometric properties?, *Proceedings, Division of Occupational Psychology Test User Conference*, BPS, Leicester

Meyer, H H (1970) The validity of the In-basket Test as a measure of managerial performance, *Personnel Psychology*, **23**, pp 297–307

Miles, D W *et al* (1946) The efficiency of a high speed screening procedure in detecting the neuropsychiatrically unfit at a US Marine Corps recruit training depot, *Journal of Psychology*, **21**, pp 243–68

Morgan, D L (ed) (1993) *Successful Focus Groups*, Sage, Newbury Park, CA

Munro-Fraser, J (1954) *A Handbook of Employment Interviewing*, Macdonald and Evans, London

Murray, H A (1938) *Explorations in Personality*, Oxford University Press, New York

Murray, H A (1943) *Thematic Apperception Test*, Harvard University Press, Cambridge, MA

Myers, C S (1920) Psychology and industry, *British Journal of Psychology*, **10**, pp 177–82

Myers, I B *et al* (1998) *MBTI Manual*, 3rd edn, Consulting Psychologists Press, Palo Alto, CA

NAHT (1991) *The Performance Management Guide*, NAHT, Haywards Heath

NIIP (1952) *The Seven-Point Plan*, Paper no 1, NIIP, London

Novick, M R (1981) Federal guidelines and professional standards, *American Psychologist*, **36** (10), pp 1035–46

Oldfield, F E (1953) *Fruitful Interviews*, Mason Reed, London

Oliveira, T (2000) Implicit logic in unstructured interviewing, *Selection and Development Review*, **16** (2), pp 10–14

O'Neill, M B (2000) *Executive Coaching with Backbone and Heart*, Jossey-Bass, San Francisco

Psychological Corporation (1988) *Assessment for Training and Employment (ATE)*, Psychological Corporation, Sidcup

Psychometric Research Unit, Hatfield Polytechnic (1992) *Graduate and Managerial Assessment*, ASE, Windsor

Ramsay, S, Gallois, C and Callan, V J (1997) Social rules and attributions in the personnel selection interview, *Journal of Occupational and Organizational Psychology*, **70**, pp 189–203

Raphael, W (1944) A technique for surveying employees' opinions and attitudes, *Occupational Psychology*, **18**, pp 165–73

Reber, A (1995) _Dictionary of Psychology_, 2nd edn, Penguin, London

Revans, R (1971) _Developing Effective Managers_, Longman, Harlow

Ridgway, J F (1977) A facet analysis of the aircrew film test, PhD thesis, University of Lancaster

Robertson, I and Smith, M (1988) Personnel selection methods, in _Advances in Selection and Assessment_, ed I Robertson and M Smith, John Wiley, Chichester

Rogers, C R (1961) _On Becoming a Person_, Houghton Mifflin, Boston, MA

Rorschach, H C (1942) _Psychodiagnostics: A diagnostic test based on perception_, Huber, Berne

Sackett, P and Harris, M (1984) Honesty testing for personnel selection, _Personnel Psychology_, **37**, pp 221–45

Saville, P (1972) _The British Standardisation of the 16PF_, NFER-Nelson, Windsor

Saville, P and Wilson, E (1991) The reliability and validity of normative and ipsative approaches in the measurement of personality, _Journal of Occupational Psychology_, **64**, pp 219–38

Saville, P _et al_ (1984) _The Occupational Personality Questionnaires_, SHL, London

Schein, E H (1985) Individuals and careers, in _Handbook of Organisational Behaviour_, ed J Lorsch, Prentice-Hall, Englewood Cliffs, NJ

Schutz, W (1978) _FIRO Awareness Scales Manual_, Consulting Psychologists Press, Palo Alto, CA

Scott, S and Kwiatkowski, R (1998) Foul or fair? Assessment centres and ethnic minorities: a study of major UK recruiters, _Proceedings BPS Occupational Psychology Conference_, Leicester

Seashore, H and Bennett, G K (1948) _The Seashore–Bennett Stenographic Proficiency Test: A standard recorded stenographic worksample_, Psychological Corporation, New York

SHL (1995) _Best Practice in the Use of Job Analysis Techniques_, Saville & Holdsworth Ltd, Thames Ditton

Smart, G H (1998) _The Art and Science of Human Capital Evaluation_, G H Smart & Co, Chicago, IL

Smith, M C and Downs, S (1975) Trainability assessment for apprentice selection in shipbuilding, _Journal of Occupational Psychology_, **53**, pp 131–38

Smith, P (ed) (1992) _Motivation and Personality: Handbook of thematic content analysis_, Cambridge University Press, Cambridge

Spearman, C (1904) General intelligence, objectively determined and measured, _American Journal of Psychology_, **15**, pp 201–93

Spielman, W (1923) Vocational tests for dressmakers' apprentices, *JL NIIP*, **1**, pp 277–82

Stott, M B (1950) What is occupational success?, *Occupational Psychology*, **24**, pp 105–12

Stott, M B (1956) Follow-up problems in vocational guidance, placement and selection, *Occupational Psychology*, **30**, pp 137–52

Strong, E K (1943) *Vocational Interests of Men and Women*, Stanford University Press, Stanford, CA

Tarleton, R (1997) *The Motivational Styles Questionnaire*, Psychological Corporation, London

Taylor, H C and Russell, J T (1939) The relationship of validity coefficients to the practical effectiveness of tests in selection: discussion and tables, *Journal of Applied Psychology*, **23**, pp 565–78

Taylor, P J and O'Driscoll, M P (1995) *Structured Employment Interviewing*, Gower, Aldershot

Thorndike, E L (1920) A constant error in psychological ratings, *Journal of Applied Psychology*, **4**, pp 25–29

Turner, S and Lee, D (1998) *Measures in Post Traumatic Stress Disorder*, NFER-Nelson, Windsor

Vernon, P E and Parry, J B (1949) *Personnel Selection in the British Forces*, University of London Press, London

Vincent, D F (1955) *Speed and Precision in Manual Skill*, Report no 11, NIIP, London

Vincent, D F (1971) Problems of test production and supply, *Occupational Psychology*, **44**, pp 71–80

Wagner, R (1949) The employment interview: a critical summary, *Personnel Psychology*, **2**, pp 17–46

Watson, G and Glaser, E M (1991) *Critical Thinking Appraisal Manual*, Psychological Corporation, Sidcup

Wechsler, D (1955) *Wechsler Adult Intelligence Scale*, Psychological Corporation, New York

Wernimont, P F and Campbell, J P (1968) Signs, samples and criteria, *Journal of Applied Psychology*, **52**, pp 372–76

Wiesner, W H and Cronshaw, S F (1988) A meta-analytic investigation of the impact of interview format and degree of structure on the validity of the employment interview, *Journal of Occupational Psychology*, **61** (4), pp 275–90

Williams, R S (1994) Occupational testing: contemporary British practice, *Psychologist*, January, pp 11–13

Wood, R (1997a) The interview: just when you thought it was safe, _Selection and Development Review_, **13** (2), pp 15–17

Wood, R (1997b) The interview: it's still not safe, _Selection and Development Review_, **13** (6), p 16

Woodruffe, C (2000) _Development and Assessment Centres_, 3rd edn, Institute of Personnel and Development, London

Wrenn, C L (1949) _The English Language_, Methuen, London

Wright, P M, Lichterfels, P A and Pursell, E D (1989) The structured interview: additional studies and meta-analysis, _Journal of Occupational Psychology_, **64**, pp 191–99

Yoakum, C and Yerkes, R M (1920) _Army Mental Tests_, Holt, New York

Further reading

Akin-Ogundeji, O (1991) Asserting psychology in Africa, *Psychologist*, **4**, pp 1–4

Albrecht, T L, Johnson, G M and Walther, J B (1993) Understanding communication processes in focus groups, in *Successful Focus Groups*, ed D L Morgan, Sage, Newbury Park, CA

Argyle, M (1975) *Bodily Communication*, Methuen, London

Arvey, R D and Campion, J E (1982) The employment interview: a summary and review of recent research, *Personnel Psychology*, **35**, pp 281–322

Baker, E A (ed) (1949) *Cassell's New English Dictionary*, Reprint Society, London

Ball, W W R (1880) *Origin and History of the Mathematics Tripos*, Cambridge University Press, Cambridge

Ballantyne, I (1996) Towards quality standards in assessment centres: practitioners' guide, *Proceedings, The First Test User Conference*, BPS, Leicester

Bartram, D (1999) Testing and the Internet: current realities, issues and future possibilities, _Selection and Development Review_, **15** (6), pp 3–11

Bartram, D (senr ed) (1997) _Review of Ability and Aptitude Tests (Level A) for Use in Occupational Settings_, BPS, Leicester

Belbin, R M (1981) _Management Teams: Why they succeed or fail_, Heinemann, London

Bellows, R M and Estep, M F (1954) _Employment Psychology: The interview_, Rinehart, New York

Blacker, K (1995) _The Basics of BPR_, Edistone Books, Birmingham

Block, J (1971) _Lives through Time_, Bancroft, CA

Block, J (1978) _The Q-Sort Method in Personality Assessment and Psychiatric Research_, Consulting Psychologists Press, Palo Alto, CA

Brindle, L (1992) The redundant executive – typical or talented, _Selection and Development Review_, **8** (6), pp 2–4, British Psychological Society, Leicester

Burnett, J (1977) What is counselling?, in _Counselling at Work_, ed A G Watts, Bedford Square Press, London

Campbell, D P (1974) _Manual for the Strong: Campbell Interest Inventory_, Stanford University Press, Stanford, CA

Carr, S and MacLachlan, M (1993) Asserting psychology in Malawi, _Psychologist_, **6** (9), pp 408–13

Cassidy, T and Lynn, R (1989) A multifactorial approach to achievement motivation: the development of a comprehensive measure, _Occupational Psychology_, **62**, pp 301–12

Cherns, A (1982) Culture and values: the reciprocal influence between applied social science and its cultural and historical context, in _The Theory and Practice of Organizational Psychology_, ed N Nicholson and T D Wall, Academic Press, London

Clarke, A D B (1996) Personal communication

Clifton, D O and Hall, E (1957) A projective technique to determine positive and negative attitudes towards people in a real-life situation, _Journal of Educational Psychology_, May, pp 273–83

Colbert, G A and Taylor, L R (1978) Empirically derived job families as a foundation for the study of validity generalisation – Study 3, _Personnel Psychology_, **31**, pp 355–64

Collins (1981) _Pocket English Dictionary_, Collins, Glasgow

Coutts, K and Rowthorn, R (1995) _Employment Trends in the United Kingdom: Trends and prospects_, ESRC Working Paper Series, Cambridge

De Groot, T and Motowidlo, S J (1999) Why visual and vocal cues can affect interviewers' judgements and predict job performance, *Journal of Applied Psychology*, **84** (6), pp 986–93

Deutsch, F (1947) Analysis of postural behaviour, *Psychoanalytic Quarterly*, **16**, pp 195–213

Dryden, W and Feltham, C (1992) *Brief Counselling*, Open University Press, Buckingham

Dulewicz, V and Higgs, M (1999a) *Making Sense of Emotional Intelligence*, NFER-Nelson, Windsor

Dulewicz, V and Higgs, M (1999b) *The Emotional Intelligence Questionnaire*, ASE, Windsor

Earl, M J (1989) *Management Strategies for Information Technology*, Oxford University Press, Oxford

Eder, R W and Ferris, G R (eds) (1989) *The Employment Interview: Theory research and practice*, Sage, Newbury Park, CA

Edwards, A L (1959) *Edwards Personal Preference Schedule*, Psychological Corporation, New York

Elliott, C D (1996) *British Ability Scales*, 2nd edn, NFER-Nelson, Windsor

England, G W and Patterson, D G (1960) Selection and placement: the past ten years, in *Employment Relations Research*, ed H G Heneman *et al*, Harper, New York

Evans, W A and Sculli, D (1981) A comparison of managerial traits in Hong Kong and the USA, *Journal of Occupational Psychology*, **54**, pp 183–86

Firth-Cozens, J and Handy, G E (1992) Occupational stress, clinical treatment and changes in job perceptions, *Journal of Occupational and Organisational Psychology*, **65**, Pt 2, pp 81–88

Fletcher, C (1992) Ethics and the job interview, *Personnel Management*, March, pp 37–39

Fletcher, C (1994) Validity, test use and professional responsibility, *Psychologist*, January, pp 30–31

Forsythe, S, Drake, M F and Cox, C E (1985) Influence of applicants' dress on interview selection decisions, *Journal of Applied Psychology*, **70**, pp 374–78

Fox, G (1999) Measuring the measures: applying standards to non-test assessments, *Proceedings, The Fourth Test User Conference*, BPS, Leicester

Frederickson, N, Urith, U and Reason, R (1997) *Phonological Assessment Battery*, NFER-Nelson, Windsor

Frisby, C B (1971) The development of industrial psychology at the NIIP, *Occupational Psychology*, **44**, pp 35–50

Gatewood, R and Field, H (2000) *HR Selection*, 5th edn, Thompson Learning, London

Gifford, R, Ng, C F and Wilkinson, M (1985) Non-verbal cues in the employment interview: links between applicant qualities and interviewer judgements, *Journal of Applied Psychology*, **70**, pp 729–36

Goleman, D (1996) *Emotional Intelligence: Why it can matter more than IQ*, Bloomsbury, London

Gough, T (1989) *Couples in Counselling: A consumer's guide to marriage counselling*, Darton, Longman & Todd, London

Guttman, L (1950) The third component of scalable attitudes, *International Journal of Opinion and Attitude Research*, **4**, pp 285–87

Hamilton, K and Kolb, C (1995) They log on but they can't log off, *Newsweek*, December, pp 60–61

Handy, C (1989) *The Age of Unreason*, Arrow, London

Heneman, H G *et al* (1975) Interview validity as a function of interview structure, biographical data and interviewee order, *Journal of Applied Psychology*, **60**, pp 748–53

Hofstede, G (1984) *Culture's Consequences*, Sage, London

Holbeche, L (1995) *Career Development in Flatter Structures*, Report no 2: *Organisational Practices*, Roffey Park Management Institute, Horsham

Industrial Relations Services (1994) *Industrial Relations Review and Report*, **556**, IRS, London

International Task Force on Assessment Center Guidelines (2000) *Guidelines and Ethical Considerations for Assessment Center Operations*, 28th Congress on Assessment Center Methods, San Francisco

James, W T (1932) A study of the expression of bodily posture, *Journal of General Psychology*, **7**, pp 405–37

Jones, J (1987) Utility analysis, in *Psychological Testing: A manager's guide*, ed J Toplis, V Dulewicz and C Fletcher, IPM, London

Krueger, R A (1988) *Focus Groups: A practical guide for applied research*, Sage, Newbury Park, CA

Latham, G P, Wexley, K N and Pursell, T D (1975) Training managers to minimize rating errors in observation of behaviour, *Journal of Applied Psychology*, **60**, pp 550–55

Leeds, D (1988) *Smart Questions for Successful Managers*, Piatkus, London

Lewis, C (1992) *Employee Selection*, Stanley Thornes, Cheltenham

Likert, R A (1932) A technique for the measurement of attitudes, *Archives of Psychology*, **140**, p 55

Mason, K, Hagues, N and Patilla, P (1998) *Mathematics 12–14*, NFER-Nelson, Windsor

McGovern, T V and Tinsley, H E (1978) Interviewer evaluations of interviewee non-verbal behaviour, *Journal of Vocational Behaviour*, **13**, pp 163–71

McHenry, R (1996) Personal communication

McLaughlin, P (1986) *How to Interview*, Self Counsel Press, North Vancouver

Mehrabian, A (1972) *Non-verbal Communication*, Aldine-Atherton, Chicago, IL

Newman, J M and Kryzstofiak, F (1979) Self-reports versus unobtrusive measures: balancing method-variable and ethical concerns in employment discrimination research, *Journal of Applied Psychology*, **64**, pp 82–85

NHS Management Executive (1992) *Women in the NHS*, Department of Health, London

Otis, J L, Campbell, J H and Prien, E (1962) Assessment of higher level personnel: the nature of assessment, *Personnel Psychology*, **15**, pp 441–46

Palmer, C (1990) 'Hybrids' – a critical force in the application of information technology in the nineties, *Journal of Information Technology*, **5**, pp 232–35

Parkinson, M (1994) *Interviews Made Easy*, Kogan Page, London

Parry, J (1951) The psychological adviser's problems, *Occupational Psychology*, **25**, pp 124–30

Peterson, C and Seligman, M E P (1988) Explanatory style and illness, *Journal of Personality*, **55**, pp 237–65

Picard, J (1995) Employees don't believe psychological contract, *People Management*, **2**, November, p 5

Prior, D H (1991) *A Perspective on Outplacement: Theory and current practice*, MSL Career Consultants, London

Prior, D H (1996) Career management – current perspectives on a new reality, in *Towards the Millennium*, ed R Heller, Sterling, New York

Robertson, I (1994) Personnel selection research: where are we now?, *Psychologist*, January, pp 17–21

Rogers, C R (1942) *Counselling and Psychotherapy*, Houghton Mifflin, Boston, MA

Rogers, C R (1965) *Client-Centred Therapy: Its current practice, implications and theory,* Constable, London

Salovey, P and Mayer, J D (1990) Emotional intelligence, *Imagination, Cognition and Personality,* **9**, pp 185–211

Schmidt, F L and Hunter, N J E (1977) Development of a general solution to the problem of validity generalization, *Journal of Applied Psychology,* **62** (5), pp 529–40

Schmidt, F L and Hunter, J E (1998) The validity and utility of selection methods in personal and theoretical implications of 85 years of research findings, *Psychological Bulletin,* **124**, pp 262–74

Schuh, A J (1978) Contrast effect in the interview, *Bulletin of Psychometric Society,* **11**, pp 195–96

Shackleton, V and Newell, S (1991) Management selection: a comparative survey of methods used in top British and French companies, *Journal of Occupational Psychology,* **64**, pp 23–36

Sheehy, N and Gallagher, T (1995) Can virtual organizations be made real?, *Psychologist,* **9** (4), pp 159–62

Sibbald, J (1992) *The Career Makers,* HarperCollins, New York

Smart, D (1983) *Selection Interviewing,* John Wiley and Sons, New York

Smith, M, Gregg, M and Andrews, D (1989) *Selection and Assessment: A new appraisal,* Pitman, London

Snaith, R P and Zigmond, A S (1994) *Hospital Anxiety and Depression Scale,* NFER-Nelson, Windsor

Spencer, L M, McClelland, D C and Spencer, S M (1990) *Competency Assessment Methods,* Hay/McBer Research Press, Boston, MA

Stephenson, W (1953) *The Study of Behaviour: Q-Technique and its methodology,* University of Chicago Press, Chicago, IL

Stutsman, R (1984) *Merrill-Palmer Pre-School Performance Scale,* distributed by NFER-Nelson, Windsor

Sworder, G (1977) Problems for the counsellor in his task, in *Counselling at Work,* ed A G Watts, Bedford Square Press, London

Task Force on Assessment Center Guidelines (1989) *Guidelines and Ethical Considerations for Assessment Center Operations,* International Personnel Management Association, Alexandria, VA

Toplis, J, Dulewicz, V and Fletcher, C (1987) *Psychological Testing: A manager's guide,* IPM, London

Ulrich, L and Trumbo, D (1965) The selection interview since 1949, *Psychological Bulletin,* **63** (2), pp 100–16

Wallbank, S (1992) *The Empty Bed: Bereavement and the loss of love*, Darton, Longman & Todd, London

Walmsley, H (1994) *Counselling Techniques for Managers*, Kogan Page, London

Warr, P B (1987) *Work, Unemployment and Mental Health*, Oxford University Press, Oxford

Wise, D S and Buckley, M R (1998) The evolution of the performance appraisal, *Journal of Management History*, **4** (3), pp 233, 249

Worden, J W (1991) *Grief Counselling and Grief Therapy*, Routledge, London

Index